THE MILITARY ESTABLISHMENT

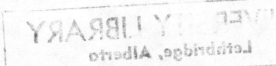

THE
MILITARY
ESTABLISHMENT

by JOHN M. SWOMLEY, Jr.

FOREWORD BY SENATOR GEORGE McGOVERN

BEACON PRESS BOSTON

ACKNOWLEDGMENTS

The author gratefully acknowledges permission to quote from the following sources: *America in Arms* by John McAuley Palmer, published by Yale University Press; "An Answer to Teller" reprinted by special permission of *The Saturday Evening Post*, © 1962 by The Curtis Publishing Company; *Army*, published by the Association of the United States Army; *Arsenal of Democracy* by Donald Nelson, published by Harcourt, Brace & World, Inc.; *The Price of Power* by Hanson Baldwin and *Arms and Politics in Latin America* by Edwin Lieuwen, published by the Council on Foreign Relations, Inc.; *Education and Military Leadership* by Gene M. Lyons and John W. Masland, published by Princeton University Press; *Japanese Militarism* by John M. Maki, published by Alfred A. Knopf Inc.; *Journal of Engineering Education; The Nation; Pentagon Politics* by William H. Neblett; *Soldiers and Scholars* by John W. Masland and Lawrence I. Radway, published by Princeton University Press.

The records and publications of the National Council Against Conscription, the Women's Committee Against Conscription, and the American Union Against Militarism, to which I have frequently referred, are in the Swarthmore College Peace Collection, Swarthmore, Pa.

Copyright © 1964 by John M. Swomley, Jr.

Published simultaneously in Canada by Saunders of Toronto, Ltd.

Library of Congress card catalog number: 64–10089

Beacon Press books are published under the auspices of the Unitarian Universalist Association

Printed in the United States of America

Second printing August, 1967

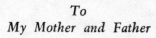
To
My Mother and Father

FOREWORD

In his "farewell address" President Dwight Eisenhower warned his fellow citizens to guard against the growing influence of "the military-industrial complex." The former President, whose life has been devoted largely to military affairs, saw in the enormous arms industry and our mighty defense establishment the danger of "a disastrous rise of misplaced power." He saw the influence of the military permeating "every city, every state house, every office of the Federal Government."

This is the central theme of this book written by a man who for many years has been deeply concerned and actively involved in efforts to prevent the militarization of American society.

Historically, the American people have understood the necessity of holding the military establishment within carefully drawn limits. When the colonies along the eastern seaboard set forth their grievances against King George, they entered a strong objection to his efforts "to render the military independent of and superior to the Civil Power."

Although Americans have rallied to the defense of the nation in time of war, they have moved with equal dispatch to "send the boys home" and convert our wartime industries to civilian production once the fighting ceased.

Since World War II, however, the United States has been following an unprecedented course. We have not only maintained the conscription of young men in peacetime, but have steadily increased our military might and the size of the arms budget.

In recent years we have been devoting over half of our federal budget directly to the armed forces. Another 30 per cent goes to such other security-related matters as atomic energy, the space effort, veterans benefits, the interest on the war debt, and the security efforts of the Central Intelligence

Agency, the Agency for International Development, and the Department of State.

Some 10 per cent of our entire national production and an equal percentage of our labor force are devoted to the defense effort. Countless communities, industries, laboratories, and universities have become intertwined with the military establishment.

As Professor Swomley tells us, this enormous military complex has not hesitated to make its influence felt in many ways in the councils of government and in civilian society.

Our military leaders have for the past two decades exerted vast influence on federal policy. Congress has appropriated enormous sums for the armed forces with far less examination and debate than is devoted to comparatively minor appropriations for such activities as education, mental health, or conservation. A $50 billion defense appropriation will slide through the House and Senate with far less floor debate than a $10 million authorization for the Arms Control and Disarmament Agency. Most Congressmen have felt that warfare in the nuclear age is so complex that both the basic and the technical judgments must necessarily be made by military experts.

But even the Defense spokesmen have not found their influence over public policy unlimited. A major portion of this book details the repeated defeats which the military leaders experienced in their efforts to establish universal military training in the years since World War II. Swomley played an important role in the anti-conscription battle and he tells that story from the vantage point, and perhaps with the understandable bias, of an energetic participant.

This is an important, timely book that will help place America's military power in better perspective.

SENATOR GEORGE McGOVERN,
SOUTH DAKOTA

PREFACE

The question of military influence over civilian authority has become the most important problem of present-day American government. This subject, which was also of real concern to Americans when our country was founded, is now a far more serious matter. Today there is military control of millions of Americans through peacetime conscription; there is military control of billions of dollars for domestic contracts and foreign aid; there is a huge military machine which cannot be fully understood or managed by the few civilian politicians who temporarily hold the reins of office.

The danger in all this is magnified by two problems: the temptation to use power, a temptation which afflicts all persons and groups who reach positions of overarching authority; and the possession of the weapons of nuclear destruction.

In the years just following World War II this writer prepared in pamphlet form a series of studies on the growth of military power in American life which were published by the National Council Against Conscription. Since then others have written about the current dangers of military control or about civil-military relationships in the light of the postwar development of military power.

This book is an attempt to trace the story of the growth of military influence over civilian American government. It is written from the standpoint of a participant in the struggle to prevent the adoption of peacetime conscription and other steps toward military control. It includes a brief summary of civil-military relationships from the beginning of our national existence and a more extensive description of the current military role in foreign policy, publicity media, education, and other areas of national life.

In describing the growth of American military power, the writer is aware of the efforts of some American civilians in key positions who have in the past attempted to subordinate

the military to civilian control. There are some who are working in this direction today. In most cases only passing reference has been made to such efforts and in other cases there
has been no attempt to describe them. In the course of doing
research and writing on this subject the author has become
convinced that such heroic efforts to regain civilian control
and the occasional graceful yielding of the military to them
are exceptional incidents. The military system is so huge and
powerful, the international situation so fraught with danger
and so capable of manipulation for military purposes, that
nothing short of total world disarmament can restore the
United States to thoroughgoing civilian control and to government by the people.

The writer is also aware that there are military leaders who
both in theory and sometimes in practice indicate their preference for civilian control. It is impossible and unjust to gen-
eralize about all military men, even though there are often
patterns of military thinking and conduct that seem to point
in that direction. Although this book does refer to specific
military leaders, it is far more concerned with describing a
group or system. Many persons who as individuals follow a
high personal code in terms of patriotism and ethics, act quite
differently when they function as agents of corporate interests.
In similar fashion, many military men tend to identify national
interests with military interests and even with the ambition
of their own particular branch of the armed forces. Power
that they might not seek for themselves they seek for the
Army or the Air Force or the Navy, sometimes at the expense
of the larger national interest.

It is out of a concern for the larger national interest and
indeed for all people everywhere that this book is written.
Americans cannot be effective workers for world peace and
world disarmament unless they understand the forces that
seek constantly to maintain and increase our dependence on
arms.

The writer wishes to record his indebtedness to many colleagues and friends who offered encouragement and advice
during the postwar campaign against universal military training, for it is out of that campaign that much of the information for and interest in writing this book have come. Among
them are Professor Alonzo F. Myers, Ray Newton, Dr. Harry
Emerson Fosdick; Richard R. Reuter, Father Allan P. Farrell,
S.J., who among others served on the National Council Against
Conscription; Alfred Hassler, A. J. Muste and John Nevin

Sayre of the Fellowship of Reconciliation; Raymond E. Wilson of the Friends Committee on National Legislation; Frederick J. Libby of the National Council for Prevention of War; Mildred Olmsted and Annalee Stewart of the Women's International League for Peace and Freedom.

But above all these is my gratitude to my wife, Marjie, for her very great help in the preparation of this book.

In acknowledging this debt to others the author nevertheless assumes responsibility for the shortcomings of this book and any errors in interpretation.

JOHN M. SWOMLEY, JR.

CONTENTS

INTRODUCTION

There is a growing body of evidence that the professional officer group in the American military establishment has been steadily expanding its influence and control over our civilian institutions and government. This group has been aided in its drive for power by civilians closely associated with the military — industrialists whose profits depend upon military contracts, and scientists and technicians whose careers depend upon the construction of military weapons. In varying degree other Americans whose prosperity or prestige derive from a large military establishment either have assisted the military in its program for expansion or have been unwilling to support measures that might curtail or limit the political and economic power of the armed forces.

Warnings about the growing military power have been issued from time to time by responsible people, but have been largely ignored by the American public. In 1948 a committee of the Commission for the Reorganization of the Executive Branch of Government, headed by former President Herbert Hoover, reported that national policy often does not now come from the civilian heads of government. Instead, "the military have picked up the ball of national policy and are running down the field with it." Congress, the report said, was "practically helpless."

In 1951 Senator Ralph Flanders (R., Vt.) asserted on the floor of the Senate: "We are being forced to shift the American way of life into the pattern of the garrison state." He charged that "Our wealth, our standard of living, the lives of our young people and our institutions are under the control of the military."

1

Representative Thomas Werdel (R., Calif.) echoed the cry: "I am reluctant to admit that I now believe that we have come to the awful day in America where we have a supreme general staff, modeled after Hitler and the Prussians, seeking military control over industry, labor, all military establishments, the economy, and the press. I am convinced that this is their plan against the expressed will of Congress."

Other civilian and Congressional leaders have expressed similar concern and alarm at the growth of military power. Perhaps the most significant statement was that of a lifelong military man, General Dwight D. Eisenhower. In his farewell address as President in 1961 he warned the American people against the "acquisition of unwarranted influence by the military-industrial complex" and stressed the danger of such "disastrous use of misplaced power." He asserted that "the total influence [of this complex] — economic, political, even spiritual — is felt in every city, every state house, every office of the Federal government."

Such efforts to warn the American people have received little space in the nation's newspapers and magazines, many of which either cooperate with the well-developed military public relations program or for other reasons believe it is not in their best interest to question or impede the growth of military influence in American life. Nor have these warnings produced a responsive concern in the American citizenry, who seem quite complacent and content, finding it hard to believe that our freedom from tyranny is really in jeopardy. Yet freedom can be eroded gradually and almost imperceptibly if we are not vigilant.

The principle of civil control of government and military power has been carefully observed by every American generation until our own. It is a principle rooted deep in both English and American history.

As early as 1628 in the Petition of Right, the British Parliament protested King Charles' military policies, including martial law and the billeting of troops among the people. Before the century was over Parliament had asserted its permanent authority over the army. The Mutiny Act, which gave disciplinary powers to Army officers and provided for the pay of the armed force, had to be renewed each year — by Parliament.

The desire for civil supremacy was evident in Colonial America, in the Declaration of Independence. One of the charges against George III was that "he kept among us in times of peace, standing armies," and "has affected to render the military independent of and superior to the Civil Power."

So strong was the fear of standing armies that the new United States government, following the Revolution, took every precaution to insure freedom from military influence and control in American life. One precaution, written into the Constitution, was to put the power to raise and support armies into the hands of a civilian congress. A condition that no appropriation might be made for the Army for more than a two-year period guaranteed periodic civilian review of military policies. No similar provision was made with respect to the Navy, partly because a permanent navy seemed essential to guard against enemies who could not reach America without crossing an ocean, and partly because there was no tradition in the Anglo-Saxon world of naval attempts to establish dictatorships, as there had been in the case of armies.

A second precaution was to provide for decentralization of military power by granting to the states authority to appoint officers and to train the militia. This Constitutional provision was in part a recognition of states' rights. But it also provided an alternative to a large standing army and a restraint on the seizure of power by a central professional military force. Alexander Hamilton reflected the mood of the time in writing that a militia "appears to me the only substitute that can be devised for a standing army and the best security against it, if it should exist."[1] In practice, from its earliest days until World War II, Congress authorized only a very small professional army that could be expanded in time of war and reduced drastically in time of peace.

A third Constitutional safeguard was to make the President, a civilian, Commander in Chief of the armed forces, without the power to declare war or appropriate money for the military establishment, these powers remaining with the Congress.

It is important to note that these safeguards against military control were tested early in the new republic's history. In 1789 George Washington's Secretary of War, General Henry Knox, asked for a federal law obligating all able-bodied men to serve in the militia. Knox wanted young men between eighteen and twenty-one years of age to receive military training; at this age, he said, "the passions and affections are strongly influenced by the splendor of military parade. The impressions the mind receives will be retained through life." [2] The request was not granted. Because of Congressional opposition, the militia law adopted in 1792 simply recognized the responsibility of the various states for enrolling male citizens and of the individual citizen for furnishing his own weapons and ammunition. No penalties were imposed for non-compliance.

After the initial struggle over military power in the new nation, there was a long period of relative calm in civil-military relationships, interrupted chiefly by four major crises.

The first crisis was the Civil War and its aftermath. The soldiers of the Union were the dynamic element in the politics of the postwar period as well as in the exploitation of the South. The counterrevolution was the Ku Klux Klan, organized by six Confederate veterans in 1865. The resistance to Federal Reconstruction was almost entirely the work of disgruntled veterans, and Confederate soldiers continued to be led by their former officers in their new status as veterans. The Civil War established the veteran as a factor in American political life.

A second surge of militarism occurred as a result of the growth of the labor movement in the 1870's. The railroad strike of 1877, which spread throughout the United States to include all major railroads, was accompanied by violence. Eleven states used almost 45,000 militia to suppress the strike, and in Pennsylvania 1,000 Regular Army troops were also used. Other Army units were on patrol in other states. It was the strike-breaking activity of the militia and the apparent dependability of the militia against their fellow-workers which was the key factor in the development of the National Guard.

The third crisis was the Spanish-American War. As a result

of the opportunity for naval and colonial expansion afforded by the war with Spain, Captain Alfred T. Mahan, the most influential American naval officer of the time, actively concerned himself with the political struggle over annexation of the Philippines. His writings were filled with derogatory statements about the anti-imperialists, who, he said, were still living in the years gone by. In the Congressional debate it was Mahan's arguments that were chiefly heard, supported by influential civilians such as Henry Cabot Lodge and Theodore Roosevelt, who were leaders in the emphasis on sea power and colonial empire.

The Spanish-American War made possible a naval expansion program and also led to a reorganization of the army. This reorganization established a General Staff modeled on the German Great General Staff, increased the size of the permanent army, and set up an Army War College. The Army reorganization made it possible to think in terms not only of large-scale warfare but also of warfare overseas. Walter Millis in *Arms and Men* speculates that without this reorganization our participation in World War I "might never have taken place at all."

The fourth crisis was World War I. Before American entry, under the impact of the war in Europe and on the urging of those involved in the Plattsburg Movement, Congress passed the National Defense Act of 1916 which authorized the War Department to establish Reserve Officers Training Corps units in schools and colleges. Shortly thereafter the War Department, without any legal right to do so, began its pressure on land-grant colleges to make military training compulsory for all first- and second-year students.

Another World War I development was a drive to increase military power in peacetime. The Army's General Staff prepared a bill which provided for a large standing army and compulsory military training for teen-age boys. Congress, in adopting the National Defense Act of 1920, rejected compulsory military training and whittled down the requested size of the standing army, but elements in the Army were successful in limiting the authority of the civilian Secretary of War. As a result, Army officers were, in effect, permitted to go over the head of their civilian superior to present their position directly to Congressional committees.

World War II marked the virtual end of military acceptance of civilian control. American generals, not willing to relinquish the great powers they had had in wartime, publicly rebuked Congress when Congress hesitated in granting their requests. The mood was strikingly illustrated by General Ira Eaker, who in a speech in Los Angeles on August 7, 1947 attacked the "appallingly bad judgment" of "the old men" in Congress, who, he said, "would have been eliminated in any other nation."[3]

More than a military criticism of Congress developed, however. A systematic campaign was begun to influence public opinion through an extensive propaganda network that made carefully planned use of the press, Hollywood, radio, television and other media. Military men began to penetrate the civil service. The chairman of the Senate Committee on Post Office and Civil Service, William Langer (R., N.D.), told the Senate in June, 1948, about "military men who were taken out of the Army by the high ranking military authorities and placed in the civil service of the United States where we cannot get rid of them without changing our entire civil service structure."

Foreign policy also came under military influence. That the Army was conscious of its new power was evident in a paragraph in a 1947 issue of the *Army and Navy Bulletin* which began: "Today the Army has virtual control of foreign affairs . . . " In 1952 A. A. Ribicoff (D., Conn.), then a key member of the House Foreign Affairs Committee, said, " . . . in the last year or two more foreign policy has been made in the Pentagon than in the State Department."[4]

It is a thesis of this book that the new influence of the military was a result of conscious planning for power. But there were at least two factors for which the Pentagon was not responsible, which nonetheless made its power drive possible.

The first was the new importance of modern science and technology, which pushed concepts of warfare beyond all traditions. Air power, atomic and hydrogen bombs, missiles, chemical and biological weapons — all necessitated expansion of the military organization and structure. The founding fathers made no provision for such developments as these; they envisioned only two armed services. Since 1947 there have been three, with the Air Force, originally a part of the U.S. Army, a separate, large and powerful group with its own hierarchy, academy and claimant voice.

The second factor was the emergence of the Soviet Union as a great power and the major rival to the United States.

Although modern science and a new great power on the international scene provide the context in which military power has grown, they do not justify the usurpation of civilian prerogatives. One by one, the historic safeguards against militarism in America are withering away. The large size of the armed forces, together with the need for long-term specialists to handle the complications of modern technological warfare, have tended to increase the size of the permanent officer group in the nation. And they have powers today that would make our founding fathers tremble.

Congress now has little control over military spending. The military has authority to let long-term contracts without Congressional review or approval. In 1951 a former Under-Secretary of the Treasury, Roswell Magill, commented that only about one-third of the President's budget was "subject to reduction by Congressional action on appropriations." A good part of the budget is of course "fixed charges," but a good part also reflects commitments to profligate military purchasing.

In addition, the very size and complexity of the budget operates against Congressional control. Said the *Combat Forces Journal* in 1952:

> It is impossible for any one Congressman or Senator, or even a group of Congressmen or Senators, to be expert on every facet of the defense budget. And so they must accept the explanations of the witnesses — and anyone who knows much about these things knows that the testimony of the experienced soldier wearing stars is the most persuasive of all.

Instead of curbing the Army or Navy, members of Congressional committees on military affairs developed a vested interest in expansion of the armed forces. This has gone so far that under Representative Carl Vinson's firm control the House Armed Services Committee has become practically the alter ego of the Pentagon. Vinson stated his philosophy in the House March 30, 1949, when he asserted that the President's decision "is not the expert military view. Our top source for military judgment is the Joint Chiefs of Staff . . . " He has given priority to the Pentagon over civilian groups of government charged with overall economic or budgetary planning. "And as between the Bureau of the Budget and the Joint Chiefs of Staff," he has said, "I will place my confidence in the latter, in regard to what our national defense needs are." This attitude of ratification of military desires is precisely what the Army has wanted and cultivated.

It was one of the aims of unification of the armed forces that a supreme General Staff be established, which, though nominally under civilian control, would have been practically autonomous. General George C. Marshall made this clear in his proposal for unification in 1947; he proposed a Chief of Staff to the President who would outrank all other military and naval officers and who might bypass the civilian Secretary of Defense on all matters relating to "strategy, tactics, operations, the preparation and presentation of the joint military budget." Although this device failed to get approval, President Kennedy in 1961 came close to implementing by executive decree what Congress had failed to accept, by appointing General Maxwell D. Taylor as Presidential Military Representative. Taylor has long advocated abolishing the Joint Chiefs of Staff and replacing them with a single Chief of Staff; on July 20, 1962, he was appointed Chairman of the Joint Chiefs of Staff.

The traditional reliance of the nation on the state militia has now passed into history. The state militia or National Guard is now largely financed by federal military money and is partially controlled by the Army. Indeed, the Army has from time to time proposed the federalization of the state militia so as to render its control of the state forces complete.

Even the Constitutional safeguard which makes the President Commander in Chief of the Armed Forces is no longer a guarantee of civil supremacy. This is especially true when a professional military officer can be elected "civilian" Commander in Chief. Yet even when a real civilian is President, the very bigness of government tends to limit his authority. He must delegate responsibility and power to heads of departments, who in turn must rely on the "career" people in the departments. A myriad of military and semi-military organizations in the Federal Government are headed by career military personnel or civilians whose short term appointments make civilian control impossible. Even in normally civilian departments there are today large numbers of military men. During General Marshall's tenure as Secretary of State, ten of the twenty ranking executive officers in the State Department were military men. In 1953 nine Army generals and 58 colonels were assigned to civilian agencies of government; in 1957 about 200 generals or admirals were serving in international or interservice agencies, with more than 1300 colonels or naval officers of comparable rank and about 6000 officers of lower grade as support.

Even though the framework of civilian control remains, the substance of American government today is increasingly that of military power.

Though today there is no effective counter-force to the military drive for power, there was in recent American history such a force, which for a time at least stood firm against the rising military tide. It was directed against the Army's campaign for peacetime universal military training, a campaign begun during World War I and revived with vigor during World War II. Universal military training (UMT) would have put every boy at an impressionable age under military indoctrination and control; it would drastically have enlarged the supervisory or professional officer group and called for large-scale production of military equipment and thus extended the allied military-industrial influence in the American economy. It would have been a long step in the direction of militarizing America.

Favoring UMT were the U.S. Army, the American Legion, the Veterans of Foreign Wars, the United States Chamber of Commerce and a few groups organized specifically to secure the adoption of the measure. Pitted against them were at first a few, then practically all of the major civilian organizations in the nation. Together the opponents waged the largest united campaign on any legislative issue in American history.

The story of the struggle over UMT will be described in this book as a case history of the expanding military influence in America. The bill for UMT was defeated but conscription was not; when the Army is loser on one front it seeks another road to accomplish the same goal and often achieves it. Other aspects of the recent military drive for power will also be examined. As one who was active in the fight against UMT, I am convinced that no nation can turn its important decisions over to the military without making its claim to democracy a mere facade; nor can the nation seriously negotiate for disarmament if the power of ultimate decision is in military hands.

CHAPTER 1

CONSCRIPTION COMES TO AMERICA

Peacetime conscription was, until recently, a notoriously un-American idea. Conscription had been used late in the Civil War but that war was really fought by volunteers and conscription, accompanied by riots, was in general so unpopular and unsatisfactory that a system of buying substitutes was accepted. General Sherman insisted that the volunteers "were the best, better than the conscripts and far better than the bought substitutes." In World War I conscription was once again employed to build the United States Army, but now there was a difference: the conscript *had* to serve if called; he could not buy a substitute.

In fact, there are several types of conscription. The two major ones are Selective Service, the method used in World Wars I and II, and universal military training (UMT). There are others as well. Perhaps an illustration is the best way to distinguish the two major types.

It is wartime; the nation needs to build an army. Joe is drafted because a local civilian committee, properly empowered, decides he can be released from his work or study without impairing the war effort. His cousin George, a skilled worker in a defense industry or a farmer engaged in producing wheat, is deferred, because the board feels he performs functions essential to the nation's health and welfare. This is *selective* service.

Were universal military training in effect, both Joe and George would be compelled to take a period of military training upon reaching the age of eighteen. Neither could be deferred except for physical disability. Following the period of training, both would be placed in the reserve forces for a period of years, giving certain nights each month and certain weeks each summer to continuation of military training.

11

Of the two sorts of conscription, universal military training is the more conducive to military control of American life, if only because it would put every fit American male under military influence for a number of the most impressionable years of his life — an army objective for many years.

The movement which culminated in the drive for enactment of universal military training legislation in America began before World War I, in 1913. In the summer of that year Gen. Leonard Wood, Army Chief of Staff, set up citizens' training camps in Plattsburg, New York. Wood saw no specific enemy and no immediate war but he believed any future land war would involve masses of men and would therefore require conscription. According to Walter Millis, his purpose in setting up military training camps was to start the process of converting the American people to acceptance of conscription and the foundations of the garrison state. Moreover, the camps were "not practical schools of war but seminaries whence propaganda for preparedness might be distributed through the civil population."[1]

The camps were soon expanded into what became known as the "Plattsburg idea." Grenville Clark, a New York lawyer who was one of the original organizers of the movement, said that "in 1915 a group of men got together" and proposed "voluntary training camps for professional and business men. These were held in 1915 for about 1,200 men under the auspices of General Wood and Secretary Garrison at the men's own expense."[2]

By 1915 the total attendance at the camps had reached 12,200. The men who participated in the Plattsburg training program formed in 1916 the Military Training Camps Association, a national organization designed to promote the idea of military preparedness. Shortly thereafter this association, which had representatives in almost every county in the country, started a campaign to educate the nation for universal military training.

The War Department's involvement in this campaign was described by Brig. Gen. John McAuley Palmer, who wrote:

> At first the movement had no official sanction from the Administration but with several other General Staff officers I did all that I could in my spare time to cooperate with its sponsors.

Finally in December 1916, the War College Division of the General Staff was ordered to prepare a plan of military organization based upon the principle of compulsory military training.[3]

A bill for compulsory military training was introduced in the Senate on December 10, 1915, by Senator George E. Chamberlain (D., Ore.). In the House, Representative Augustus P. Gardner (R., Mass.) had also proposed compulsory training. But Congress at that time was not in a mood to accept any form of conscription. Nor did President Wilson back universal training. However, as a result of the pressure of the Plattsburg group, the National Defense Act of 1916 provided for continuing the voluntary military camps of the Plattsburg movement with the Federal government paying transportation and subsistence for those participating.

The Plattsburg men were not daunted, but continued their campaign for universal military training. They initiated the formation in Washington in 1917 of the National Committee of Patriotic Societies. This committee set up a central bureau in the nation's capital with a card index of local leaders enabling it to communicate directly in every section of the country with leaders eager to promote universal training and other moves for military preparedness.

Although the Plattsburg movement failed to achieve its central goal in 1916, the work done on behalf of universal military training affected the passage of a wartime conscription law a year later.

The United States broke diplomatic relations with Germany on February 3, 1917. The following day President Wilson called at the War Department and after a thirty-minute conference with Secretary of War Newton D. Baker, it was agreed that the United States wartime army should be raised by conscription. The bill for conscription which eventually became law was drafted by a team headed by Gen. Enoch Crowder within the next twenty-four hours. It incorporated some of the plans which had been drawn up in the War Department to produce a peacetime compulsory training program.[4]

When Secretary Baker testified in behalf of the bill before the House Military Affairs Committee on April 7, 1917, he said:

> A policy ought to be adopted which, without becoming the beginning of the practice of universal training or service and without committing the Government to a present decision of that problem . . . would . . . spread the strain over the entire country and at the same time reach men of ages within the limit of those who could be spared from the industrial uses of the country.

In this way it was clearly understood that, although both systems were compulsory, selective service was not universal training or service and was not to be considered as a precedent for a postwar universal program. On the other hand, President Wilson stressed the idea of a "universal obligation to service" even though some would serve in their capacities as farmers, miners or businessmen.

Throughout the legislative discussions of the Selective Service proposal, the feeling was expressed that compulsion for military service was incompatible with the American spirit of freedom. But the Wilson administration persisted in holding that any volunteer system would dislocate industry, and in the end the House Military Affairs Committee approved the selective system. The Selective Service Act became law on May 18, 1917.

During World War I the campaign for postwar universal military training was pressed by the National Security League, organized in 1914 by industrialists, New York lawyers and financiers. With such backing, legislation was introduced in the Senate to amend the Selective Service Act to provide not less than six months compulsory training for boys between 19 and 21, though they could not be called for military service until they were 21. President Wilson was reported opposed to a compulsory military training program which would extend into peacetime, and Senator John Sharp Williams (D., Miss.) on March 29,

1918 vigorously attacked the proposal in the Senate, saying that he did not want the United States

> . . . to sink to the level of the Prussians and Austrians and Bulgarians, to the level of the condition of the continent of Europe, living in armed camps, one against the other, suspecting one another every day, prepared to pounce upon one another every week . . .

When the measure was brought to a vote on March 29, it was defeated 36 to 26, with 33 not voting.

So long as the war continued there was no further effort to secure universal military training. It would have been impossible in any event so long as both people and government held to the view that the war would end all militarism and conscription. There was also a feeling that such a proposal would mean acceptance of the system the nation was then fighting. But because of the attempt to push universal military training in Congress, the leading anti-military organization in the country, the American Union Against Militarism, voted unanimously at its annual meeting on February 26, 1918 to re-open its office in Washington and decided to "direct all its energies against the propaganda for compulsory military training."

The Union was composed of leading anti-war liberals such as John Haynes Holmes, Stephen Wise and Max Eastman. Although leading the attack, it was by no means the only organization opposed to compulsory military training. Oswald Garrison Villard, publisher of the *New York Evening Post* and *The Nation;* and the Women's Peace Party, of which Jane Addams was the president, were also active. The American Federation of Labor was opposed to conscription and in its 1919 convention reaffirmed its position. Both the National Farmers Union and the National Grange were on record against universal military training. Hundreds of newspapers also opposed it. In 1918 the American Union Against Militarism reported that about two hundred newspapers had opposed compulsory military training before the war, and that currently about seven hundred papers were using its materials.

The *Des Moines Register* said: "Universal military training is a scheme to Prussianize America and is promoted by men who have always been converts to the Prussian theory of the state." The Springfield (Mass.) *Republican* asked: "If England will not stand for such a system, why should America, which is carrying a war debt of thirty billions?" The *New York Evening Post,* the *Pittsburgh Sun,* the *Jacksonville Times-Union,* and the *Sun* and *New York Herald* were among the papers opposing universal training. On the other hand, *The New York Times,* the *New York Herald Tribune,* the *Washington Post,* the Boston *Evening Transcript,* the *El Paso Times,* the *Topeka State Journal,* and the *Seattle Times* favored it.

As soon as the war ended, the War Department resumed active preparation for universal military training. The bill drafted in the War Department and transmitted by Secretary Baker to Congress on August 3, 1919 provided for universal military training for eighteen- and nineteen-year-old boys. Some other bills providing for universal military training were introduced about the same time, including one prepared by National Guard officers and one prepared by the Military Training Camps Association.

The American Union Against Militarism, opposing all three bills, proposed a course of action for opponents of universal training through its executive secretary. After pointing out that the Republicans, who "take their cue on these matters from business organizations," have "swallowed the entire program of 'preparedness' and 'universal military training,' " the secretary wrote:

> But, Republican politicians are politicians . . . and as politicians they want to know just how popular they would be in the country if they endorsed universal military training. There are a whole lot of them who have discovered that universal military training is intensely unpopular. Suppose you sat down and wrote, utterly at random, to two or three Republican politicians — the National Committeemen from your state, or your Republican state chairman, or your local Republican chairman or even a member of Congress of that political faith — and wrote a brief note commenting on the action of the

New Jersey Republicans in endorsing universal military training and remarking . . . that if the Republicans were going
in for universal training . . . they were as good as dead.
[*Bulletin 17*, July 18, 1919, published by the American
Union Against Militarism.]

In spite of growing public opposition to any form of postwar
conscription, Chairman James W. Wadsworth (R., N.Y.) of the
Senate Military Affairs Committee pressed for immediate action
and in August, 1919 opened hearings on the reorganization of
the Army. There was little evidence in the hearings of effective
organized opposition to peacetime conscription. Only two Quakers
from the Ohio Yearly Meeting of Friends and two National Guard
generals opposed it. A National Guard officer, asked during the
hearings to appraise public sentiment on universal training, said:
"The employer and the man who appears prominently before the
public is in favor of it, but the employed man is not and the
farmer is not, and they are in the majority."

When the bill was reported out of committee, Senators
Kenneth McKellar (D., Tenn.) and Morris Sheppard (D., Tex.)
issued a minority report. Their chief argument against the bill
dealt with the unnecessary and enormous expense of training new
soldiers when there were already available for any emergency
four million men who had been trained during the World War.

The American Union Against Militarism, as soon as the
Senate bill had been reported out of committee, called for letters
to senators and to Republican politicians. Brigadier General
Palmer, in reporting the reaction to the Senate bill, wrote: "Every
senator was overwhelmed by a flood of letters and telegrams from
agitated constituents."

By a superior strategy the American Union Against Militarism overcame its opponents. It concentrated on the Republicans while the American Legion, which felt certain of Republican
support, was working on Secretary of War Baker, the key to
President Wilson, and on the Democrats. When Baker succumbed
to the Legion pressure and endorsed the Wadsworth bill for
universal military training, the Republican floor leader in the
House denounced the bill which Baker had just endorsed. The

Democrats in the House, alarmed by the Republican denunciation, hastily called a caucus and by a vote of 106 to 17 decided to oppose any action on universal training in that session of Congress.

Wadsworth began Senate debate on the bill in spite of a decision by Republican leaders to delete the compulsory training feature. In time Wadsworth finally yielded and supported a substitute proposal for four months voluntary training that several weeks earlier had been quietly drafted by the military personnel on his own committee staff when they foresaw the defeat of compulsory training.

The National Defense Act of 1920, finally approved by the President on June 4, 1920, was adopted in the form of amendments to the National Defense Act of 1916. Although the Act did not provide for universal military training or the substitute of four months' voluntary training, it did provide for a Reserve Officers Training Corps which extended military training in universities and colleges and introduced it into the public high schools. It also provided for Citizens' Military Training Camps which any youth could attend in the summer at government expense.

In spite of the fact that Congress rejected universal military training, a number of those responsible for American military policy endorsed the National Defense Act of 1920 as sound. Their appraisal of it indicated that they by no means regarded universal military training as indispensable or even necessary. General John J. Pershing in 1920 wrote "this act gave us, for the first time, a sound national defense system . . . "[5]

General Douglas MacArthur, when he was Army Chief of Staff, wrote in his Annual Report for 1932:

In 1920, with the lessons of the World War fresh in mind, the Congress devised a practical program that constituted the first real attempt in the United States to adjust military preparation accurately to defensive needs, and so framed that program as to assure other nations of its non-aggressive purpose. . . . Tradition and public sentiment have always precluded conscription as the basis of a peacetime defense policy . . .

The establishment of this conservative system of land defense was unquestionably one of the most constructive measures evolved by any government in recent years. In it are combined efficiency, economy, and respect for American ideals and traditions.

Even James Wadsworth is reported as having said in early 1940: "After surveying the success of our National Guard and Reserve Training for the last twenty years, I am not now so convinced that universal training is a necessity."

In spite of general approval of the National Defense Act of 1920, the Military Training Camps Association, in cooperation with the War Department, kept the idea of universal military training alive between wars. The executive committee of the Association in the Second Corps area met in New York City after the invasion of Norway on May 8, 1940. One of the committee, Grenville Clark, insisted on mobilizing their organization to press for the adoption of compulsory military training and service. A committee headed by Clark worked closely with General Staff officers, headed by Lt. Col. Lewis B. Hershey, who were responsible for War Department conscription plans.

As a result of the Clark committee's proposal "that the draft should take effect at once instead of after the occurrence of a state of war," a conscription bill was introduced in the Senate by Edward R. Burke (D., Neb.) and in the House by former Senator James W. Wadsworth (R., N.Y.). The bill was more comparable to the Selective Service Act of World War I than to universal military training.

The attack on the bill was led by a number of peace organizations. Working together against the bill were Edwin C. Johnson of the Committee on Militarism in Education, John Nevin Sayre of the Fellowship of Reconciliation, Frederick J. Libby of the National Council for Prevention of War, and Dorothy Detzer of the Women's International League for Peace and Freedom.

In the Senate the most vocal opponents were Senator Arthur Vandenberg (R., Mich.); Bennett (Champ) Clark (D., Mo.);

George Norris (Ind. Republican, Neb.); Rush Holt (D., W.Va.); Burton K. Wheeler (D., Mont.); Edwin C. Johnson (D., Colo.); Arthur Capper (R., Kan.); and Robert A. Taft (R., Ohio).

No labor union, no church group except the Methodist Church and the Society of Friends, and no group of educators appeared in the public hearings in opposition to the bill. Following the hearings, this writer, who testified against the bill for the Methodist Church, joined two Quakers, Paul Comly French and E. Raymond Wilson, who had been steadily interviewing Congressmen about the bills. The team discovered that although some members of Congress were opposed to conscription because it would create in the United States an atmosphere of militarism, most Congressional opponents were united by the hope that a defeat of the draft would halt or reverse the Administration tendency toward military intervention in World War II.

In spite of such work and the efforts of a much wider "Keep America Out of War" movement led by Norman Thomas, the veteran Socialist candidate for President, the Burke-Wadsworth bill was adopted. It was passed in the House by a vote of 233 to 124 and in the Senate by a vote of 47 to 25 and became law on September 16, 1940.[6]

America now for the first time had a peacetime conscription law.

CHAPTER 2

THE BATTLE IS DRAWN

In the early stages of World War II the energies of the armed forces and the civilian population were largely absorbed in the organization of the tremendous military-industrial machine that was to win the war. Before long, however, Army leaders and their civilian colleagues in finance and industry began to think of the postwar scene. They did not want World War II to end as did World War I, with the Army drastically cut back and the industrial-military ties severed. They agitated, therefore, for a large peacetime army, since a small military establishment meant diminished influence, reduction in rank for officers, fewer orders for industry.

But top officers feared that they could not indefinitely maintain a large military establishment without some type of continuing military conscription. Universal military training thus became the key to their planning. As an instrument for expanded military influence it had certain advantages over Selective Service. Under UMT every fit male, not merely selected ones, would be subject to military training and indoctrination. And, once accepted, UMT would be a permanent system, not subject to renewal year after year by a civilian Congress. A permanent system made planning easier, avoided cutbacks in men and weapons and supplies.

Proponents of universal military training blamed their defeat following World War I upon the fact that UMT had been brought up in Congress after the war when the atmosphere of crisis had passed and the people wanted a return to normalcy. Not wanting to experience a similar postwar mood, a group of officers in the War Department began as early as the spring of 1943 to make preparations for postwar compulsory military training. By early 1944 planning had developed to the point where the War Department was encouraging friendly Congressmen to establish a special House Committee on Post War Military Policy. *Newsweek,* in describing the resolution by James W. Wadsworth (then a Congressman from New York), said it called for a "special 23-man committee to see that the postwar military mistakes of the last war are not repeated." *Newsweek* also noted that the special committee "had the full support of the War and Navy Departments." Top military leaders, the report continued, "fear that unless definite policies are formulated now, the military may some day" find its plans blocked.[1] Lieutenant Colonel Roscoe Conkling, who served on the national Selective Service headquarters staff, reported that a group of officers "charged with urgent duties pertaining to the daily progress of this war" nevertheless "spent most of their time" during July and August, 1944, in planning and "drafting legislation for compulsory military training." [2]

By August 1944, Gen. George C. Marshall, Army Chief of Staff, was ready to make universal military training the key to all postwar planning. He "directed the General Staff and all other planning agencies under his jurisdiction to adapt their plans to the citizen-army formula." [3] In his initial directive and thereafter, General Marshall assumed that Congress would enact a law providing essentially for the kind of military training the Army wanted. So certain was he that the Army campaign would succeed, that he directed the Joint General Staff Committee studying the problem of reserves to operate on the assumption that UMT would be enacted.[4]

The Army had no hope of getting peacetime universal military training unless it could be sold to the American people. To this end Secretary of War Henry L. Stimson called its importance to the attention of American Legion officials and he also wrote a letter of endorsement to Archibald G. Thacher, upon the formation of a Citizens Committee for Universal Military Training of Young Men. This Citizens Committee, which coordinated its planning with the Army, was largely made up of business leaders whose connections were either with war industries or in Wall Street. A number of its members had also been actively associated with the Plattsburg Training Camps and the Military Training Camps Association which had advocated universal military training following World War I.

Within a month after General Marshall and Secretary Stimson had launched the Army drive for UMT, James Forrestal, Secretary of the Navy, in an address to the National Convention of the American Legion, emphasized the "primary importance" of compulsory military training and the "necessity to deal with this question speedily."

War Department planning not only called for the involvement of veterans' organizations and business groups but for support from the millions of soldiers then fighting the Germans and Japanese. The National Commander of the American Legion, Edward N. Scheiberling, was "permitted" to speak in favor of UMT to soldiers in Europe, but inquiries directed to Secretary of War Stimson revealed that no organization or individual desiring to present an opposite point of view would be permitted to speak to members of the armed forces. Stimson indicated that the Army would continue to grant representatives of veterans' organizations the right to speak in this fashion.[5]

In addition to encouraging Legion speakers, Army officers themselves tried to persuade their wartime armies that they should favor universal military training. But the Army's official policy prohibited officers and enlisted men alike from opposing UMT. Sergeant James T. Donnelly, after an honorable discharge, told the House Military Affairs Committee of the "many speeches by high-ranking officers in favor of peacetime training." He became alarmed at this and decided to oppose UMT. Permission was denied when he wanted to write a letter to his Congressman against it.

Donnelly indicated that he did nevertheless send a letter to Senator Hawkes (N.J.) which was returned, without delivery, by the Army censor. Donnelly added: "The office of the Judge Advocate General stated that in the future under threat of court martial I could not write anything against compulsory military training according to Army Regulation 600-10, paragraph 5." [6]

The Army also conducted an extensive propaganda program among civilians. In Washington there was a full-time staff working under the direction of Maj. Gen. Edward Weible to carry the program forward. In addition, one officer in each corps area office was assigned to work with the public on this issue.

Leaders of national and regional civilian organizations were cultivated in "off-the-record" meetings called by Secretary of War Stimson. Those attending were asked to keep the meeting and its information secret, the implication being that if the public were to know about it, it would jeopardize national security. Mr. Stimson and Army generals then proceeded to impress upon those present the need for universal military training.

Numerous other techniques were used to sell the public. War Department writers prepared articles for publication in popular magazines. For example, the August, 1945 *Woman's Home Companion,* with over three million circulation, carried an article by Under Secretary of War Robert P. Patterson entitled "Now or Never." In a box in the center of the article the editor urged readers to write to their Congressmen asking for compulsory military training.

Army leaders did not overlook the direct local appeal. General Jacob Devers, Commanding General of Army Ground Forces, for example, asked a Colorado Springs, Colorado group to support universal military training. He implied that it would be good business for the community when he said that nearby Camp Carson would go at "full blast" if UMT were adopted. Such training, he said, would be particularly valuable "in this community where specialist training would develop youths. This would be a top asset to them and the community."

A major effort was made to sell Congress and the country on UMT during the public hearings before the House Committee on Post War Military Policy. The Army, wrote one Washington columnist, "staged a spectacular performance, producing favorable testimony from high ranking officers and civilian officials." He added, "It had been expected that these sessions, deliberately held in the aftermath of German surrender and in the re-deployment of our forces against Japan, would stimulate great public interest and make black headlines." [7]

Although the Army was the driving force in the campaign for UMT the American Legion and the Citizens Committee for the Universal Military Training of Young Men were also vigorously pressing for its adoption. National Commander Warren Atherton carried the Legion's campaign to educators by addressing the National Education Association in July, 1944. He predicted a greater interest in education on the part of high school and college students "if the educators and the military coordinate their training and their plans." The Legion sought to influence other groups through messages addressed to labor, to the churches, to Congress. At a dinner in Washington for members of Congressional committees dealing with military affairs the National Commander of the Legion told those present that the American Legion wanted "action now." It should, however, be noted that the American Legion, though strongly favoring UMT, wanted UMT to be supervised and largely handled by groups other than professional military officers, and thus never gave wholehearted support to the UMT plan proposed by the Army.

The Citizens Committee and a Women's National Committee for Universal Military Training set up local chapters in big cities across the country, sent out press releases, and distributed leaflets. Among the officers and members of the Women's Committee were Mrs. Winthrop W. Aldrich, Mrs. Vincent Astor, Mrs. E. Roland Harriman, Mrs. Robert P. Patterson, Mrs. Archibald Roosevelt, Mrs. Kermit Roosevelt.

Long before the campaign for universal military training moved into full stride, opponents of peacetime conscription were also organizing. One group formed as early as 1942 began as a Committee to Oppose Conscription of Women. It was led by Mildred Scott Olmsted, a Philadelphia Quaker. Another group, the National Council Against Conscription Now, was started in 1943 by the Post War World Council, in which Norman Thomas and Oswald Garrison Villard were active. It was headed by Dr. Alonzo Myers of New York University and eventually merged with a third group, called the National Council Against Conscription, which was organized in the height of the campaign, in the fall of 1945, by two staff members of the American Friends Service Committee. The NCAC was led by Mordecai Johnson, President of Howard University, with Dr. Walter Sykes and Carlyle Adams as co-directors.

But the most active group was an informal cooperative or joint staff provided by a number of peace and pacifist organizations, including the American Friends Service Committee, the Church of the Brethren, the Fellowship of Reconciliation, the Friends Committee on National Legislation, the National Council for Prevention of War, and the Women's International League for Peace and Freedom. This joint staff began functioning in November, 1944.

The American Friends Service Committee, in addition, hired a special staff which included a minister to work with church groups, former labor organizers to visit unions, former officials of farm organizations to work with farm groups, as well as additional persons in education and other fields. These men, functioning under the overall direction of Ray Newton, the secretary of the Peace Section of the Friends Service Committee, encouraged national and regional organizations throughout the United States to take a position against UMT and to educate their members.

One staff member assigned by the Fellowship of Reconciliation was the present writer, who served as editor of *Conscription News,* which became the regular weekly organ of the anti-conscription forces and ultimately the coordinating center of the movement. Although it was not intended to be an impartial paper, it sought to present the news both for and against conscription on the assumption that opponents needed to be fully informed on all developments. With each issue of *Conscription News* there was a separate "action sheet" which outlined the strategy and tactics of the campaign and called for weekly action. The influence of *Conscription News* reached beyond its maximum circulation of 7,500, since thousands of additional copies of particular issues were ordered for use by various cooperating church, farm, labor and education groups.

Neither the American Friends Service Committee nor the Fellowship of Reconciliation engaged in legislative work. E. Raymond Wilson of the Friends Committee on National Legislation served as a legislative liaison with the legislative staffs of the church, farm, labor, and education groups on record against UMT, and also organized the opposition testimony in the many public hearings before Congress. Frieda Lazarus of the War Resisters League compiled a record of the attitudes of Congressmen on UMT, while Dorothy Detzer and subsequently her successor Annalee Stewart of the Women's International League and Albion Beveridge of the National Council for Prevention of War engaged in lobbying.

It was these peace groups on the one hand and the Army-Legion combination on the other who provided over a period of eight years the leadership for the most dramatic struggle in civil-military relationships in American history. Both groups were acutely aware that the real issue was civil versus military control of the postwar society, and that peacetime conscription had larger implications than the immediate claims officially made in its behalf.

CHAPTER 3

THE END OF WORLD WAR II

During the closing months of World War II, the Army had a tremendous advantage in its campaign for UMT. Few organizations or individuals were prepared to take a stand against peacetime conscription as such: to many it seemed almost unpatriotic to take such a stand while the war was being fought. It was, however, much more possible to speak against hasty action during the heat of war. "Wait 'til the war is over" was an attractive argument. Except for the American Legion and the army, few groups were willing to do otherwise than wait.

Indeed, many groups were on record for delay in consideration of UMT. A joint statement in March, 1944 by committees of the American Council on Education and the National Education Association and the American Association of School Administrators asserted that "until the postwar national situation is clarified, it seems to us extremely unwise and even dangerous to commit the nation to such a revolutionary change in fundamental national policy."

Several other influential groups also went on record for delay in 1944. The General Conference of the Methodist Church (May 6), the National Congress of Parents and Teachers (May 25), the Northern Baptist Convention (May 26), the General Assembly of the Presbyterian Church, USA (May 30) and the United Council of Church Women (June 16) all took action to ask Congress to delay until after the war any action on the question of compulsory military training. By autumn, other groups, including the National Commission on Christian Higher Education of the Association of American Colleges, the Federal Council of Churches and the Roman Catholic Bishops, had also opposed immediate enactment of a permanent compulsory military training program.

Several newspapers of influence spoke similarly. "Midway in the heat and exertion of the greatest war in history," said the Boston *Globe* on November 20, 1944, "is scarcely the time for making such momentous decisions and shaping them intelligently." The Louisville *Courier Journal* advised its readers: "We are inclined to agree . . . with the organizations which have . . . counselled a cautious policy . . . There is no hurry now."

The major wartime strategy of the anti-conscription campaign was therefore to capitalize on such pronouncements, to urge postponement of all action on UMT until after the war was ended.

As the joint campaign of the peace movements began to pick up momentum in 1945, opponents of postwar conscription had a central place to get up-to-date information and assistance in developing opposition to UMT on state and local levels. Stimulation from this central source, together with the direct work of the American Friends Service Committee with various groups, resulted in a steady stream of resolutions against conscription from a wide variety of organizations. Farm groups, as well as the Catholic War Veterans, the National Council of Labor Union Legionnaires, and some local Legion posts, declared themselves opposed to universal military training. When the war ended the newly-formed American Veterans Committee took a similar stand. In time almost every major church, farm, labor and educational organization in the United States had taken action opposing UMT. (So numerous were the actions against UMT that in 1947 a booklet containing the major statements which had been gathered by the Friends Committee on National Legislation numbered 236 pages.)

But military and Legion pressures forced Congressional leaders to think in terms of early consideration for postwar UMT measures, and on January 3, 1945, Chairman Andrew J. May (D., Ky.) of the House Military Affairs Committee introduced a bill requiring a year of military training for all males at eighteen years of age, or within four years thereafter. The bill provided that after a year of training in the Army or Navy the men would be enrolled as reservists for six years, though not subject to further training except in an emergency declared by Congress.

Shortly thereafter, President Roosevelt, in his first message to the Seventy-ninth Congress on January 6, called for the establishment of a United Nations Organization and then said: "I am clear in my own mind that as an essential factor in the maintenance of peace in the future we must have universal military training after this war and I shall send a special message to the Congress on this subject."

The military, however, were not content with pushing UMT; they wanted control over a much wider group. As a result of their insistence, President Roosevelt on January 6, 1945 also asked Congress for a draft of nurses and a draft of labor. He justified his position by quoting a joint letter from the Secretaries of War and the Navy dated January 3 which had the "support" of Gen. George C. Marshall and Adm. E. J. King. The letter called for "total mobilization of our manpower by the passage of a national war service law" and asserted that "the recognition by law of the duty of every citizen to do his or her part in winning the war, will give complete assurance that the need for war equipment will be filled." The President also asked that "Congress immediately enact legislation" to draft for labor purposes "the 5,000,000 men now classified as 4F" who by virtue of physical or other defects were not qualified for military service.

Representative May, a loyal supporter of the Army's General Staff, accordingly introduced a "work or fight" bill which would include all males between the ages of eighteen and forty-five. Those inducted could be assigned to special service units and could be put, under military discipline, into jobs in war production plants. May then announced that hearings would begin on his bill January 10 in the hope of completing them within two days and getting early action on the floor.

The Army's drive for a labor draft had two unexpected results. The first was a postponement of congressional action on UMT. On January 10 Chairman Clifton A. Woodrum (D., Va.), announced that hearings on peacetime UMT scheduled before his Select Committee on Post War Military Policy would be postponed in order to concentrate full attention on compulsory labor legislation.

The second unexpected result of the request for a labor draft was the subsequent support by organized labor of all efforts against conscription, including universal military training.

Labor and also industry opposed a labor draft. William Green, President of the American Federation of Labor, said that "free labor is more efficient and productive than slave labor." The Congress of Industrial Organizations also opposed the proposal. The National Association of Manufacturers joined the opposition to the labor draft, blaming the army for last-minute schedule changes and asserting that "an overall view discloses that war production in general is up to or ahead of schedule." The situations where production was lagging, they said, could "be corrected only by specific treatment and . . . general statements of policy do not contribute to their correction."

Actually there was no production shortage and the Army General Staff knew it. Donald Nelson, head of the War Production Board, later revealed the Army's technique in connecting its own supply and logistics problems in Europe with labor and industry at home:

> The Army's technique was to go into great detail about shortages at the front . . . then, in the same breath, to draw attention to the fact that war production programs at home were behind schedule. No one would ever say actually that there was a direct connection between the two facts, but the inference was there, and the attempt to have the people believe that the connection existed was certainly made. But the record shows that in not a single instance, after the critical early period of 1942, did an American fighting man at the front have to go without munitions because of any failure in production. Front line shortages in the summer of 1944 were a question of logistics, and were not due to production shortages. The Army's deliberate attempt to create a contrary impression was one of the most dangerous bits of double talk I ever heard of.[1]

The Army conducted what Nelson called "a very intensive campaign" to create the impression that a labor draft was needed. This was not a minor propaganda effort designed to blame Army mistakes in supply on some scapegoat; it was, Nelson felt, plainly and simply an effort to get control of the nation's economy.

The chief non-governmental support for a labor draft came from old friends of the Army who had been active in the Plattsburg camps and who were also supporting UMT. Grenville Clark, who had been active in these movements, was chairman of the Citizens Committee for a National War Service Act, and Ernesta Barlow was chairman of the Women's Division.

The joint anti-conscription staff and other executives of the peace organizations involved in the campaign against UMT were quick to act on the Army's proposal for a labor draft and a nurses' draft. Their vigorous opposition not only prolonged consideration of those measures, thus aiding in delaying consideration of UMT, but it also helped cement ties with some key labor leaders. Labor groups became much more conscious of the threat of peacetime conscription, since its proponents also sought labor conscription and its opponents fought any labor draft.

In January, shortly after a labor draft had been proposed, a Michigan Labor Committee Against Peacetime Conscription was formed by a group of CIO leaders. Victor Reuther, assistant director of the War Policy Division of the UAW-CIO, was named president of the committee, and Barney Hopkins, secretary-treasurer of the Michigan CIO Industrial Union Council, was named secretary-treasurer of the Committee. Officers of this committee and other CIO leaders signed a statement against UMT which said: "We are convinced from the records of the Congressional sponsors of this proposed legislation and of many of its public sponsors, that one of its unstated purposes is to regiment our youth on a mass basis for use as a military strike-breaking, union-busting force." [2]

In late January the United Automobile Workers-CIO announced its intention to campaign actively against the adoption of peacetime conscription. Other unions also became active. H.

W. Brown, president of the International Association of Machinists (AFL) wrote in the February *Machinist's Monthly Journal:* "I urge every local and district lodge, individual members, mothers and wives to each write to your national lawmakers in your respective states and demand they oppose any form of compulsory training after the war."

In spite of such opposition, the House passed the May labor draft bill February 1 by a vote of 245 to 165. The House-approved bill placed the penalties on the employees who left a war job or refused to take one. The Senate, however, passed 63 to 16 a bill which imposed penalties on employers who violated the ceilings on workers imposed by the War Manpower Commission. A House-Senate conference committee bill, which was a compromise of the two bills, was defeated April 3 in the Senate by a vote of 46 to 29, thus laying the labor draft issue to rest.

When President Roosevelt called for a nurses' draft, he spoke of a need for 18,000 additional nurses in the Army and 2,000 in the Navy. In response to his plea, the House on March 7 passed a nurses' draft bill by a vote of 347 to 42. In the Senate both the chairman, Elbert D. Thomas (D., Utah) and the next-ranking Democratic member, Edwin C. Johnson, of the Senate Military Affairs Committee, refused to press for enactment of nurses' draft legislation. They not only doubted that there was a great shortage of nurses but they also feared that a nurses' draft was an entering wedge for a draft of women.

By April 1, 1945 the Navy Nurse Corps quota was filled, and the Army quota was gradually being met. Figures demonstrating that there were available 2,000 male nurses, 1,500 Negro nurses, 1,438 Cadet Corps nurses and nurses from other sources were placed in the hands of Senator Johnson and other Senators by Mrs. Alexander Stewart of the Women's Committee to Oppose Conscription. From this point on the nurses' draft had no chance of passage, and the Army in a letter to the Senate Military Affairs Committee on May 26 withdrew its demand. These figures discovered by the peace group's joint anti-conscription staff, together with the campaign they directed, not only gave prestige to their work but built morale among conscription opponents throughout the country. If conscription of labor and nurses could be demonstrated to be either unnecessary or unwise in the heat of war when the War Department termed such legislation essential, postwar conscription, they felt, might also be prevented.

One further result of the Army's effort to conscript labor and nurses was the resentment against the Army felt not only by organized labor but also by Congressmen and others. The *San Francisco Chronicle* of January 9, 1945 spoke to this mood: "There is the more reason to fear rule by the military because it is known that in Army and Navy alike there is a group of officers, some of them highly placed, who believe this country needs discipline for discipline's sake alone."

Phelps Adams, in the February 5 *New York Sun,* reported "resentment toward the legislative activities of the Army" when it was learned that "men on the fighting fronts have been told that unless" the labor draft is passed "they cannot hope for replacements necessary to give them respite for the battle." Some Senators thus felt coerced into voting for labor conscription "as a means of bolstering service morale."

The *Portland Oregonian,* in a strong criticism of the Army's conduct, asserted on February 8 that the "War Department has gone entirely outside of its proper field of activity" in calling for a labor draft.

In spite of the resentment against the Army and its defeat in the effort to get a labor draft, military efforts to control the economy continued. In an article entitled "The Army Takes Over," which appeared in the May, 1945 *Harper's Magazine,* John Fisher asserted that "During the early months of this year, the military finally succeeded in seizing possession of most of the machinery which controls the nation's economy." The Army had succeeded in one way or another in getting rid of most of the civilian administrators who were directing war production. They "either surrendered or fled the field," he said.

After the defeat of the labor and nurses' draft bills, the House Select Committee on Post War Military Policy, in response to pressure from the American Legion, scheduled public hearings on universal military training from June 4 to June 16, 1945. The hearings were intended to present an impressive military case to the public. But in fact their major significance lay in the parade of witnesses against conscription. An overwhelming majority of the non-governmental witnesses either opposed UMT or favored delaying its consideration.

The proponents of postwar conscription included Colonel Jay Cooke, director of the Citizens Committee for Military Training of Young Men, Inc.; Mrs. Ernesta Barlow of the Women's Committee for Universal Military Training; Dunlap C. Clark, chairman of the United States Chamber of Commerce National Defense Committee; Carl McIntyre of the small American Council of Churches; and spokesmen for the American Legion and Veterans of Foreign Wars.

The Committee either heard the testimony of leading generals or admirals or encouraged them to send letters to be incorporated in the record. General Dwight D. Eisenhower was among those writing in favor of postwar compulsory training. No letter from any high-ranking officer was introduced in opposition to post-war UMT, but the absence of a letter from General Douglas MacArthur led to inquiries and subsequent reports that he had refused to endorse peacetime conscription.[8]

Among the groups testifying against universal military training were the Federal Council of Churches, the National Catholic Welfare Conference, the Rabbinical Assembly of America, the National Grange, the National Farmers Union, the American Federation of Labor, the Congress of Industrial Organizations, the National Parent Teachers Association, the Catholic War Veterans, the American Council on Education, the National Association for the Advancement of Colored People, and a number of other church, education and labor groups. Josephus Daniels, World War I Secretary of the Navy and editor of the Raleigh, N. C. *News and Observer*, appeared as an individual opponent.

The Woodrum Committee on July 5, 1945, by a vote of 16 of its 22 members, recommended "as a matter of broad policy" the adoption of a system of universal military training, but did not specify the details of such a policy. Three members of the committee, L. C. Arends (R., Ill.), A. L. Bulwinkle (D., N.C.), and M. J. Bradley (D., Pa.) urged postponement of legislation until postwar defense needs were known and until the men in the armed forces were home and able to express their opinion. Representatives Leo Allen (R., Ill.) and Dewey Short (R., Mo.) were undecided; one member, Harry R. Sheppard (D., Calif.) was absent.[4] Chairman Andrew J. May of the House Military Affairs Committee then announced that his committee would take up the matter of specific legislation as soon as the House returned from its summer recess.

During the 1945 summer recess the war with Japan ended. Opponents of UMT were immediately confronted with the need for a new strategy to replace their earlier one of "Wait 'til the war is over." Their new emphasis, which had been carefully worked out as early as May, 1945, was built around the formation of the United Nations and the hopes of millions that the world might be organized for peace rather than for war.

At a meeting of executives of peace organizations on May 14, 1945, Dorothy Detzer of the Women's International League for Peace and Freedom had proposed as a serious legislative alternative to UMT a resolution calling for the international abolition of conscription. With the approval of the group Miss Detzer encouraged Representative Joseph Martin, the House Republican leader, to introduce such a resolution. His resolution, introduced on July 17, 1945, called upon the President and other United States leaders "to work unceasingly for an immediate international agreement whereby compulsory military service shall be wholly eliminated from the policies and practices of all nations." The resolution asked that this be done "before the United States adopts compulsory military service." *The New York Times,* which was editorially in favor of the immediate passage of compulsory military training, assailed the resolution, saying that "the first effect of the Martin resolution would be to postpone consideration of universal military training in this country."

Administration leaders, including leading proponents in the House of Representatives, attacked the Martin proposal as "unworkable," but Republicans rallied to its support, declaring: "It's just as practical as the peace agreements reached at the San Francisco Conference." Martin, himself, pointed to more than 1000 letters and telegrams he had received by August 1 favoring his plan. Only 22 had opposed it.

The choice of Joseph Martin as the one to be asked to introduce the resolution was a happy one, for it was an important step in the direction of preventing Republican support for universal military training. If UMT had received bi-partisan support there would have been little chance of defeating it. Not long after Martin's introduction of the resolution, Leslie Arends, the Republican whip and a member of the House Military Affairs Committee, endorsed the resolution, By February, 1946, Martin's support had grown to the point where the *Washington Post* referred to it as a Republican effort to side-track universal military training.

CHAPTER 4

CONSCRIPTION EXTENDS INTO PEACETIME

On August 7, 1945, one day after the dropping of the first atomic bomb, Edwin C. Johnson, the ranking member of the Senate Military Affairs Committee, said: "The atomic bomb ought to blow up peacetime conscription as well as bring the war with Japan to a speedy conclusion." The decision to drop the atom bomb was a brutal one, but at first glance it seemed that such atomic power spelled the end of the armies built on masses of men and indicated a return to smaller and more select groups of highly trained volunteers.

Yet in spite of the atom bomb and the ending of the war President Truman in a letter to the House and Senate Military Affairs Committees on August 27, 1945 asked Congress for a peacetime draft for an indefinite period of men eighteen to twenty-five years old. He gave as the reason for this request the need for replacement of overseas veterans.

Anti-conscription forces quickly spoke to this issue. *Conscription News* charged that the army wanted to continue drafting teen-age boys to accustom the country to peacetime conscription. It pointed to an Army announcement that it intended to discharge by July 1, 1946 about 6,050,000 men out of a total of 8,050,000, thus leaving an army of 2,000,000. It also pointed to the controversy between the War Department and General MacArthur: Army leaders who were advocating conscription insisted that 830,000 men should occupy Japan, whereas MacArthur stated that only 400,000 to 500,000 troops would be needed.[1] On September 17 MacArthur announced in Tokyo that "the occupation force would probably be cut to 200,000 Regular Army men within six months." His use of the term

"Regular Army men" was generally interpreted as indicating he did not want a conscript army. He even declared that within six months all drafted men in the Pacific area could be sent back, and, on October 11, he announced that by the end of March, 1946 he would need only about 60,000 combat troops in Japan and not more than 200,000 for both Japan and Korea.

Further doubt about the need for conscription was raised by a September 21, 1945 Associated Press dispatch from Berlin which stated: "Generally, officials look for the United States occupation army, already scheduled to be reduced to fewer than 400,000 men by Spring, to be a mere token force of a few thousand, a year hence." Meanwhile, Congressional opposition to extension of the wartime draft beyond its May, 1946 expiration date resulted in the passage of a bill to encourage voluntary enlistments, which President Truman signed on October 6, 1945.

General George C. Marshall, who was aware of the mounting opposition to continuing the wartime draft, revived the campaign for universal military training by emphasizing it in his biennial report as Chief of Staff released on October 10, 1945.

On the day the report was issued, Marshall's Navy counterpart, Admiral Chester Nimitz, was asked at a press interview in New York City if he favored universal military training. At first he said, "No," but after a hurried consultation with an aide, he qualified his negative answer to apply only to the Navy.

President Truman in an address to a joint session of Congress on October 23, 1945 again asked for a compulsory military training law. He proposed a year of military training for the physically fit. Those not fit for military service would be trained in other skills "so that if war came they could take their places in shipyards, munitions factories and similar industrial plants." At the end of the year's training each trainee "would become a member of the General Reserve for a period of six years."

Within two days after the President's appeal, Chairman Andrew J. May of the House Military Affairs Committee announced that public hearings on the proposal would begin on November 8.

The opposition to the Truman proposal was immediately evident. Just one day after his address the National Board of the United Council of Church Women, meeting in Washington, voted to oppose compulsory military training. The Machinists' Executive Council blasted the proposal. "There is a sinister implication in the idea of military supervision of training of youth for jobs in industrial plants, shipyards, and munitions factories," the Council said.

Roman Catholic Archbishop Richard J. Cushing of Boston on October 28, 1945 declared that compulsory military training "would mean the end of the American way of life," and on November 2 Cardinal Dougherty, Archbishop of Philadelphia, stated that "future national security does not require universal military training."

On November 8, the first day of the public hearings on UMT, there was a revolt against committee leadership, led by Dewey Short, a key Republican member, which blocked hearings until November 13. Short and others wanted to wait until the Senate acted. They recalled that the Senate by not passing the labor draft and the nurses draft had left many House members with a pro-conscription stigma without the consolation of having supported successful legislation.

When the hearings resumed it soon became apparent that the Veterans of Foreign Wars, the Regular Veterans Association, and the American Legion were not supporting the army's plan for UMT. Each group had its own private plan and all were hesitant to turn boys over to a year's supervision by Regular Army officers. The National Guard spokesman favored a year of training but thought the Legion proposal of only four months Army training preferable to that of the War Department because it provided for an additional period of training in the Guard. General E. A. Evans, the executive secretary of the Reserve Officers Association, showed a similar suspicion of the army by indicating that the American Legion plan "embodies the principles we feel are essential."

The opponents of UMT represented the large education, labor, and religious organizations as well as some veterans and peace groups. There were so many opponents that representatives of many influential groups were denied an opportunity to be heard. All attempts to get a hearing for the Martin bill for the international abolition of conscription were equally unsuccessful. Dorothy Detzer said to the Committee: "What we are asking for . . . is the substitution of a constructive alternative to the measure that is before you. We are asking that, before action is taken on this pending bill, you take up the Martin resolution which is in this committee."

Martin, in a letter to Chairman May, also called for public hearings "on the Resolution, unless you have already concluded it is so eminently right that you can report it without a hearing."

During the hearings a group of Congressmen on the committee who had earlier favored postponing action on UMT persisted in seeking delay. They stressed the wisdom of waiting until after January 1 because the "President is engaged in discussions with Prime Minister Atlee concerning the atomic bomb . . . " They felt that "the details of the President's negotiations and the possibilities of universal agreement" might "make the draft unnecessary."

Partly in response to this pressure from within the committee, and the heavy flow of letters from UMT opponents to the chairman and other Congressmen, the hearings were recessed on December 19. That same day President Truman in a message to Congress asked for passage of UMT "at the earliest possible moment." He said: "A grave responsibility will rest upon the Congress if it continues to delay this most important and urgent measure."

The President then turned to the people and on January 3, 1946 appealed to them to ask Congress to enact his legislative program including UMT.

In spite of Presidential pressure, generally attributed to the unusual influence General Marshall had with Mr. Truman, the House Committee did not give its approval to the pending UMT bill. Instead, Chairman May yielded to the pressures of organizations opposing UMT who had not previously had a chance to testify against the bill. He reopened hearings in mid-

February and also permitted testimony from Representative Joseph Martin and others who favored the international abolition of conscription. That the Martin resolution had created a serious problem for the Army's UMT program was evident from President Truman's statement on February 21 that he was opposed even to attempting to get an international agreement to abolish conscription. A few days later Hanson Baldwin, the *New York Times* military writer who was trained at the U.S. Naval Academy, wrote: "The Martin resolution deserves enthusiastic support."

When the hearings ended the Committee was sufficiently divided that it failed to report to the House either the Martin resolution or a bill for universal military training. The Army, temporarily frustrated in its effort to get a permanent peacetime conscription program, asked the Committee for a renewal of Selective Service.

As the Army began its drive for draft extension, Congress was already being faced with mounting pressures for demobilization. Soldiers overseas were complaining that Army leaders were holding up demobilization as a means of pressure to get soldier support of UMT. In a front-page article in the January 16, 1946 *New York Times,* 400 enlisted men at an Army Air Forces depot in Germany were reported as having cabled their opposition to the Army's demobilization policy. Stating that Army policy was designed as "pressure" to win support for UMT, they urged that the Regular Army be unhampered by drafted men but made attractive to volunteers of all intelligence levels. In charging the Army with pressure tactics the men said: "All of the recent War Department announcements are seemingly aimed to arouse public opinion via the soldier resentment to push through legislation calling for compulsory peacetime military training . . . " They added that "such tactics, with possible resultant actions and decisions, are neither the true expression or desire of the enlisted men here."

In reporting the story, the *Times* pointed out that "The entire enlisted strength of the depot unit apparently joined in sending the message" which was more than 1,600 words and cost more than $100 to send.

One Washington newsletter reported that "The G.I. demonstrations around the world created a profound impression in Washington and Congress . . . " The newsletter added that "On one of the many pairs of baby shoes sent to the House Committee was this tag: 'We are all worn out waiting for my daddy to come home.' " [2] Part of the pressures on Congress had come from parents who received letters from the War Department stating that their sons could not be demobilized unless Congress extended the draft. Some of them had assumed that this also meant UMT.

In March, 1946, Secretary of State James Byrnes and Secretary of War Robert Patterson asked the House Military Affairs Committee to extend the draft which was due to expire in two more months. The announced basis for their plea was the Soviet refusal to pull its troops out of Iran in accordance with allied agreements. The State Department, in support of the request for draft extension, issued a report that Russian troops were moving into Iran in the direction of Teheran and also toward the Turkish border. Other stories designed to foster a mood of crisis followed. On May 17, 1946 the nation's press reported that Byrnes asked compulsory military training as a "warning to aggressor nations." On March 22 Byrnes warned that the "world situation" justified draft extension. On April 7 President Truman was reported as asking a draft "to prevent conflict in the Middle East." On April 9 the House Military Affairs Committee reported its approval of draft extension.

Only a few newspaper correspondents revealed the true picture. Frederick Kuh of the *Chicago Sun* reported March 16 from London that "British authorities have admitted there is no evidence whatever indicating that Red Army forces have moved beyond the Soviet Area in Iran." From Iran came denials of any increase of Russian troops in the country. C. L. Sulzberger, in a *New York Times* story written from Berlin on March 21, said: "Certain diplomats believe that this crisis may have been delib-

erately seized upon by the United States Government to crystal-
lize public opinion . . . " Mr. Sulzberger added,

> . . . the momentum of pro-Soviet feeling worked up during
> the war to support the Grand Alliance had continued too
> heavily after the armistice. This made it difficult for the Ad-
> ministration to carry out the stiffer diplomatic policy required
> now. For that reason, these observers believe, a campaign was
> worked up to attain a better psychological balance of public
> opinion to permit the Government to adopt a "harder line."

Although the Soviet Union and Iran agreed on the withdrawal of Russian troops before the House and Senate were able
to act on the proposal for draft extension, Army spokesmen continued to press for it. Their request for draft renewal was not
based on actual need, though some military spokesmen such as
Maj. Gen. Lewis B. Hershey asserted that the ending of the draft
would seriously affect recruiting because enlistments were almost
entirely from those liable to military service. But the Adjutant
General of the Army, Maj. Gen. Edward Witsell, revealed that
81.3% of all recruits were veterans and hence not liable under
the draft.

The Navy director of recruiting indicated, "We do not need
the draft either now or in the future to recruit for the peacetime
Navy," and added that current Navy enlistments were not caused
by the threat of the draft.

Even Army statistics presented something less than a case.
General Eisenhower told the House Military Affairs Committee
on March 21, 1946 that the army would be short 165,000 men
on July 1, 1947 if the draft were not renewed, but on April 3
General Textor presented another set of figures showing that
the Army would be short only 51,000 men on July 1, 1947.[3]

A reluctant House, hesitating to buck the Army, passed a
nine-months draft extension, but only after the bill had been
amended to eliminate the drafting of teen-age boys and to suspend
all inductions from May 15 to October 15, 1946, in order to
give voluntary enlistments a real chance. One significant factor
in the House vote was an "Analysis of Army Figures if Draft is

not Extended" which conscription foes made available to each lawmaker. Using only official Army figures, the anti-conscription staff demonstrated that the Army would have on a volunteer basis more than the number it said it would need on July 1, 1947.

Conscription proponents were alarmed. The Citizens Committee for Military Training of Young Men, Inc. sent telegrams to supporters throughout the nation stating that "there will be no chance of favorable action by the Congress on a Universal Military Training Bill if the draft is not extended." Their supporters were urged to concentrate on their Senators asking extension of the draft "for 12 months without crippling amendments."

An uncertain Senate tried to buy time for longer consideration by passing a six weeks stop-gap draft extension, but the House refused to cooperate without inserting its own amendments. Even President Truman got into the act by demanding a labor draft so that striking workers could be drafted.

The draft extension was finally passed after a coalition of Senate Republicans and New Deal Democrats by a 70 to 13 vote knocked out the labor draft. Various amendments eliminated fathers and boys of eighteen from the draft and held the extension to less than a year.

The draft extension was never needed. The Army tried to make use of it in order to demonstrate need but had to violate the law in doing so. There was a provision in the law forbidding the Army to issue a draft call if enlistments during the preceding three months were sufficient to keep the Army at its authorized strength. In order to issue draft calls for September and October, 1946 the Army ordered the discharge of about 300,000 men six months before the expiration of their enlistment term and then indicated it needed to draft men as replacements.[4] The public revelation of this did not help the Army's case. Thereafter the Army announced the cancellation of all draft calls for the rest of the year.

While the armed forces were working for peacetime conscription they were also expanding their program in the nation's schools and colleges. Between January and September 1946, 121 new Reserve Officer Training Corps (ROTC) units had been set up by the Army. The Navy also expanded its program through the Holloway Plan by which a maximum of 14,000 students in fifty-two colleges and universities would receive full tuition, fees, books, laboratory expenses, travel expenses and an additional retainer pay of $600 a year while in Naval ROTC.

Students in Army ROTC units were not paid so well. The Army, however, decided that after six months in Army camps boys could as an alternative to further Army training or service enroll for four years in an Army ROTC unit in some college. On the surface this seemed like just another way students could work off their military training if UMT were adopted. Practically, it would force the nation's colleges to install ROTC units if they wanted male students.

Dr. Francis Brown of the American Council on Education called this Army proposal "insidious" when he attacked the Army's UMT proposal November 30, 1946 at a conference of educators. "It is an admission that it is not the military skills that are important but the indoctrination of attitudes," he said. "And even more, it enlisted the cooperation of established educational institutions in the indoctrination . . . " Dr. Brown pointed out that "no comparable plan has been devised to identify, much less subsidize, capable youth for education, for leadership in our social, economic or political life."

The military also moved to control scientific research in the nation's schools. *Business Week* of September 14, 1946 summarized the problem:

> Partly by design, partly by default, federal support of pure science is today almost completely under military control. Its general direction is being set by military needs; its finances are coming from military funds. The odds are getting better all the time that pure scientific research will become permanently a branch of the military establishment.

It was not only a desire to penetrate educational institutions that led the Army to propose a new UMT program. It believed that it could also win the support of the American Legion, the

National Guard and the Reserve Officers Association if it modi-
field its earlier one-year program to provide for six months training in Army camps and the equivalent of another six months in
other military activity such as National Guard drills or Reserve
Officers training in college for four years. Secretary of War Patterson described it to the Legion Convention on October 2, 1946,
but on October 4 the Legion responded by reaffirming support
of its own plan which limited training in Army camps to four
months.

The Army nevertheless decided to press forward with its
new program. It even decided to abandon any further fight to
extend Selective Service in order to concentrate on its campaign
to get UMT — and indeed the draft did lapse, in March 1947.
President Truman in support of the Army's decision asked Congress for UMT in his State of the Union message on January 6,
1947. A day earlier he appointed as Secretary of State General
George C. Marshall, the nation's leading advocate of universal
military training. The *Army and Navy Bulletin* on November
24, 1945 indicated that President Truman was considering
General Marshall as his personal Chief of Staff because he "is the
leading sponsor of universal military training." One Washington columnist spoke of the influence Marshall had over Truman.
"Some of Truman's own civilian advisers are complaining that
General Marshall can overrun them on almost any issue. They
point out that twice — on the atomic bomb and on military
training — Truman has accepted the general's view against
strenuous cabinet opposition." [5]

Marshall's whole conviction about peace had been summarized in his report to the nation as Chief of Staff in 1945. After
expressing his doubt that peace was possible he wrote: "We must
enforce our will for peace with strength . . . " He added,
"What then must we do to remain strong?" and his answer in the
atomic age was George Washington's "program for the peacetime
training of a citizen army."

It was not surprising, therefore, that in his first major
policy statement as Secretary of State, General Marshall called
for the adoption of universal military training. Marshall per-

sistently used his new office to promote UMT. On March 17, 1947 Senator Elbert D. Thomas, former chairman of the Senate Military Affairs Committee, described to a meeting of Methodist ministers at American University some of Marshall's activity on behalf of UMT. He reported that at a recent conference designed to brief members of the Senate Foreign Relations Committee on world problems General Marshall had spent three-fourths of his time asking for Universal Military Training and won over a majority of the Committee.[6]

Shortly after Secretary Marshall made his February 7 appeal for UMT, the Army made public its offer to the House Military Affairs Committee to cut the Regular Army to 875,000 if Congress approved UMT. *Conscription News* was quick to point out that in November, 1945 Secretary of War Patterson had offered to cut the Army to 500,000 if it got UMT, and that the Army Chief of Staff, General Eisenhower, had in July 1946 told the same committee the Army needed only about 800,000 men. Thus, said the anti-conscription newsletter, "The Army is offering the House Committee something that it expects will happen whether or not universal military training is passed."

The fall of 1946 had been a crucial period in the anti-conscription movement. The peace organizations who had contributed the services of the joint anti-conscription staff could scarcely afford to have their executives devote a major part of their time to UMT when there were other important problems such as those relating to the United Nations, atomic energy and disarmament which needed attention. In addition, the only group organized specifically to deal with conscription problems, the National Council Against Conscription, had been unable to raise enough money for staff salaries and soon lost the services of Carlyle Adams, its director. In June, 1946, the co-director, Walter Sykes, also resigned. It was finally decided to merge the National Council Against Conscription with *Conscription News,* whose editor, this writer, would also become the Council's Director. The officers of the Council included the following: honorary chairmen: Dennis Cardinal Dougherty of the Roman

Catholic Archdiocese of Philadelphia; Dr. Harry Emerson Fosdick, pastor of Riverside Church, New York; President Frank Graham of the University of North Carolina; Chester H. Gray, former Master of the National Grange. Alonzo Myers, chairman of the Department of Higher Education of New York University, served as chairman and Richard Reuter, an executive of CARE, served as treasurer.

Except for strictly organizational matters, the real strategy decisions for the campaign against conscription were made informally in meetings where the representatives of the farm, church, labor, education and peace groups gathered on call. In this fashion the National Council Against Conscription became the formal vehicle for decisions which were frequently made by its staff or by staff members of other organizations. This reorganization of the anti-conscription forces in 1946 and 1947 thus paved the way for more effective resistance to the Army's new hard-hitting UMT campaign.

The National Council Against Conscription not only had to face the opposition of the Army and the American Legion, but also that of the Communist Party. During World War II the Communist Party and its various "front" groups favored universal military training. "We firmly believe with the President," said a February 8, 1945 *Daily Worker* editorial, "that a postwar world security policy must be accompanied by universal military training, and we think Congress should act on this at once." [7] The American Youth for Democracy, the successor to the Young Communist League, also endorsed UMT. Its national secretary, Carl Ross, favored universal military training "within the framework of a system of United Nations cooperation. That cooperation is directed against the re-emergence of Germany and Japan as aggressors . . . " [8]

In June and July, 1945, it became apparent that the Communist Party was preparing for a shift in its line on UMT. The first indication appeared during the hearings on universal training before the House Select Committee on Post War Military Policy. The American Youth for Democracy had asked for time to appear in favor of universal military training and was scheduled to appear on June 14, 1945. Although there had been no national convention or interim committee meeting which had changed its policy, American Youth for Democracy notified the House Committee that it had decided not to appear since it was no longer certain of its position on universal military training.[9]

The Communist change was further revealed on July 7, 1945, when a *Daily Worker* editorial agreed that there would have to be some method of military training after the war that did not exist before the war, but insisted that "there is . . . no need to rush the issue."

Finally on October 24, 1945, the *Daily Worker* announced that it was "opposed to President Truman's proposal of universal military training for all of America's young men." Instead, it urged a "policy of Big Three unity" claiming that "if President Truman were to return to this policy advocated by his great predecessor and stop using the atomic bludgeon of American military might, the fever chart of international relations would quickly subside."

A few months before that October 24 editorial, *Conscription News* warned its readers of the probability that "the Communists are preparing to change their party line" and suggested that "state and local committees and other groups opposed to peacetime conscription will be well advised to be on the lookout for the customary efforts of Communist or Communist front groups to form united fronts with organizations of the Communist Party."

The Youth Division of the Communist Party published leaflets and prepared "an outline on Universal Military Training which we recommend for discussion in all Party clubs, including the youth and student clubs." [10] The real effort of the Party, however, was made by united front groups in which Communists worked, or by attempts on the part of Communists to infiltrate non-Communist groups.

In early December, 1947, one of the officers of the United Christian Council for Democracy approached this writer in the office of the Fellowship of Reconciliation in New York to ask for the names and addresses and some type of introduction to the well-known persons who had worked with the National Council Against Conscription in opposing universal training. He mentioned the formation of a National Youth Assembly Against UMT and indicated that there were in it a number of persons who had worked with Communist front groups and who themselves were Communists. He hoped, however, to get enough others to work with it so as to take the Communist curse away from it. In the course of the discussion it was made clear that the National Council Against Conscription would not cooperate in any way with an organization influenced by Communists.

Nevertheless, the December 19, 1947 newsletter of the National Youth Assembly Against UMT listed the National Council Against Conscription as a source for further information on universal training. This led to a discussion in Washington in which individuals from the Grange, National Education Association, Friends Committee on National Legislation and others associated with the informal formulation of strategy against universal training met. It was agreed that members of the National Council Against Conscription and leaders of cooperating groups should be kept informed of Communist efforts and of the Council's opposition to any collaboration with united fronts.

At a subsequent meeting a representative from the Youth Assembly told A. J. Muste and this writer he was not opposed to universal military training in Russia and would not be opposed to it in a "socialist" America. Again it was made clear that the forces opposing conscription could not collaborate with those who favored building up Russian military strength while advocating a different policy for the United States.[11] Nevertheless the National Youth Assembly began to invite sponsors of the National Council Against Conscription to serve also as sponsors of the National Youth Assembly Against UMT. This development and plans announced to the press that the National Youth Assembly would hold a large conference in Washington February 15 and 16, 1948, led the National Council Against Conscription to issue a further warning to its sponsors, its local committees and its entire mailing list.[12] In response to this warning none of the sponsors or local committees supported the Youth Assembly.

A second result was the formation of a Youth Division of the National Council Against Conscription with William Leuchtenburg, executive secretary of Students for Democratic Action, as its national chairman. Leaders from the National Conference of Methodist Youth, the National Federation of Catholic College Students and Newman Clubs, the American Veterans Committee, the Student YMCA, Division of College Work of the Protestant Episcopal Church, Student League for Industrial Democracy, Young People's Socialist League, and a number of national religious youth organizations such as the Baptist, Presbyterian, and Congregational-Christian churches participated.

The warnings of the National Council Against Conscription were of value to a number of organizations whom the Communists sought to involve. For example, "the National Administrative Committee of AVC [American Veterans Committee] recommended early in January that AVC units refrain from any association with the National Youth Assembly Against UMT which the National Council Against Conscription charged was 'to all practical purposes a Communist-front group.' "

The National Youth Assembly held a public meeting February 15, 1948 but in its continuing activities found it extremely difficult to win any non-Communist support. The anti-conscription campaign was so effectively organized under the leadership of the National Council Against Conscription and so active that the Communists had nothing to offer in terms of competition. The National Youth Assembly soon passed out of existence. Thereafter, except for three abortive efforts to infiltrate youth groups in Boston, Philadelphia, and Los Angeles, the Communists largely avoided anti-conscription activity. On one or two occasions they did try to keep non-Communist national youth organizations, where their fellow travelers had gained a foothold, from cooperating with anti-conscription forces. During the rest of the UMT campaign the National Council Against Conscription was free to concentrate its energies on opposition to Army and Legion efforts to secure the adoption of a permanent system of universal military training.

CHAPTER 5

NEW PROGRAMS FOR PEACE AND WAR

The Army's postwar campaign for universal military training was a major one, made up of three programs. The first was a drive to win the support of many influential persons, especially leaders of national organizations. The Army, impressed with the way Congressmen had listened to organizational leaders who had opposed UMT, held a great many "off the record" meetings in the Pentagon for invited groups of educators, club leaders and others, so that they might be "sold" on UMT by Army generals. The *Army and Navy Journal* of February 1, 1946 in reporting such luncheons and conferences added: "Top level speakers have presented these programs in several cities and before diverse civilian groups. These tours have been supplemented by other Army speakers appearing throughout the country."

Such appearances were frequently initiated by the Army. Instead of waiting for invitations, the War Department asked requests to be issued for generals to speak to important civilian groups. In some cases officers appeared, uninvited, to work behind the scenes in an effort to get delegates to vote for a compulsory military training resolution.

When military men spoke at civilian conventions they captured the nation's newspaper headlines. But, in addition, Army public relations officers found other ways to keep UMT constantly before the public. The Railroad Brotherhood's paper, *Labor*, commenting on the Pentagon's "manufactured" flood of news, said on January 4, 1947, "Even old General Peyton C. March, the Army's boss during the First World War, was dragged out of retirement to speak as an 'elder military statesman' in favor of conscription."

A second program intended to "sell" UMT to Congress and the people was the appointment by President Truman on December 19, 1946 of a nine-member Advisory Commission on Universal Military Training. He charged it with the responsibility of "studying the basic need as well as various plans for universal military training . . . " Although the White House release implied that the Commission would make an impartial study, it was clear from the outset that with two exceptions members of the Commission were either close to the Army or had long records of public support of UMT.

The executive secretary of the Commission was John Ohly, the special assistant to the Secretary of War. Truman Gibson, the only Negro on the Commission, was a former aide to the Secretary of War. The religious leaders on the Commission were Dr. Daniel Poling and Father Edmund Walsh, both committed advocates of peacetime conscription. Dr. Karl Compton, the chairman of the Commission, had also been an outspoken advocate of UMT. Others on the Commission were Joseph E. Davies, Harold W. Dodds, Anna M. Rosenberg, Samuel I. Rosenman, and Charles E. Wilson.

The nation's leading Protestant periodical, *The Christian Century,* said of the Commission: "The kind of study in which such men will engage is not the open-minded examination of this question of great public importance which is needed and which their appointment as a Presidential Commission seems to portend." The *Journal* of the National Education Association said that the President "selected a fine and able group of men whose views were well known in advance to agree essentially with his own and that of the military hierarchy."

The Commission's report, which was made public in June, not only recommended compulsory military training, largely according to the War Department plan, but urged the nation to vote additional billions in military preparation for future war. The report was so clearly a recommendation for preparation for war that some newspapers featured it in that fashion. The June 2 *New York Daily News,* for example, carried banner headlines "Prepare for Atom War, U.S. Warned."

As soon as the report was made public, a critical analysis was made by this writer as director of the National Council Against Conscription. Twenty leading citizens joined in sponsoring the 28-page analysis including Senator Edwin C. Johnson of Colorado; Henry I. Harriman, past president of the U.S. Chamber of Commerce; Josephus Daniels, former Secretary of the Navy; Father William J. Millor, President of the University of Detroit; and Robert Hutchins, Chancellor of the University of Chicago. Other university presidents, Jewish, Protestant and Roman Catholic leaders, and spokesmen for farm and educational groups were among the sponsors. Practically every newspaper in the country carried a story about this "Analysis" and a number gave it front-page space. More than thirty thousand copies were purchased and distributed by such groups as the American Council on Education and the Presbyterian Church, U.S.A.

The prompt refutation of the Presidential Commission's report did not completely offset the gains for UMT which the report achieved, but it caused real doubt about the Army's role. From time to time cracks in the solid military front also cast doubt on the Army's motives. Brigadier General Merrit A. Edson, winner of the Congressional Medal of Honor, stated on June 14, 1947 that he was returning to civilian life because of what he called "the assumption of power" by the military in Washington. "Some people feel," he said, "that we will never properly organize the country until an overall top command completely controls everything." [1] Earlier, on May 7, Edson had testified before the Senate Committee on Armed Services, stating that "National emergency can be used time and time again to insist that the budget, the money, or the bills proposed by the armed forces are required in the defense of the nation; that unless they are passed our national security will be endangered."

The third major program in the Army's campaign was the establishment in January, 1947 at Fort Knox, Kentucky of a model or demonstration unit of universal military training. The first trainees who arrived at Fort Knox were told by Brig. Gen. John Devine: "It is our mission to demonstrate that military training as proposed by the War Department is beneficial to the youth of

the nation, as well as necessary to the security of the country."
One of the thirteen Army Public Relations officers stationed at the
unit later said: "We have one purpose — to sell Universal Military Training to the public."

This model unit had 664 boys aged seventeen to nineteen,
all of whom had volunteered for Army service. They were trained
by a force of 482 enlisted men, 75 officers and three warrant
officers who were hand-picked, the best the Regular Army could
offer. Good food, luxurious club facilities, girls whom the Army
brought from nearby towns for the post dances, the hobby shop
and educational program, all helped make this a different kind of
Army camp. The *Washington Star* said that "The Army is clearly
working under ideal rather than typical conditions."

Army publicity on the unit, extensively carried in magazines
and newspapers, portrayed the unit as different from an Army
camp. There was no swearing, no drinking, no immorality and
last, but not least, they said, the boys had better health, discipline,
education and religion than they could possibly get at home or in
civilian life. An Army pamphlet entitled "The Fort Knox Experiment" stressed the importance of accepting "the responsibility
for developing the 'whole' man" which meant "developing personality, character and mature manhood. The Army today is
the only organization in America equipped to conduct this kind
of efficient training of our citizenry."

In order to avoid unfavorable publicity the unit discharged
a number of boys who became ill, including two for reasons of
mental health, as well as anyone who committed a serious crime.
In this way the unit's health and morality record was kept high.

After the morale of the model UMT unit had been built up
to the point where the "trainees" did not swear or drink liquor
in public and were ready to deny participation in practices normal
to Army camps, the Army began a large-scale visitation program.
Letters like the following were sent over the signature of Robert
P. Patterson, Secretary of War, to leaders of influential organizations in labor, education, religion and other fields:

Dear ————— :
As you are doubtless aware, the Army Ground Forces have

organized a Universal Military Training Experimental Unit at Fort Knox, Kentucky to test the War Department plan for training on a national scale. This experiment has progressed far enough to make it possible to see how the system would work in training camps throughout the country if the plan as recommended to Congress should receive legislative sanction.

The War Department would like to have you or your representative visit Fort Knox in the near future and witness the operation of this Experimental Unit. Air transportation from Washington to Fort Knox and return will be provided by the War Department for this purpose if desired. An Army plane will be made available for your visit on May —, subject to your acceptance of this invitation. If this date should conflict with other engagements, and you will let me know when you could conveniently make the trip, I will try to fit it into our schedule. The trip would require two days. . . .

Please let me have your answer as soon as possible, and if you cannot go give me the name of the person who will represent you and your organization.

The Army's propaganda in connection with the Fort Knox unit and its many other approaches to the public were so effective that *Conscription News* began in early 1947 to call attention to the Army public relations budget which in the fiscal year 1946 amounted to $5,715,690, exclusive of pay and allowances of military personnel.

Readers of *Conscription News* were urged to ask members of the House Appropriations Committee "for elimination of, or at least drastic cuts" in the War Department's Public Relations budget. Shortly thereafter opponents of UMT were encouraged to "ask the Congressman to whom you write to tell you how much money the War Department wants for public relations activities. Ask why the War Department should be given money and personnel to propagandize the people for UMT."

The National Council Against Conscription then called for letters to Congress asking for an investigation of the Army's propaganda for universal training. It also asked selected individuals to write members of the House Committee on Executive Expenditures, the logical group to conduct such an investigation. *Conscription News* collected affidavits from listeners to radio programs and those attending meetings where Army leaders spoke, as well as documented other illustrations of military propaganda. Armed with a letter from a friendly member of the House Military Affairs Committee, the editor of *Conscription News* went to Fort Knox to gather information on the Experimental UMT Unit there. This information was published and became the basis for letters to the Committee. It was also presented to the Executive Expenditures Committee staff and to Representative Forest Harness (R., Ind.), chairman of the Committee's Subcommittee on Publicity and Propaganda.

In response to the many letters it received, the Harness Committee decided to hold public hearings on War Department propaganda. The Committee staff, led by Frank T. Bow, conducted its own investigation and discovered that General J. Lawton Collins, in speaking to a group of women invited to the Pentagon, had asked their support in winning the Republican leadership "to support a non-partisan national military security program" which included UMT.

The Committee also discovered that the War Department had employed civilians to travel around the country propagandizing for UMT. One of them, Mrs. Arthur Woods, not only told Girl Scouts and other women's groups of the "great spiritual benefits to be derived" from compulsory military training, but also planned the testimony that the Women's Committee for Universal Military Training would present to the President's Commission. The Harness Committee staff uncovered War Department office memoranda which included the following note from Mrs. Woods to Colonel Huntley: "Thought you would be interested in reading this account of the group of women Mrs. Barlow took before the President's Commission. The group was set up. Each was to cover a certain aspect as you suggested. I mapped it all out along those lines." [2]

The Committee discovered many other activities, especially in connection with the Fort Knox unit. Moving pictures of the Experimental Unit had been made and widely distributed at taxpayers' expense. The Committee also learned of the War Department's internal organization designed to get citizens to influence

Congress to vote the legislation the Army wanted. There was, for example, a Women's Interest Unit. The mailing list of the unit "contained more than 3,000 names and addresses of the leaders in women's activities in every section of the United States." In one bulletin sent to this list was the suggestion: "Your legislative committee can be asked for a report on the bill for universal military training which died with the Seventy-Ninth Congress."

A great deal of evidence presented during the hearings and discovered by the Committee staff made it obvious that the Army was trying to bend Congress to its will. The Committee's report to the House stated that "the War Department was using Government funds in an improper manner for propaganda activities supporting compulsory military training." [3]

The law which the Army had violated was quite specific. "No part of the money appropriated by any Act shall . . . be used directly or indirectly to pay for any personal services, advertisement, telegram, telephone, letter, printed or written matter or other device intended or designed to influence, in any manner, a member of Congress to favor or oppose by vote or otherwise any legislation or appropriation by Congress . . . "

The penalty for such influence was, among other things, removal from office of "any officer or employee of the United States" who "violated or attempted to violate this section . . . " [4]

Top Army officers were so uniformly involved in violating this law that it would have been extremely difficult to remove them from office without emasculating the entire military establishment. Two civilians hired to promote UMT resigned as a result of the investigation, and a Fort Knox publication, the *UMT Pioneer,* was reduced to 3,000 copies per issue. But aside from a few similar concessions to the Committee, the Army continued its propaganda drive. The fact of the investigation, however, was important because Congressmen became aware that at least a portion of their pro-UMT mail had been stimulated by the Army.

At the same time that the Harness Committee hearings were being held the House Armed Services Committee, which replaced the former Committees on Military Affairs and Naval Affairs, began new hearings on universal military training, now thought to be more urgent since the extended wartime draft law had been allowed to lapse in March. The Committee had given those favoring UMT a full hearing, but instead of hearing all the opponents, it bypassed many major organizations, permitting instead some smaller and less influential groups to appear in opposition. Then the hearings were peremptorily closed and the bill was reported out of committee.

Twenty members of the committee voted for the UMT bill. Thirteen members stayed away from the meeting at which the vote was taken because they wanted to protest Chairman Walter Andrews' (R., N.Y.) high-handedness in rushing action on the bill without any committee study.

Shortly after the Committee reported its bill, known as the Towe bill for its sponsor, Rep. Harry L. Towe (R., N.J.), Congress recessed for the rest of the year. During the recess an effort was made to get the American Legion and other veterans groups to engage in an all-out drive for UMT, since, for the first time, a bill sponsoring it had actually been reported out of committee and had a chance of coming to the floor of the House for a vote. Army leaders spoke to the Legion Convention, urging a drive for UMT. Representative Towe told the Legion that opponents of the bill "are going to raise a hell of a rumpus." He urged the Legion to inform the people of the country about the bill. The Legion's publicity director responded with an announcement of "an all-out UMT publicity campaign . . . designed to reach its climax when Congress reconvenes in January."

When the Legion announced its campaign, John Thomas Taylor, national legislative director, declared, " . . . it will be the most extensive and aggressive campaign in all Legion history." The Hearst Press, in reporting Taylor's statement, said: "Five million members of the American Legion and American Legion Auxiliary on December 1 will launch a smashing 'do or die' crusade to secure enactment of universal military training." The Hearst Press joined the Legion in seeking to collect 10,000,000 signatures to petitions, and facsimiles were reproduced in Hearst newspapers.

Nevertheless, the February 1948 American Veterans Committee *Bulletin* reported, "the high pressure American Legion campaign for passage of UMT was seen as falling flat . . . and prospects of defeating the compulsory training program seemed good." The *Bulletin* concluded by noting, "Some Congressmen report that the Legion campaign has had a negative effect since Congressmen who were led to expect a deluge of pro-UMT mail have been getting only a dribble."

Although the Army had sparked the Legion campaign, it was in no sense prepared to rely on the Legion's efforts. The Army had worked and hoped ever since 1945 for a program of compulsory military training, but each year something had happened to prevent its adoption. Selective Service had been terminated on March 31, 1947, and yet Congress had recessed in the summer of 1947 without adopting universal training. One Reserve officer, Colonel William Neblett, who had been a member of MacArthur's staff in the Southwest Pacific and later served on a high staff level at the Pentagon, described the military reaction to its failure:

> When the bill did not pass the Pentagon was thrown into complete confusion. . . . The Pentagon turned on the heat. The huge professional officers corps was converted into a propaganda organization the like of which the world had never seen. Generals and admirals, colonels and captains, spoke throughout the land at every meeting to which they could wangle an invitation. Reams of statements . . . for press and radio were ground out for them by the civilian publicity experts, employed at the Pentagon and the several hundreds of headquarters, camps, posts and stations . . . throughout the nation. The Pentagon line was that we were living in a state of undeclared emergency; that war with Russia was just around the corner, and that the safety of the nation was dependent on the speedy rebuilding of the lower ranks of Army, Navy, and Air with the Pentagon form of UMT.[5]

Colonel Neblett, who was National President of the Reserve Officers Association of the United States during 1947-1948, added: "I know from my own knowledge of the men who worked up the fear campaign that they do not believe what they say.

Their propaganda has always had the single objective to build a huge conscript professional military force of 10,000,000 men under the command of a professional General Staff."

As a result of the Pentagon buildup of an atmosphere of crisis, the Towe bill was an immediate issue when Congress convened in January, 1948. The bill, however, had to clear the powerful Rules Committee or be discharged from that committee by a petition signed by a majority of the House. The Republican chairman of the Rules Committee, Leo Allen (Ill.) and a majority of the committee were hostile to UMT and had no intention of sending the bill to the floor of the House for a vote. In the Senate the Republican leader, Robert Taft, had declared his opposition to the measure. His influence was also strong in the House, where another opponent of UMT, Joseph Martin, was serving as Speaker.

In spite of this formidable opposition, a number of Representatives began to circulate a discharge petition. The American Legion, which was in the midst of its UMT campaign, began a tactic of local pressure on selected members of the Rules Committee. In Indiana, for example, the Legion went after Forrest A. Harness. Harness had served as State Commander of the Legion and also as Commander of Kokomo Post 6. Post 6 wrote Harness asking him to change his vote in the Rules Committee and added "Your future activities in this matter will be watched closely by this post of more than 2,200 honorably discharged veterans."[6]

In order to counteract such pressure, the National Council Against Conscription not only tried to give a more balanced picture of the international scene but also called for letters to Congressmen asking that the Towe bill be recommitted so that the national organizations which were denied a hearing before the House Armed Services Committee might be heard. As a result the bill remained bottled up in committee.

While this particular fight over universal training was in the headlines, other issues were also being fought out in Congress.

Among them was the question of economic aid to Europe. Most of the organizations that were opposed to UMT were in favor of helping rebuild Europe. The Army was also in favor of aid to Europe but for different reasons. Moreover, the Army was putting pressure on Congress for such aid by means of the same crisis atmosphere it was using to secure the adoption of UMT. The Army reasoned that for the foreseeable future only Russia was capable of being a military adversary of the United States. In the event of conflict with the Soviet Union the Army wanted not only allies but also military bases on European soil from which to operate. But Europe had been so largely destroyed or exhausted in World War II that no military alliance seemed feasible without rehabilitation of the European economy. On this basis Army leaders felt that the Marshall Plan for aiding Europe was necessary if the Western European union or alliance which was to precede NATO had a chance to succeed.

One columnist pointed at the time to the fear held "by our foreign policy makers that the Western Europeans would seek to declare themselves neutral in event of war between the world's two giants." He described the "clamor in Britain, France and the Lowlands for a neutral status, similar to that enjoyed by Eire during the late war and against granting the United States bases should conflict occur." Finally he indicated that "by helping those countries to build up their economy, health, trade, and business and improve their living conditions, our policy makers believe a fighting spirit can be regained."[7]

Early in the 1948 session of Congress, military leaders put strong pressure on Congress and the people to approve General Marshall's plan for aiding Europe. Newspapers of January 15 and 16, 1948 carried headlines asserting: "Draft, Big Boost in Budget Hinted if Aid is Refused." The news story that followed this particular headline said:

Two top United States military leaders, Defense Secretary James Forrestal and Army Secretary Kenneth G. Royall, told Congress today that if the United States did not go through with the Marshall plan for European recovery, it would be forced to spend an equal or greater amount of money on military preparedness. Royall flatly told the House Foreign Affairs Committee that as he saw the choice it was virtually between the Marshall Plan and a return to Selective Service.[8]

By the beginning of March, however, the Army was linking the Marshall Plan and UMT as *both* necessary to defeat Communism. The United Press reported an effort "to make universal military training a 'companion measure' to the stop-Communism foreign aid program." In order to get some action on UMT in view of the House's refusal to bring it to the floor, General Marshall, Secretary Forrestal and others pressed the Senate Armed Services Committee to take action in the Senate. Military leaders were prepared to go before the Senate committee to discuss the need for UMT to back up the Marshall plan. The Army even went so far as to hand to President Truman an intelligence report which "pictured the Soviet Army as on the move" when "actually the Soviets were redistributing their troops to Spring stations . . . "[9]

The Hoover Commission, which in 1948 was, by Presidential direction, investigating the various departments of the executive branch of government, later said that this intelligence report "stimulated recommendations which if followed might well have had serious consequences," by which it presumably meant war.

President Truman, taking the intelligence report at face value, went before a joint emergency session of both Houses of Congress on March 17, 1948. In a crisis speech he asked for immediate passage of the things the Army and General Marshall as Secretary of State most wanted, the Marshall Plan, Universal Military Training, and in addition Selective Service which the Army felt it could also get in such a "crisis." President Truman and Congress could easily believe the Army's report because the Communist coup in Czechoslovakia had taken place just three weeks earlier. Although Russian soldiers had not actually invaded Czechoslovakia, Zorin, the Soviet deputy foreign minister, then in Prague, had dropped hints that the Red Army might back the Czech Communist Party. No political or military support seemed in the picture from the United States because

Churchill and Roosevelt at Teheran had agreed with Stalin that Czechoslovakia should be in the Soviet military sphere and American policy had not yet moved beyond such agreements.

Not long after the President's address to Congress, the Central Intelligence Agency evaluated the Army's report as false. On March 25, Secretary of the Army Kenneth Royall told the Senate Armed Services Committee that war was not imminent.[10] But neither the President nor military leaders told the people of the false report. Instead they continued to let the people believe that there was a state of continuing crisis. General Omar Bradley kept alive the idea of war with Russia by saying in late April that "we are not sure" that "there is no war right away." [11] Again in June he warned the nation that war with Russia is a "plausible possibility."

It was not until the *Chicago Tribune* on June 19, 1948 reported the "Inside Story of Phony Red War Scare" that the public had any access to what happened. Other newspapers evidently did not consider it news of importance. But later Hanson Baldwin, in the December 2, 1948 *New York Times,* spoke of the huge military program which Congress passed "on the heels of a war scare partially inspired in Washington where predictions were then being made that there would be 'war before the harvest.' "

In this atmosphere of crisis the House and Senate took steps to build up the National Military Establishment and increase the power of the military. In describing the situation the *United States News and World Report* on May 14, 1948 said:

> President Truman is somewhat disturbed by the way the idea of imminent war with Russia hangs on in the country even after the official line has changed from war scares to more emphasis upon the prospect of peace.
>
> Gen. Omar Bradley, Army Chief of Staff, was out of step with the Government's new policy when he expressed the opinion that war prospects had risen in recent days. Both at the White House and in the State Department there is a backing away from that attitude now that the Marshall Plan is law . . .
>
> War scares, encouraged by high officials only a few weeks

ago, so alarmed the 144,000,000 U.S. public that top planners
now are having to struggle hard to keep Congress from pouring
more money into national defense than the Joint Chiefs of
Staff regard as wise or necessary. It is proving more difficult
to turn off than to turn on a war psychology.

The Army's talk of war and its outspoken hostility toward
the Soviet Union during 1947 and 1948 were a cause rather
than a result of tension between the United States and Russia.
The Army's talk of war preceded the Czech *coup d'etat*, which
of course generated additional tensions. But there is ample evidence that the war scares were synthetic. For example when
Congress offered to increase the Air Force from a 48- to a 70-
group force instead of adopting UMT, President Truman and
Army leaders felt such an increase was unnecessary, thus con-
firming the analysis that they did not regard the Czech coup as
a forerunner of war with Russia.

It seems difficult in retrospect to believe that Congressmen,
who presumably should have been aware of the way in which
the war crisis was created, could be deceived as many of them
were. Some who knew of the problem were ready to use any
occasion to promote measures they personally favored. Others
were swept along with the general hysteria. Only on the UMT
issue was there any effort to hold the line, and this was due to
the unwavering public expression of opposition to it.

CHAPTER 6

THE RESUMPTION OF SELECTIVE SERVICE

The creation of a mood of international crisis was only one step in the Army's effort to sell peacetime conscription to Congress. The Army tried also to convince Congress that the Army and its reserves were unable to fill the ranks without conscription. It was of course difficult to demonstrate such a need because Congress had already provided for a postwar reserve establishment and voluntary recruiting had been running so high that the Selective Service law had already been allowed to lapse.

The Army's first decision was to weaken the reserves. Universal military training was designed to provide a reserve establishment; if the reserve force were adequate there would then be no need for it. The Army therefore had to decide to undercut its own reserve program. But in order to weaken its reserve force it had to violate the law. The Selective Service Act of 1940 provided that all World War II veterans should be transferred to some reserve component for ten years upon leaving active service in the regular forces. Instead of complying with the law the Army decided to discharge veterans and not place them in the reserves. Although this decision was made in the War Department, the Judge Advocate General concluded that the President had the authority under another act of Congress and this was the technical justification as reported to the House Armed Services Committee on April 22, 1948.

General Marshall was responsible for the decision that the National Guard and Reserves were to be reorganized and brought up to strength only after UMT was adopted. General Milton A. Reckord, president of the National Guard Association, told the House Armed Services Committee on April 22 that Marshall had directed that the planning for the reserve establishment and the Guard should be "based on the fact that Congress would give us UMT. . . . " Apparently Marshall assumed that Congress would simply do what he asked.

General Reckord, who was chairman of the Joint General Staff Committee studying the reserve problem, added that on that basis "we went ahead and set up the National Guard and the reserves . . . based on the fact that eventually we would get UMT with which to fill the Guard up to strength with men who had basic training."

General E. A. Evans, executive director of the Reserve Officers Association, testified in response to a question from Representative Dewey Short that "if the Army had done its duty and supported the Guard and the Reserves, having made a sincere, earnest, determined effort to build them up, we would not have this legislation [for UMT and Selective Service] here." General Evans also made quite clear his agreement with the statement that any "lack of defense has been brought on by the failure to develop the reserves."

These two generals also revealed that while the Navy had gone ahead with plans for its reserve program, the Army had not planned for constructing armories for the reserves nor done much in the way of providing equipment.

As of September 30, 1947 the Army had not given one reserve unit adequate equipment, although millions of rifles and other material were lying idle. Only 189,998 of the 509,255 reserve officers had been assigned to units and only 71,668 out of the 631,039 ex-soldiers who had signed up with the reserves had been given assignments. Nor had the Army even issued a directive on reserve training policies.[1]

The Army's second decision involved recruiting and the regular Army force. The Army wanted conscription not only for the reserves but for the Regular forces as well. Therefore, since volunteers were ample for the authorized strength, the Army pressed for an increase in the size of the Army after the false intelligence report had "justified" the need for such an increase. President Truman in January, 1948 had set the Army's strength at 560,000 men for the year beginning July 1, but in order to justify Selective Service the Secretary of Defense on March 25, one week after the Army had produced the synthetic war scare, announced that it needed 782,000 men for the coming year. The Navy and Air Force asked for more moderate increases but these two branches made it clear that they intended to rely on voluntary recruiting.

As early as 1947 when the Army saw that it might not get either UMT or Selective Service, it raised the passing grade for volunteers on the Army General Classification Test. During World War II the passing grade was 59. After the war it was raised to 70, but the Army continued to get all the volunteers it needed. It was then raised to 80. The *New York Times* reported that the Army recruiting chief indicated that as a result of raising the passing grade to 80 the Army had been turning down "about 50% of those who apply for enlistment." [2] The Army tried to make a case for an 80 grade because of the need for specialists, but General Eisenhower and others admitted in Congressional hearings that many jobs in the Army did not require persons with the education that a grade of 80 signified. Nevertheless, longshoremen, cooks, truck drivers, section hands and others all had to make an 80 grade.

The Army also did certain other things which kept volunteer enlistments low. Rep. Paul Shafer (R., Mich.), a member of the House Armed Services Committee, told the House on June 15, 1948 of a recruiting officer who was limited to only twelve recruits a month. Since he got these during the first week of each month he had nothing to do the rest of the month. The Army set a limit on the number of Negroes and Puerto Ricans who might enlist, as well. The quota set for Negroes, for example, was ten per cent of the Army's strength.

In addition to such devices the Army transferred uniformed personnel to civilian jobs. The *Washington Post* indicated that "Thousands of jobs such as hospital attendants, fire fighters, guards, skilled trades, and even typists and file clerks were filled by military men."

In spite of such devices, recruiting remained high. One

columnist reported in the April 7, 1948 *Washington Post* that "A sudden spurt in recruiting after the first of the year almost upset the Pentagon's plan to high-pressure Congress into a new draft act and universal training." He indicated that the monthly recruiting total "wasn't publicized" but recruiting for the Army ground forces hit "a postwar high, just a little short of its assigned goal."

The anti-conscription forces publicized the information about the Army's policy of weakening the reserves, raising educational standards and imposing racial quotas. But although they received some support in Congress, they were powerless to stem the tide set in motion by the false war scares.

These scares and the carefully built atmosphere of international crisis immediately preceded the opening of the public hearings on UMT in the Senate on March 17, 1948. A week later, as we have noted, Secretary of the Army Kenneth Royall assured the Senate Armed Services Committee that war was not imminent, but he did not dispel the sense of crisis nor indicate that the emergency measure of Selective Service was unnecessary. As a result of the mood of continuing emergency the public hearings were largely a formality. The bill which came out of committee provided both for a two-year term of Selective Service for those nineteen through twenty-five and also for a one-year term of compulsory military training for boys of eighteen.

The vote on this bill, however, was by no means unanimous. The committee was divided not only because two Senators opposed the compulsory training section, but because four Southern Senators, led by Richard Russell (D., Ga.) wanted to preserve racial segregation in the armed forces by providing an option for persons wishing to serve in units solely of their own race.

The problem of racial discrimination and segregation in the armed forces was a great source of trouble to those advocating universal military training. Some of the most vocal supporters of UMT in Congress were those most committed to the maintenance of segregation. In the Negro community on the other hand it was virtually impossible for anyone to support a compulsory military program that would continue the racial segregation experienced by so many Negroes in World War II.

In World War II Negro soldiers were humiliated, persecuted, lynched, and shot. At Fort Benning, Georgia on May 2, 1941 the body of a Negro private was found hanging from a tree, arms and legs bound. In Arkansas in August, 1941 Negro soldiers were slapped and otherwise attacked by white civilians. This led forty-three Negro soldiers to go A.W.O.L. from Prescott, Arkansas and return to their former station in Michigan. In Savannah, Georgia on June 10, 1942 Negro troops were forced to march behind garbage trucks at the tail end of the Army Day parade. There were many other glaring illustrations of hardship and abuse. But in some respects the most galling aspect of segregation was the experience of having to do menial jobs with little or no chance of advancement or change of status.

The wartime racial practice of the armed forces was actually a violation of the Selective Service Act of 1940 which stated: "In the selection and training of men under this act and in the interpretation and execution of the provisions of this act there shall be no discrimination against any person on account of race or color." But in October, 1940 President Roosevelt formally accepted the Army and Navy decision to continue their traditional discriminatory practices. In a release dated October 9 the White House indicated that except for three regiments all present and future Negro units would have white officers. "This policy," said the release, "has proven satisfactory over a long period of years, and . . . it is the opinion of the War Department that no experiments should be tried with the organizational set-up of these units at this critical time."

Negro leaders protested the Presidential approval of such segregation. President Roosevelt, who was unwilling to buck General Marshall and other top military figures, was facing re-election and needed the Negro vote. He tried to meet the issue by appointing three Negroes to high posts in the military organization. These appointments, however, didn't alter Negro resentment about segregation.

The resentment continued to mount so that in 1944 after the drive for UMT was underway, the National Association for the Advancement of Colored People came out against it. In December, 1944 an editorial in the N.A.A.C.P.'s periodical, *The Crisis*, stated: "We must not have this without a fight. *The Crisis* is opposed to compulsory military training for other reasons than its bolstering of segregation and its perpetuation of the discriminatory treatment of our men in uniform, but we are most opposed to it on the racial angle."

Again in January, 1945 *The Crisis* carried an editorial against UMT which asserted: "There is untold danger in this conscription bill and it should be fought with every weapon at the race's command."

Following World War II a halting step in the direction of modifying segregation in the armed forces was taken as a result of the Gillem Board report in November, 1945. This report, "The Utilization of Negro Manpower in the Postwar Army," led to a policy announced in 1946 that instead of having segregation in a large-scale unit, such as a division composed entirely of Negroes, there would be smaller all-Negro units grouped with white units in a division. The Gillem report also established a quota system for Negroes. Since about one-tenth of the nation's population was Negro the ratio of one Negro to ten whites would be maintained in the armed forces. In addition all personnel were to be given equal opportunity for promotion.

The recommendations of the board, headed by Lt. General A. C. Gillem, Jr., were so biased in the direction of maintaining the caste system that the report was thoroughly discredited in Negro circles.

An investigation in 1947 by the President's Committee on Civil Rights noted that Negroes "are faced by an absolute bar against enlistment in any branch of the Marine Corps other than the steward's branch . . . " The Committee reported that "almost 80 percent of the Negro sailors are serving as cooks, stewards and steward's mates . . . " In the Army, said the Committee, "less than one Negro in 70 is commissioned, while there is one white officer for approximately every seven white enlisted men. In the Navy there are only two Negro officers in a ratio of less than one to 10,000 Negro enlisted men," whereas "there are 58,571 white officers, or one for every seven enlisted whites."

The continued drive of Negro organizations to end segregation in the armed forces and the continued Army drive for compulsory military training of all males on a segregated basis seemed a natural opportunity for cooperation between Negro groups and opponents of UMT. If desegregation of the armed forces led segregationists in Congress to vote against UMT this would be a solid gain. In any event the staff and administrative committee of the National Council Against Conscription and other cooperating peace groups were opposed to segregation as well as to UMT. In the fall of 1947, the director of the National Council Against Conscription, in consultation with two Negroes active in the peace movement, Bayard Rustin and William Worthy, initiated discussion looking toward the formation of a Committee Against Jim Crow in Military Service and Training. The National Council Against Conscription would finance the organizing of the committee and give it every encouragement, but aside from suggestions on strategy the proposed committee would function on its own.

When the committee was started in November, 1947 it was called the Committee Against Discrimination in Military Service and Training. Grant Reynolds, a New York State Commissioner of Correction, served as chairman and A. Philip Randolph, president of the Brotherhood of Sleeping Car Porters, A. F. of L., was the treasurer. They announced on November 24, 1947, a campaign "to insure inclusion of equality amendments in pending legislation for universal training." They indicated they did not plan to go beyond this to deal with the problem of segregation in all of the armed forces.

When the Republican chairman of the House Armed Services Committee, Walter Andrews, indicated he was in favor of "limited segregation in keeping with Army policy," Grant Reynolds asserted: "If this is a representative sample of Republican thinking it is well that Negroes know it now. If compulsory military training is adopted without proper safeguards for Negroes, the Republican Party will alienate the Negro vote beyond recall." [3]

Soon thereafter, a delegation from the committee, which had changed its name to the Committee Against Jim Crow in Military Training and Service, called on Congressional leaders. Senator Robert Taft, Speaker Joseph Martin, and House Rules Committee chairman Leo Allen all pledged opposition to universal military training and support of any amendment "in that bill barring all racial distinctions."

The *New York Post's* "Washington Memo" on January 16, 1948 said that "continued discrimination against Negroes as a factor in American life is now threatening to reduce the already slim chances of approval of a system of universal military training."

President Truman, who was evidently aware of this problem, instructed Secretary of Defense Forrestal in early February, 1948, to eliminate racial and religious discrimination in the armed forces. But six days later, Secretary of the Army Kenneth Royall, a North Carolinian who had to work with key Southern members of the House and Senate Armed Services Committees, announced that after careful review, segregation of Negroes "was considered to be in the interest of national defense and both the staff and I feel that this is still the case."

Negro leaders were angered by such expressions of a continued segregation policy. One result was the announcement by A. Philip Randolph in a public hearing before the Senate Armed Services Committee that millions of Negroes would conduct a "civil disobedience protest" against any segregated universal military training. He indicated that he would "recommend that Negroes take no part in the Army."

Grant Reynolds, who was a former Army officer, told the same committee: "I personally will not re-enter a Jim Crow army if the age categories should include me." He demanded insertion into any universal military training or Selective Service bill of "very specific, unequivocal, anti-segregation and civil rights amendments."

A few months later, following a poll of 2,200 Negro college students on 26 campuses which revealed 71 percent to be in favor of civil disobedience, the National Association for the Advancement of Colored People announced that it would give legal aid to all civil disobedience resisters against any Jim Crow military program.

This controversy over segregation had a real influence on the UMT struggle. In spite of the stand by Secretary Royall, Southern Senators on the Armed Services Committee were worried by the thought that every boy under UMT might be trained in a desegregated army.

In May, 1948 Senator Richard Russell introduced an amendment which would preserve racial segregation in the armed forces by providing an option for persons wishing to serve in units solely of their own race. Other Southern Senators in the Armed Services Committee backed Russell and demanded a guarantee in the draft and UMT legislation pending in the committee that white boys would not be forced to serve with Negroes.

This "mutiny" by conscription supporters brought Secretary of Defense James Forrestal and Secretary of the Army Royall to the Capitol for a hurried conference. Forrestal tried to point out that an amendment giving drafted men the right to serve only with members of their own race would be "unworkable from an administrative point of view." Russell insisted and referred to the President's instruction to the Secretary of Defense "to take steps to have the remaining instances of discrimination in the armed services eliminated as quickly as possible." Forrestal said there was no reason to be alarmed. Royall added "I don't believe that was in the mind of the President. If such a provision is put into operation I will no longer be Secretary of the Army." [4]

When the vote was taken the Committee was divided. Four Senators backed the Russell amendment but seven others opposed it. Three of the four Southern Senators then simply voted "present" on the final bill. The *New York Times* of May 12, 1948 stated: "Another factor concededly behind the Russell move in Committee today was the recent starting of a 'civil disobedi-

ence movement' against the draft — a pledged refusal by either
Negroes or whites to serve in a 'Jim Crow army' even under a
selective draft system."

The Committee vote was only a hint of more moves to
follow. The Republican leaders, especially Senator Taft, who
had given a pledge to Negro leaders that they would support
amendments against segregation in any UMT bill, now entered
the picture. Before the debate began on the Senate floor, there
were behind-the-scenes maneuvers to enlist Democratic Party
support to kill UMT in return for no anti-segregation moves by
the Republicans, who controlled the Senate and its committee
structure.

On May 24, Chairman Chan Gurney (R., S.D.) of the
Senate Armed Services Committee, and a vigorous proponent of
universal military training, introduced an amendment to the
Senate bill killing the universal training proposal of a twelve-
month draft of eighteen-year-old boys. Gurney, who had en-
countered strong opposition to UMT in top Republican circles,
polled his committee, reaching eleven out of the thirteen members.
They too agreed to drop the UMT proposal.

Further proof of the effectiveness of the campaign against
racial segregation became evident in the course of the Senate
debate. Senator William Langer, a Republican who often broke
party ranks, introduced a series of amendments against racial
segregation at the suggestion of the Committee Against Jim Crow
in Military Training and Service. All but one of these was rejected. Senator Scott Lucas (D., Ill.), the minority whip,
according to the *New York Times* of June 8, accused the Republican leadership in effect of violating " 'a general agreement' that
Senator Langer's whole series of amendments would be knocked
out." Although the press did not reveal what the Democrats had
promised in return for the Republican agreement on the Langer
amendments, it was obvious to the careful observer, because the
Senate decided on June 14, without a dissenting vote, to eliminate
from the bill the new universal military training program for
eighteen-year-old boys.

Though the introduction of the racial issue into the Congressional discussions of UMT played an important part in the various decisions, there were two other factors that led the Senate to eliminate UMT. One was the attitude of the House. The House leadership had opposed both Selective Service and UMT and gave no signs of changing. The Senate Committee decision to drop UMT was, therefore, a move which the *New York Times* said "might bring the Senate and House into harmony and speed enactment of the draft at this late stage of the session."

A second factor was the opposition of Senate Republican leaders to UMT. In January, 1948 a Democrat, Edwin C. Johnson, took advantage of the President's Air Policy Commission Report to urge a larger Air Force instead of UMT. Senate Republican leaders such as William F. Knowland whose home state, California, had many aircraft industries, urged an emphasis on air power as an alternative to UMT. The Air Force, which had never been enthusiastic about UMT and had been giving lip service to it because the Army wanted it, was now in a mood to change its position. It finally did so when the President talked in terms of not going along with the expanded or 70-group Air Force. Secretary of the Air Force Stuart Symington "behind closed doors" told the Senate Armed Services Committee that a 70-group air force was more important than universal training. " 'It is true,' Symington continued, 'that we testified for universal military training. We did that before we knew the Air Force was going to be cut.' "

The Senate Republican Policy Committee approved a 70-group Air Force and was prepared to approve Selective Service if it was not tied to UMT. The Army program for universal military training was thus a victim of the divide and conquer strategy. Southern and Northern Senators were divided over the question of racial segregation in any such program, and the Air Force and Army were divided over the issue of concentrating on air power or a big army training program.

After the section on universal training had been deleted, the Selective Service bill passed the Senate on June 10 by a vote of seventy-eight to ten. In the House there was more opposition.

The House Rules Committee had earlier decided by a seven to five vote to keep the bill in committee. But Robert A. Taft, the Senate Republican leader, decided to put pressure on the House Republicans. Taft was a staunch opponent of UMT. His staff in the Senate majority leader's office regularly cooperated with the National Council Against Conscription staff in preparing and exchanging information. When Taft became the Senate majority leader after the election of a Republican Senate in 1948, his staff not only took the initiative in establishing contact with the National Council Against Conscription but made it clear that opposition to UMT was one of Taft's priorities. He also spoke against it in his campaign speeches throughout the country. But Taft was a politician who hoped to get the Republican nomination for President. If he rejected Selective Service and there were a genuine war crisis before his nomination or election it might hurt him politically. Perhaps it is more accurate to say that Taft too had been influenced by the war psychology carefully built up in the Pentagon.

Taft succeeded in "persuading" Speaker Joseph Martin, who was very reluctant to let either UMT or Selective Service become law. Martin in turn put pressure on the Rules Committee, which on June 14 by a six to four vote released the bill to the House floor.

In a stormy debate with frequent parliamentary threats to suspend rules, the House on June 16, 1948 voted 156 to 88 to reduce the period of military service from two years to one and voted 145 to 38 that final responsibility for drafting men should rest with the President. The House voted another amendment which indicated how well the anti-conscription forces had educated Congressmen about the Army's efforts to make the voluntary system ineffective. That amendment provided that inductions should be delayed until January 31, 1949 and, in the meantime, the Army had to initiate a whole-hearted volunteer enlistment program permitting two-year original enlistments and one- or two-year reenlistments, with monthly reports on recruiting methods and progress being made to a special Congressional committee.

The House approved the Selective Service bill by a vote of 283 to 130, and because it differed from the Senate bill, sent it to a Senate House conference committee. Usually House members of such a committee are picked so as to get the best possible bargain from the Senate members. But Speaker Joseph Martin picked a committee that, with one exception, Dewey Short, would agree with the Senate bill. Short pointed this out on the floor, stating, "My hands are tied. There are six against one."

The bill that became law on June 24, 1948, was largely the Senate bill. It was to expire in two years instead of the five originally proposed, and the draft term was to be twenty-one months instead of two years. In this way there was fastened on the nation a peacetime conscription program that has steadily been renewed from June, 1948 to the present time.

THE ARMY NEVER GIVES UP

In spite of the Congressional rejection of universal military training, the Army decided to try again. When Congress convened in January, 1949, President Truman in his State of the Union message backed the Army position by asking again for UMT. The American Legion was again prepared to do battle for it but decided that the name had been a handicap and the program should thereafter be referred to as "National Security Training."

One reason for the Army's new push for UMT was its fear that Selective Service might not be renewed in 1950 and there would be no conscription law of any kind. The *Washington Star* reported on January 20, 1949 that "The present draft law may never be used again if enlistments continue high enough to keep the Army at its present strength." The *Star* indicated that Secretary of Defense Forrestal had "said the armed forces on December 31 had reached the full quota set by President Truman as his goal for the year ending June 30, 1950, which also is the date the draft law dies."

A favorable recruiting picture did not, however, lead to abandonment of the draft. Instead it led the General Staff to find ways of reducing enlistments. The Army even ordered recruiting officers as early as October 1, 1948 to stop accepting first enlistments by men with dependents. The Army also decided to curtail volunteering by ending two-year enlistments. Hereafter, said a January 13, 1949 Associated Press dispatch from Washington, "only three-year volunteers will be accepted." In addition, the Army raised its physical standards and decided to accept only men scoring 90 or above on the mental test. To cap it all, it proposed a reduced advertising budget for recruiting for the next fiscal year amounting to a drop of more than two million dollars. Still other measures were taken by Army directives which the *New York Times* said were expected to "cut re-enlistments and new enlistments, both of which have been running at high levels."

Well before the Army made its appeal for draft renewal it released stories to the press indicating that enlistments had declined. A typical news report was the statement in the June 18, 1949 *Washington Daily News* that the Army had dropped below its authorized strength and that therefore "drafting for the Army may start again this fall."

In an effort to make the Army more palatable the military public relations staff began to tell the people of reforms that had resulted in a "New Army." These reforms were, according to the publicists, designed to convince people, especially those in the churches, that the Army was really a character-building agency and that a draft term would be a spiritual experience.

One California reporter lampooned the Army's effort to improve its public image. In describing the induction ceremonies at a nearby Army camp the reporter described the new religion program:

> A rough old Army sergeant stood out in front of his young men and said: "General says he wants you all to go to church. So you are going, see! Any atheists in the house?" Nobody raised a hand. "Okeh, that's good. Cause any of you guys would have to listen to an hour lecture on religion — by me." That was new Army.[1]

In addition to the "New Army" public relations program, the General Staff decided to ask Congress for an army of 837,000. Since this was a substantially larger army than the one then authorized, there would be no assurance that it could be raised by the volunteer method.

While the Army was laying its plans for renewal of the draft, it was also actively involved in laying the groundwork for a Western European military alliance which had become a political possibility when the Marshall Plan had been adopted. Well before Congress had given any green light for a military alliance the Anglo-American Joint Chiefs of Staff had planned for the standardization of military equipment and training for fifteen European countries as a step in the direction of an alliance. Thereafter, the American military gradually worked to encourage a Western European Union and finally a North Atlantic military alliance.

Many questions were raised about the proposed alliance. It "draws the lines more clearly for the contest between East and West," asserted a *New York Times* reporter. Others insisted it would result in countermoves by the Soviet Union, or lead to the eventual rearmament of Germany or weaken the United Nations.

In terms of its effect on the growing power of the American military three things were clear. The Alliance would give the Defense Department a greater voice in the molding of American foreign policy. It would require a larger army if American bases were set up throughout Europe and if American troops were to garrison these bases. It would also require more foreign military aid and involve the military more directly in American economic policy.

In April, 1949, after initial U.S. success in promoting the alliance, eight European Pact nations appealed to the United States for financial and military assistance to back up the military alliance. European leaders also asked that the number of American troops on the European continent be increased.

Months later, in January, 1950 when the Secretary of Defense, Louis Johnson, presented the case for renewal of the Selective Service Act, he said: "Failure on our part to extend the Act might seriously undermine the position of the military establishments of other signers to the North Atlantic Pact who are maintaining mandatory national service over considerable opposition within their countries." In various ways thereafter, military leaders on both sides of the Atlantic reinforced military expansion in their respective countries.

The Army used other arguments for draft renewal, pointing

out that Selective Service would be needed for mobilization if, as General Lawton Collins put it, Washington should be attacked "with possible disruption of government processes . . . " General Hershey objected to a proposal that Congress might adopt Selective Service in principle but retain the authority to determine when men might actually be drafted. Hershey said, "I'm not so sure we're going to have orderly government in a war emergency."

The chief military argument for the draft was the international scene. In spite of press reports from Moscow and elsewhere that there was no evidence of a Russian military buildup for war, American military leaders continued to talk about war. A Navy plane exploring Soviet coastal defenses in the Baltic area was shot down by the Russians. On May 3, 1950, General Omar Bradley told the House Armed Services Committee that "the shooting down of an American plane" together with other items such as the Russian demand that the Western Powers withdraw from Trieste, the "continued trouble in Indo-China," and in Bulgaria and Hungary, indicated that the situation was worse in recent months. On May 4 Secretary of Defense Louis Johnson, Army Secretary Frank D. Pace, Jr., George F. Kennan of the State Department, and all members of the Joint Chiefs of Staff met with the Committee in secret session. That same day, under such pressure and with talk of war, the Committee unanimously voted to extend the draft for another two years. President Truman, however, refuted the war scare. According to a report in the May 4 *Washington Times Herald* he said that "the cold war situation is improving, that he sees no prospect of armed conflict in the near future, and is optimistic about peace." One member of the House Armed Services Committee, W. Sterling Cole (R., N.Y.) said: "If Mr. Truman had made his statement prior to the Committee meeting this morning more than one member would have voted against the draft extension."

Under military pressure the House then approved a bill extending the registration and classification features of Selective Service for two years but so strong was the opposition to peacetime conscription that the bill forbade inductions without the consent of Congress. Because the Senate bill provided for three years extension of the draft, a compromise was necessary. The final bill which the President signed simply renewed the draft for a year and a few days.

Just three days before he signed the draft renewal bill, President Truman on June 27 ordered General MacArthur to aid South Korea in defending itself against North Korean invading troops. The resulting Korean War made possible a further drive for military power. General Marshall, who had resigned as Secretary of State in 1948, came back to Washington as Secretary of Defense. The very day he took this position, September 21, 1950, he appealed for a universal military training law and set in motion a new drive in its behalf.

In the course of the new campaign for UMT, Army leaders felt they had a chance, during the heat of war, of getting a more drastic conscription program than they had earlier thought was possible. They therefore demanded both compulsory training and a period of 27 months of compulsory service, to be followed by eight years in the reserves. Even the physically unfit would be drafted "to fill the military and civilian needs of the nation, including civil defense." The bill which the Army submitted to the Senate Armed Services Committee on January 17, 1951 had no termination date and was designed as a permanent peacetime law. It was so drawn as to permit the drafting of persons for defense jobs or other necessary work. A group of labor leaders including Philip Murray and John L. Lewis tried on February 1, 1951 to get a clear statement from Defense Mobilizer Charles E. Wilson that he was not thinking of drafting labor. Wilson refused. "He would give no assurance that it wouldn't come to the point . . . where the government directs labor in and out of jobs." [2]

The bill also authorized the President to remove from the armed forces after their initial basic training 75,000 persons who would be selected by government agencies "to engage in study or research in medicine, the sciences, engineering, the humanities and other fields determined by him to be in the national interest." Thereafter such persons would be re-ordered into the armed forces unless they performed an equivalent of twenty-seven months of military or civilian service in the national interest. In this way military influence would be extended into education, government service, research and other fields.

General Marshall and the Army had gauged the temper of the country well. Many groups who had earlier opposed peacetime conscription did not continue their opposition during the Korean War. Both the National Catholic Welfare Conference and the National Council of Churches failed to testify at the public hearings on the bill. The major labor groups opposed making the bill permanent but did not oppose it as such. The American Council of Education, under the influence of its new president, Arthur S. Adams, a formal naval officer, endorsed the bill even though Council members had "reservations regarding certain provisions . . . "

The chief opposition to universal training came from the National Grange, the National Farmers Union, the Methodist, Baptist, Presbyterian and smaller Protestant groups. This opposition was not able to convince the Senate, which by a vote of seventy-nine to five approved the bill. The Senate had previously defeated sixty-eight to twenty a move led by Senators Edwin C. Johnson and John W. Bricker to eliminate UMT from the bill.

Opponents of UMT had much more influence in the House. There was so much opposition there that Chairman Vinson of the House Armed Services Committee barely got the bill out of committee with the UMT feature in it. When debate began in the House, Vinson was faced with a Republican-Democratic coalition led by Dewey Short and Graham Barden (D., N.C.), who aimed at eliminating UMT. Speaker Sam Rayburn, in an unusual procedure, took the floor to warn members of "terrible danger" facing the nation. He implied that Russian troops were massing in Manchuria and that a third world war might be near.

In spite of Rayburn's pleas the opposition coalition held firm. Vinson, in order to avoid defeat, proposed an amendment that would require specific approval of a detailed plan for universal training before it could be put into effect. "Thus," said the *New York Times,* "the UMT battle would have to be fought again in Congress before the proposed long range training program could be activated."

The House approved the amended bill by a vote of 372 to 44. In the Senate-House compromise the draft term became twenty-four months instead of twenty-seven, and the draft was to be terminated on July 1, 1955 instead of being of indefinite duration as the Army had asked. The final bill also provided for the establishment of a National Security Training Commission of three civilians and two military men who were asked to submit recommendations for a UMT program to Congress, following which Congress would again vote on UMT.

When the National Security Training Commission, of which former Senator James W. Wadsworth was chairman, re- ported to Congress on October 29, 1951 it called for the passage of UMT for the purpose of building the reserves. But it also recommended that persons with poor eyesight and body deformi- ties "which did not prevent their following a 'useful vocation in civil life' " should be given military training in spite of the fact that they would not be useful in the reserves. Theological students and others who would be deferred in the event of war would also be forced to take military training. "The theory be- hind this proposal, with which we do not disagree," said the Commission, "is that a period of military training for every young man is of intrinsic benefit to the nation, even if a percentage of those trained cannot qualify for the reserve." [3]

Opponents of UMT promptly charged that "psychological indoctrination with its result of regimented thinking is one of [its] major purposes." [4]

During the next public hearings in the House it was evident that a number of education groups on record against UMT were not going to testify before the Committee. Under pressure from the Teamsters Union, the A. F. of L. supported UMT provided that it have a terminal date. James Carey of the Congress of In- dustrial Organizations, on the other hand, said, "My organization

believes that the enactment of this bill . . . would be a tragedy."
He added, "Frankly, some of us feel that this kind of loose talk
about UMT as a morale and character builder almost smacks of
a military cult."

The chief opposition continued to come from the farm
groups and the Protestant social action groups. Every Protestant
denomination except the Episcopal Church was on record against
UMT and many were militantly opposed to it. The Roman
Catholic Bishops with the one exception of Cardinal Spellman,
who broke ranks in the synthetic war crisis of 1948, were opposed
to UMT but were far less vocal about it in 1952 than they had
been during the forties. Among Roman Catholic groups the
Jesuits were its most consistent and vigorous opponents.

Following the public hearings, the House Armed Services
Committee approved a detailed UMT program by a vote of twenty-
seven to seven. The vote was taken in closed session, but the
New York Times revealed that the seven opposing votes were all
cast by Republicans under the leadership of Dewey Short.[5]

In the crucial month of February, 1952, a number of things
happened which made it difficult to predict whether the House
would accept or reject UMT. Informal polls of Congressmen
revealed a majority who were personally in favor of it. At a
House Republican conference on February 25 Representative
Sterling Cole presented arguments in favor of the bill, while
Dewey Short presented the case against it. At the conclusion,
"Representative Joseph Martin . . . said that sentiment appeared to be about evenly divided and that it obviously was
impossible to make a party issue on the bill."

Graham Barden who in 1951 had opposed UMT, had in
the meantime told Raymond Wilson and Annalee Stewart that
he was no longer certain that he would oppose such legislation
when it came up again. But on February 17, 1952, not quite
two weeks before the House debate began, he attended an American Forum of the Air debate on universal military training which
was televised and broadcast from the Wardman Park hotel in
Washington where the Bardens were living. The Forum speakers

were Lt. Gen. Raymond S. McLain, Maj. Gen. Lewis B. Hershey, E. Raymond Wilson, and this writer. When the debate was over Mr. Barden told this writer that he had been thoroughly convinced that the opponents had the sounder case and that the generals, especially General Hershey, had resorted to humorous parries instead of facts when challenged in the course of the debate. Barden then asked this writer to spend the following Tuesday in his office discussing all angles of the UMT problem. Following this session Mr. Barden began talking to various Democratic Congressmen, especially those from the South. He estimated that about seventy Democrats to whom he had spoken would vote to recommit the bill.

On March 2, 1952, two days before the debate began, the Associated Press indicated that forty votes might hold the key to universal military training.

When the UMT bill was brought into the Committee of the Whole in the House, opponents of the measure followed a secret but carefully planned strategy. Included in this strategy was a highly interesting parliamentary maneuver. Representative William H. Bates (R., Mass.), a veteran of nine years in the Navy, moved to strike out the enacting clause. If this had prevailed the bill would have been shelved automatically. Speaker Sam Rayburn, however, left the Speaker's desk to come down into the well of the House to plead with Administration forces not to kill UMT in this fashion. Following his plea there were enough votes to defeat the motion, 196 to 167, and, judging from appearances, to win in the final vote.

Chairman Vinson of the House Armed Services Committee was nevertheless uncertain of winning and offered a motion he had refused to accept in his committee. His amendment would have terminated universal military training on July 1, 1958, and would have forbidden its application at any time the Selective Service system was actually drafting men for military service. Although denounced by opponents as a trick to get the bill through the House so the Senate could revise it as the Army wanted, the amendment was easily passed 126 to 9.

Omar Burleson (D., Tex.) proposed as a substitute that

military training be offered in the colleges. This was amended
by Charles Brownson (R., Ind.) who, according to plan, proposed
a measure acceptable to the American Legion but not to the
Army. It provided for training in the last two years of high school
with two six-week periods of summer camp for gunnery and
other items not easily taught in school. The Committee of the
Whole by a vote of 133 to 128 adopted the Brownson amendment and then by a vote of 150 to 145 substituted it for the
Army bill.

Under House rules, when a substitute was adopted, the
Committee of the Whole would rise and report its action to the
House for a record vote. On the roll call a number of opponents
who, as a matter of strategy, had voted in the Committee of the
Whole for the Brownson substitute switched sides and defeated
it by a vote of 255 to 155.

The House then had before it the original or unamended
universal military training bill as it had come from the Pentagon,
since the Committee of the Whole had not approved the amendments of the Committee on Armed Services. The House, thus
having before it the bill in its least acceptable form, approved
Dewey Short's motion to recommit the bill for further study. The
bill was sent back to committee by a vote of 236 to 162.

Among the eighty-one Democrats who followed the strong
lead of Representative Graham Barden, instead of Speaker Rayburn or Carl Vinson, were forty-two from the South. Without
these votes the bill would not have been recommitted. Behind
the scenes Barden had quietly organized this group. By agreement, when he spoke vigorously against the bill no one of those
prepared to vote with him applauded, although tremendous applause came from the Republican side. Their strategy was to
keep the Speaker and other party leaders from learning their
position in advance, since they would otherwise have had strong
pressure exerted upon them. Army lobbyists were circulating in
the corridors and the Administration looked upon universal military training as "must" legislation.

Prior to the House vote the *Des Moines Register* said: "The
opponents of UMT are so vigorous, determined and emotional

that they've convinced many members of Congress that when they go to the polls they actually will vote to oust any member who votes for the bill."

The recommittal of the bill to the House Armed Services Committee killed UMT. Chairman Carl Vinson said he would not ask his committee to consider the question again during that session of Congress. As a result the Senate Armed Services Committee decided not to press for action on the bill it had reported to the Senate.

That UMT was in fact dead for a time became evident when the House in April voted to strike out of the military appropriations bill the $75,000 earmarked for maintaining the National Security Training Commission. The Senate, however, restored the appropriation and a compromise figure of $37,500 for the fiscal year 1953 was approved by both Houses.

The reaction of the Pentagon and the White House to the new defeat of UMT was very strong. General Lewis B. Hershey proposed that the armed forces launch a universal military training program without authorization from Congress. He said such a program could be set up under the authority of the draft law then in effect. Nothing came of the Hershey proposal. After all, the Army would have another chance in the new Congress if, as seemed likely, General Eisenhower could get the Republican nomination for President and then be elected.

THE ARMY NEVER LOSES

General Dwight D. Eisenhower, who had willingly supported the Army line on UMT, was nominated for the Presidency in the summer of 1952. His chief rival for the Republican nomination was Senator Robert A. Taft, a strong opponent of UMT. Most of the other leading Republicans were also opponents of it. Something of the mood of the Republican Convention was reflected in the tremendous applause given former President Herbert Hoover when he vigorously assailed UMT in his address.

In the light of such Republican commitments, Eisenhower did not immediately endorse UMT. It was widely rumored at the time that when Eisenhower and Senator Taft composed their differences after the nomination the former agreed for the time being not to press for universal military training. In the course of his campaign and while the Korean War was being fought, General Eisenhower stated that "so long as we are forced to employ the draft, because of actual combat requirements we cannot at the same time establish any form of training for our young men." The press in reporting this interpreted it as a move in Taft's direction. "Tonight," said the September 26 *New York Daily News,* "he aligned himself directly with Senator Taft's arguments against UMT."

During Eisenhower's first year as President, however, he reconstituted the National Security Training Commission and instructed it to begin work immediately so as to report to the President by December 1, 1953. The Commission, as had been expected, recommended UMT, calling for six months of comulsory training followed by seven and one-half years in the reserves. The Army wanted a longer period of military training and service but the American Legion and the National Guard backed the Commission plan. The compromise which President Eisenhower sent to Congress included extension of the draft law under which men would serve a two-year term, followed by six years in the reserves. It also authorized the Army to enroll volunteers for six months of basic training, after which they would be transferred to a National Guard or Organized Reserve unit. They would then attend weekly drills and summer camps for a period of seven and one-half years. Failure to comply would lead to re-induction in the Regular Army for another eighteen months.

By this legislation the Army hoped on a semi-volunteer basis to secure a program that would eventually include every boy at the age of 18. The legislation as drawn actually provided for a "national security training corps" as one of the groups to which young men could be assigned.

In the course of Committee consideration, Dewey Short's amendment to remove any reference to UMT and to strike out the national security training corps was adopted by an eighteen to thirteen vote. When the measure went before the House on May 17, 1955, Dewey Short called it a move to "get a foot in the door" for universal military training. He said he was sorry to turn his back on his President, but contended that "the six-month plan to give youths a chance to escape the two-year draft" was comparable to offering an Ozark jackass an ear of corn in order to get the critter close enough to slip a halter over his head.

The Eisenhower recommendation, which also included a compulsory reserve, was sidetracked in the House by an amendment which would have barred personnel from being assigned to military units where segregation was enforced. Since the National Guard in the South does not admit Negroes this would have changed Southern policy. When Carl Vinson could not rescue the bill by a further amendment, he moved that the House cease consideration of it. It was then laid on the Speaker's table.

In the meantime President Eisenhower began summoning

Republican members of the House Armed Services Committee to
the White House to force them to shift their position on the bill.
Some of those called to the White House reported intense pressure
comparable to a military order. The President would not even
listen to any objections to the bill, but insisted on complete support for his position, in spite of a long-standing public commit-
ment of the Congressman to oppose it. Confidential reports of
some of these meetings with the President were given at a dinner
at the Hamilton Hotel, April 25, 1955, attended by three members of the House Armed Services Committee and one staff
member each from the Friends Committee on National Legislation, the Women's International League for Peace and Freedom
and the National Council Against Conscription. According to
these reports only one Congressman braved the President's wrath
to assert his independence as a legislator. Not all of them
succumbed to Presidential pressure when the bill was brought
again before the House in May, 1955. But by July 1, Dewey
Short, who had led the fight against the measure in May, changed
his position and urged its adoption.

Eisenhower, who never used his presidential power decis-
ively to get agreement within his Administration on a disarmament proposal or any other peace measure, was a devoted Army
man. He criticized the Army upon occasion, but as he said in
a press conference after resigning as Chief of Staff, "I shall
belong to the Army as long as I am above ground."

Without his pressure it is doubtful if the Reserve Forces
Act of 1955 would have passed. Only if Senator Taft had lived
and opposed the President would there have been a reasonable
chance of building a voluntary rather than a compulsory reserve.

The new compulsory reserve program was not very successful during its first year of operation. It was attacked by writers
on military affairs as having a military value "close to zero." [1] The
President of the National Guard Association, Major General
Ellard A. Walsh, said he was convinced that the only reserve
training program that could be sold to the people was a three
months voluntary one. The National Security Training Com-

mission, in its first annual report to Congress on September 16, 1956, on the reserve program, looked upon it as a failure which should be "fundamentally revised."

A few months later, in December, the Defense Department announced that it was drafting a plan to cut the reserve program and "place emphasis on quality rather than quantity." The *New York Times* reported that "The Defense Department revision of the reserve program represents a change of emphasis from the agency's stand when the reserve law passed in 1955." Nevertheless, the six months plus seven and one-half-year voluntary reserve program for those wanting to avoid the draft remained.

The Army's mood, however, was reflected in the National Security Training Commission suggestion in a letter to the President that the Commission should be abolished since there would be no clear purpose in its continuation. There seemed to be little likelihood of a renewed drive for UMT. The Army apparently now was content with Selective Service even though it got only a portion of each generation of young men.

President Eisenhower on March 28, 1957 agreed that there was little likelihood of Congress approving universal military training and abolished the Commission as of June 30, 1957.

It might well be asked, then, what the years of opposition to UMT accomplished in the light of the fact that the Army succeeded in getting and renewing a Selective Service law from 1948 to date. The record reveals that the Selective Service Act of 1948 had been incorporated into the Universal Military Training and Service Act of 1951. In spite of the title of the Act, Congress had refused to adopt UMT. Instead it laid a general military obligation of eight years on males between the ages of eighteen and one-half and twenty-six, at least two years of which would be spent on active duty and the remainder in the reserves. Since there was no compulsion to engage in reserve training and since the armed forces could use the draft only to fill vacancies in their authorized strength, military training and service was in fact selective rather than universal.

The Reserve Forces Act of 1955 made reserve duty compulsory for all who enlisted or were drafted and extended the draft to June 30, 1959. In 1959 it was again extended.

The record also reveals that although many were drafted, a significant number were deferred who would not otherwise have escaped universal military training. By early 1957, for example, out of a draft pool of about 5 million, 2.3 million, or 46 per cent, were physically or mentally unfit for military service by the artificial standards of the armed forces. An additional 1.4 million were deferred by executive order because they were fathers. Certain other deferments granted to students, conscientious objectors and others resulted in well over 60 per cent of those of draft age not being drafted. The campaign against UMT thus prevented millions of teen-age youths from being drafted just for the sake of an Army desire for compulsory military indoctrination.

There was another value in the campaign. It exposed the weakness of the American Legion and some other organized veterans groups. These groups had tried for years to maintain a position of great political power and prestige. In effect they had staked their position on their ability to get UMT through Congress. One of the spokesmen for veterans in the House, James E. Van Zandt, a former National Commander of the Veterans of Foreign Wars, told the Maryland VFW on June 7, 1952: "Whether UMT is right or wrong, in my opinion the defeat suffered by organized veterandom at the hands of civic, church and pacifist groups definitely presents to the various veterans' organizations the greatest challenge to their prestige and influence." He indicated that "the individual members . . . showed little interest in the UMT bill . . . " In other words, they tended to follow the lead of the other groups to which they belonged. This was evident in the fact that the United Auto Workers-CIO Veterans Conference representing 213,000 veterans, the American Veterans Committee, and the Catholic War Veterans were on record as opposed to UMT.

The *Washington Star* on January 27, 1955 reported that one Legion leader pleaded with the Legion auxiliary, "For God's sake don't sell your national president down the river . . . " He added: "I beg of you, plead with you, if you do have

any qualms of conscience about UMT please keep them to your-
selves. Don't brunt them around as you have been the last few
days in Washington."

The UMT campaign did not in any sense alter the basic
pro-military orientation of the Legion. But it did reveal to Congress and to many others that the Legion was not the great
political power on the American scene that it had claimed to be.

Still other values from the organized effort to defeat UMT
were the defeat of the various attempts to adopt a draft of labor
and nurses and to make Selective Service a program without any
terminal date. The mere fact of the unwavering opposition to
UMT for boys made it impossible for any military campaign to
register or draft women to have any real effect on Congress or
the people.

Another major value in the campaign against UMT was the
attention it called to the military drive for power. On January
19, 1948 the *Washington Post* and the *New York Herald
Tribune* reported on their front pages, as did many other newspapers throughout the nation, a 32-page study called *The Militarization of America*. This study was prepared by this writer as
director of the National Council Against Conscription, but was
released to the press by a group of twenty-one distinguished persons including Albert Einstein, Ray Lyman Wilbur and various
leaders of national organizations. *The Militarization of America*
described the military penetration of the State Department and
similar efforts in the fields of science, education and industry.

A year later a 64-page report entitled *New Evidence of the
Militarization of America* was prepared by the director of the National Council Against Conscription and issued by eighteen
persons including Pearl Buck, Louis Bromfield, Albert Einstein
and others.

These studies, which were distributed to Congress, were
followed by still others such as *Militarism in Education, Press
Agents of the Pentagon* and *Our Military Government*. These
publications, involving substantial research and documentation,
were the first postwar publications to reveal the pattern of increasing military power.

But the mere fact of the UMT campaign illustrated more clearly than any published research that the armed forces had become the most powerful pressure group in the country. Civilian groups opposed to UMT formed the largest coalition on any single issue in American history. Yet it took more than ten years of constant effort by these groups to defeat UMT. The top officers of the armed forces did not face similar opposition on any other issue, and therefore were able to expand military influence almost at will into other branches of government and into other normally civilian activities. The *United States News* as early as March 21, 1947 described the problem in these words: "Never before have the Army and Navy been so powerfully placed in government controls, and never before has the United States adopted so stern a foreign policy." Speaking about the military men who were expanding their influence throughout the government, the magazine said "The group as a whole have been operating as a team."

Although public attention has most frequently been focused on such pressure groups as labor unions or veterans groups or business organizations as the "invisible government," these groups in their periods of greatest effort cannot muster for their policies the financial support, lobbying, or public relations activities that the armed forces can. In addition to their resources, prestige and bigness, the armed forces can overtly or subtly play upon the fears of the nation in seeking adoption of a desired policy.

It is difficult for Congressmen and even the President to oppose military demands, because such opposition can easily be interpreted by the military and their civilian supporters as opposition to national security itself. Even the normal Congressional power to investigate and publicize abuses of power is limited by the ability of the armed forces to classify as top secret certain items that they do not want exposed to public gaze.

From 1944 through 1952 the military party was constantly the concern of the large coalition of civilian groups who had come together to oppose peacetime military conscription and who also opposed the expanding military influence at certain other points. With the formal defeat of UMT and a minor effort to prevent the subsequent renewal of Selective Service, this coalition of groups fell apart. Except for such occasional resistance to military demands as the small peace and pacifist groups are able to muster, there is no organized opposition to military power and not even a watchdog group or publication to expose military encroachments.

The problem of military power is therefore more dangerous today than it was when there was some check on that power. Practically every area of our national life has overtly or subtly been affected by military ideas and organization, as we will now see.

CHAPTER 9

THE ECONOMIC POWER OF THE PENTAGON

No activity of the military is more dangerous to American democracy today than its economic program. This program, which President Eisenhower briefly described in referring to a "military-industrial complex," is an illustration both of "creeping militarism" and of the military's conscious planning for power.

Military planning for economic control over the nation began during World War II. In the early stages of the war the energy of the armed forces and the civilian population was largely absorbed in the organization of the tremendous military-industrial machine that was to win the war. But before long Army leaders and their civilian colleagues in finance and industry began to think of the postwar scene. They did not want World War II to end as did World War I, with the Army being drastically cut back and the industrial-military ties being severed.

At first the Army itself sought to control the economy and only later thought in terms of collaboration with industry as equal partners. Donald Nelson, the prominent business executive who headed the War Production Board, revealed that "from 1942 onward the Army people, in order to get control of our national economy, did their best to make an errand boy of the WPB." [1]

A Bureau of the Budget report, *The United States at War,* published in 1946, said that during World War II the Army sought "total control of the nation, its manpower, its facilities, its economy." When a particular effort to seize control was frustrated by the President or by Donald Nelson "the military leaders took another approach to secure the same result; they

99

never abandoned the sincere conviction that they could run things better and more expeditiously than the civilians." [2]

Unfortunately, a combination of Congressional willingness to let military men run the war and a tendency of President Roosevelt to deal directly with the Joint Chiefs of Staff resulted in a weakening of civilian control. The Secretaries of War and the Navy were not only uninformed about important matters of strategy, but were not even put on the routine distribution list for the papers of the Joint Chiefs of Staff. Roosevelt also excluded the State Department so that it had only a peripheral role even in matters that might determine postwar foreign policy. The Joint Chiefs of Staff became so accustomed to power and to formulating major policy that they were unable to accept being overruled with good grace.

Donald Nelson, concerned with this drive for power, warned in the concluding sections of his book *Arsenal of Democracy* that "the question of military control will confront us not only in war but in peace. The lesson taught by these recent war years is clear: our whole economic and social system will be in peril if it is controlled by the military men." [3]

When the war ended, the military took advantage of the unsettled condition of the world to consolidate its power. Charles E. Wilson, president of General Electric, had pointed the way by suggesting both an alliance of big business and the military, and "a permanent war economy." In an address to the Army Ordnance Association in January, 1944, he warned that "The revulsion against war not too long hence will be an almost insuperable obstacle for us to overcome in establishing a preparedness program and for that reason I am convinced that we must begin now to set the machinery in motion." Wilson went on to suggest that every big company appoint a special executive to act as liaison man with the armed forces, with the commission of a colonel in the reserve. He added:

> First of all such a program must be the responsibility of the federal government. It must be initiated and administered by the executive branch — by the President as Commander-in-Chief and by the War and Navy Departments. . . . Of

equal importance is the fact that this must be, once and for all, a continuing program and not the creature of an emergency. In fact one of its objects will be to eliminate emergencies so far as possible. The program must be insured and supported by the congress. Industry's role in this program is to respond and cooperate . . . in the execution of the part allotted to it; industry must not be hampered by political witch-hunts, or thrown to the fanatical isolationist fringe tagged with a "merchants of death" label.[4]

As a result of this reasoning and its own desire for power, the military entered a marriage of convenience with big business. Secretary of the Navy James Forrestal served as another of the matchmakers. In 1944 he organized the National Security Industrial Association, a group of industrial firms with significant military contracts in order to insure that "American business will remain close to the services."

In the decade following World War II the Defense Department built itself into the biggest business of the entire world. Any one of its separate branches was bigger than any existing corporation. In 1952, less than five years after it became a separate branch, the Air Force was boasting of being "the biggest business in the world today" with "money available to it many times the aggregate of the biggest of the great American corporations." Air Force Secretary Thomas Finletter called "the value of our plant facilities," including equipment, greater than "the 1950 total compiled assets of General Motors, Standard Oil of New Jersey, United States Steel, and American Telephone and Telegraph combined."

By 1952 the *U.S. News and World Report* described the military's economic holdings as a $200 billion investment which is, "more than four times the present book value of all the plants and equipment of all U.S. manufacturing corporations."

By 1957 the Department of Defense owned or controlled a total of 34.9 million acres of land throughout the world, of which more than 32 million acres were in the United States. This acreage is greater than the areas of Rhode Island, Massachusetts, Connecticut, Vermont, New Hampshire, Delaware, Maryland and New Jersey combined.

Far more important than its economic holdings is the yearly budget and financial activity of the Pentagon, which enables it to be the biggest employer, contractor, purchaser, owner and spender in the nation. In June, 1950 the Defense Department had 1,460,000 military and 753,000 civilian employees. Taking advantage of the unforeseen Korean War, the military was able to persuade the nation to increase and maintain in succeeding years a much larger establishment, numbering almost 2,500,-000 military and 1,078,000 civilians in June, 1959. Even this was not large enough.

Under the impact of a threatened Russian peace treaty with East Germany which might cut Berlin off from the West, the military was able again to increase its size. Even after the crisis had subsided and the mobilized reserves were being sent home, military manpower was not cut back and the military budget was actually increased. For years the Army had wanted an army of at least 1,000,000 men. President Eisenhower had kept it at 870,000 during his last two years in office. But President Kennedy's budget for 1963 increased it to 960,000 men. The grand total for the armed forces was 2,684,000 in the aftermath of the Berlin crisis.

In addition to the civilian and military employees of the armed forces, about 40,000 people are engaged in government activities which directly support the Defense Department, such as the Atomic Energy Commission, Selective Service and the National Aeronautical and Space Administration, bringing the total number to almost 3,800,000. Since the total labor force in the United States averages about 73 million persons, the military sector of government supports directly one-twentieth of the nation's total labor force.

Every state of the Union profits directly from this military payroll, which in 1959 was well over 11 billion dollars in the United States. "This payroll alone," says a government report, "is equal to 1½ times the combined payrolls of the iron and steel industry and of all other basic metal producers. It is more than double the payrolls of the automobile industry." [5] Still other military money is poured into the American economy, some of it sent back by the hundreds of thousands of soldiers and sailors stationed overseas, some of it from the thousands of paid reserves, and about $1.4 billion which goes into local labor and materials for military construction projects.[6]

All of this can be translated briefly into political terms. In 1958, Chairman Vinson of the House Armed Service Committee, in presenting a military public works bill which amounted to about a billion dollars, said to the House: "My friends, there is something in this bill for every member." Representative J. L. Whitten (D., Miss.), in reminding the House of this on May 3, 1960, added, "And sure enough, when you read the requests for military construction they had them listed by states so you could see every Member had a monetary interest in passage."

It is no wonder that Congressmen concerned about employment in their districts want to keep the military budget high. Most Congressmen have been unenthusiastic about disarmament or any other program that might require drastic changes in the economic health of their districts.

An even more ominous picture is that of the military tie to big business. In 1961 fifty large corporations succeeded in getting 65.4 per cent of the prime contracts offered by the Defense Department, or $14,850,000,000. A five-year analysis shows these same companies receiving a total of almost $67 billion, or 62.5 per cent of all Defense Department contracts awarded from 1957 through 1961. In 1959 Representative Whitten pointed out on the floor of the House that the "Defense Department spent $50 billion with 10 corporations in 5 years and their stocks increased in value from an average of $58 per shaare to $149 per share in that period."

The aircraft industry, which is dominated by about thirteen large companies, sold $9,496,000,000 worth of goods in the peacetime year of 1956, a year's turnover exceeded only twice during World War II. Well over three-fourths of this total was sold to the Defense Department. These companies make enormous profits on their capital investments. A major reason for this is that the Pentagon provides a subsidy to industry in the form of capital investment. In the aircraft industry the government furnishes about 70 per cent of all productive facilities. A Congressional subcommittee headed by Rep. Hebert reported in 1956 that twelve of these companies were using $985,000,000 worth of government-owned plants and equipment as compared with their own total private investment of $394,000,000.

The furnishing of these facilities has led almost automatically to the awarding of contracts year after year to the same companies, since idle equipment would result in the Air Force (or other branch) carrying the heavy maintenance costs. The extra maintenance costs would then reduce the funds available for procurement of new weapons. The net impact of this logic has been to build monopolies in the defense industry. The Pentagon provides a major part of the productive facilities, pays for the production and a "reasonable" profit. Only "excessive" profits are subject to renegotiation. It should be no surprise that such arrangements produce a mutual vested interest which lead the Pentagon and the big munitions industries to support each other and therefore a huge armaments system.

The profits of these companies, which are enormous, are known not only by the high officers in the armed forces who furnished the contracts, but also to Congress. On May 22, 1962 a Senate investigator told a Senate Investigations subcommittee that the Boeing company's profits since 1951 had ranged from a low of 36 per cent in 1951 to a high of 108.6 per cent in 1953 when measured by the company's net investment. Boeing's contracts had totaled $11,818,900,000 since 1951, whereas company costs had totaled $10,911,200,000. The gross profit was $907,700,000. Even after taxes, according to Senate testimony, profit averaged 35.68 per cent on the government contracts. This was over three times the 10.73 per cent average net profit for all manufacturing industries in the United States as computed by Government regulatory agencies against net worth in the same years.

The Senate investigator indicated that Boeing does not dispute the accuracy of the figures. Boeing does, however, prefer to have profit percentage figured on the basis of sales volume rather than on the amount of its own investment in production.

Other companies with lush military contracts have also been investigated by the Senate Investigations subcommittee. The Douglas Aircraft Company, said the committee's chief counsel, was awarded contracts for the Nike guided missile totaling $599,000,000, of which it subcontracted $496,000,000 to other firms. The costs Douglas incurred in managing and supervising the subcontracts were repaid with profit by the Pentagon. Yet the committee spokesman said Douglas negotiated total fees of $45,600,000 on the production, which is 44.3 per cent of the $103,000,000 work on the Nike missile which Douglas itself did. One charge levelled against the company was that profits were taken not only on the work performed by Douglas but also for the work done by subcontractors who themselves made a substantial profit.[7]

The Senate subcommittee investigation of Douglas also revealed that on a military contract for Nike launcher-loaders the entire cost to Douglas for one order was $3,316 because the work was actually done by the Consolidated Western Steel Company on a subcontract basis. Yet Douglas collected $1,211-790, chiefly for subcontracting this order. Even stranger is the committee evidence that the Army contract in the first place had been given to Western Electric Company. That company had passed it to Douglas, which passed it to Consolidated Western Steel Company. Out of the total Army bill for $16,408,800, $1,733,286 went to the Western Electric Company.

The Senate subcommittee also noted in April, 1962 that in seventeen similar contracts which Douglas sublet to Consolidated Western, Douglas added a profit of $10,000,000 for itself on top of a $9,200,000 profit received by Consolidated Western. Senator McClellan indicated that Western Electric then got an additional $9,800,000 profit or profit plus expenses. [New York Times, April 11, 1962]

The Pentagon with its industrial or big business sympathies continues to award fat contracts to industry. But in 1962 there were a number of strikes at missile bases because of labor troubles.

The *New York Times* of April 5, 1962, in reporting this, indicated that Major General W. T. Thurman, Air Force Director of Procurement Management "said the Air Force had adopted a tougher attitude toward labor, based on a directive by Robert S. MacNamara, Secretary of Defense, that 'we will take a strike before we will pay unreasonable payments or subject ourselves to unreasonable demands.' " In other words the Pentagon concerns itself with labor's demands for an increase in a few cents or dollars per hour but raises no similar objection about industry when millions of dollars of unwarranted profits are involved.

Calculated as a part of expenses in government contracts with industry are the very large salaries of top company executives and board chairmen. Six companies that were dependent exclusively on government contracts paid in 1955 $694,000 to their six presidents, not including dividends and stock options.

These big munitions industries provide a convenient source of employment for retired generals and admirals. A Special House Subcommittee commissioned to investigate the employment of retired officers in defense industries revealed in 1960 that 261 generals and admirals and 485 retired officers above the rank of colonel and Navy captain are employed by the companies that manufacture 80 per cent of our armaments. General Dynamics, which ranked first among the top fifty defense suppliers from 1957 to 1961, had 186 retired officers on its payroll. The chairman of the board of General Dynamics was former Secretary of the Army Frank Pace. Boeing Aircraft, which during the same period ranked second among the top defense suppliers, employed 72 retired officers. Lockheed Aircraft, the third in rank, employed 171 retired officers.

These retired officers have a great influence in the Pentagon just because they retired early. "A great number of the top ranking generals and admirals," wrote Colonel Neblett, "exercise overpowering influence upon the high rankers left behind who could not be promoted to the grades they now hold until those who retired had gotten out of the way." Neblett, in pointing out that the munitions makers send "General A. to the Pentagon to see General B. who succeeded him," revealed that often there is an effort to "talk General B. into continuing the manufacturer's contract to make obsolete equipment" if only because "the companies they represent are tooled up to make" these weapons.[8]

Admiral H. G. Rickover has testified that these military lobbyists have exerted pressure on high Navy officials "to undertake new projects which we consider not worthwhile." Another admiral, William Fechteler, a former Chief of Naval Operations, told a House subcommittee that upon retirement he went to work for General Electric Co. at a yearly salary of $30,000 plus incentive pay which amounted to $8,500 in 1958. As is true of all other retired officers, he also drew his military retirement pay which amounted to $1,014 a month. Fechteler described himself as a "convenient, glorified messenger boy" for General Electric. By this he meant he took company officials to meet the Secretary of the Navy and key admirals. Admiral Fechteler let the company officials talk contracts. In a statement that must have been highly amusing to the Congressmen present the Admiral said: "I studiously avoid even being in the room when anybody talks about a contract." Congressman Hebert added, however, "you had the key to the door and you opened it."

These retired officers are especially effective in getting contracts since about 95 per cent of the defense contracts are negotiated rather than let as a result of competitive bidding.

Aside from this question of the military-business alliance, there is a question as to how much ex-officers for business reasons influence or determine Army, Navy or Air Force policy at crucial points.

Each company not only does its own lobbying in its own way, but also joins forces with other manufacturers to lobby in the general interests of their whole industry. The Aerospace Industries Association, headed by a retired Air Force general, Orval Cook, looks after the general interests of that industry. Each industry is assessed on the basis of its gross contracts. In 1958 such companies as Boeing, Lockheed, General Dynamics, Curtis Wright, Douglas and North American were each assessed $75,000. The Aerospace Industries Association which receives these sums calls itself a non-profit organization. Therefore, as

Representative Hebert pointed out, the aircraft company "is allowed a tax deduction because it has contributed to a non-profit organization, and the non-profit organization takes that money to advance the interests of the contract."

One of the activities of the Aerospace Industries Association is entertainment parties for the press. This may not be the reason for the small amount of publicity in the press given to the industrial-military tie. But rarely does the press report such charges as those made on the floor of the House on April 6, 1960 by Carroll Reece (R., Tenn.). Speaking of the missile program and the use of retired officers as agents of the aircraft-missile industry, Reece said: "The Army's efforts have not been directed exclusively to the defense of our country. They have been directed almost solely toward benefiting financially a few very large corporations who are in almost complete control of the Army's missile program." Reece added, "That the purpose of this policy has or will benefit certain highly placed Army personnel is all too obvious."

In effect Reece was saying that military officers who expect to retire and get high salaries in jobs created for them in defense industry thus develop a vested interest in those industries. His statement was also reminiscent of President Eisenhower's June, 1959 assertion that "political and financial consideration . . . rather than merely military ones were influencing decisions for a higher military budget."

Another Congressman, J. L. Whitten, noted on May 3, 1960 that "most of the top people in our Defense Department came from big business." The "companies doing huge contracting business with the Department" have "large numbers of retired military personnel working for them. This makes it hard to determine just what is what or rather who is who." This interlocking directorate of the military and big business not only controls the prosperity but the jobs in each Congressional district. This in turn produces Congressional support. Joseph Alsop has suggested that defense contracts "are now vastly more important than both pork [porkbarrel legislation] and patronage put together." In mid-October, 1960 he reported that Richard Nixon, then a presidential candidate, had persuaded President Eisenhower to authorize an additional $190 million to be spent on the B-70 project in California. The publicity about this and the "contract quite certainly helped carry California for Nixon by the narrow margin of about 30,000 votes." [9]

It is of course no accident that Georgia has nineteen military installations and in 1959 ranked fourth in the nation in the military payroll. Georgia is the home state of Carl Vinson and Richard Russell, chairmen respectively of the House and of the Senate Armed Services Committees.

It is not the big corporations alone which are involved in defense industry. Many small businesses are kept alive by the military. The Air Force alone provided an average of $200,000 in 1958 for each of 1,116 firms having fewer than 100 employees and $910,000 average for each of 1,952 firms employing 100 to 500 persons.

In 1958 $756.5 million was poured into small businesses by the Air Force. Nor is this a haphazard development. The Air Force kept 41 small business specialists on duty full time around the country to be sure that there was proper care of small business.

Labor is also tied into the military system through the cooperation of the Department of Labor which supplies the Pentagon with a list of areas where there is unemployment. In 1958 there were 292 areas designated by the Department of Labor as areas of substantial unemployment. In October-December 1958, the Pentagon awarded $3,224,000,000 in contracts of $10,000 or more to firms in these areas of unemployment, or a total of $9,060,000,000 for the calendar year 1958.

In discussing this problem, Representative Whitten said: "As long as the employment is tied to military spending and the local economy is dependent upon military bases' spending, it may lead to what we see in the press . . . a competitive situation amongst various members of Congress and Senators as to who can be for the highest level of defense spending."

This, in turn, means that there is very little chance of getting real support in Congress or from business or labor for a disarmament program. In practice the military, who have a vested interest in maintaining the war system, have control over the economy.

Control over the economy is in part maintained by the creation of real or artificial crises so that there is some seeming justification for a high rate of military spending. The process by which this is accomplished was described in the April 14, 1950 *U.S. News and World Report:* " 'Cold War' tends to heat up and spy scares tend to become active each year at about the time that Congress is getting ready to decide the size of military appropriations . . . " On May 19, 1950 the same magazine pointed out that "Business won't go to pot so long as war is a threat, so long as every alarm can be used to step up spending — lending for defense at home and for aid abroad. Cold war is almost a guarantee against a bad depression."

Dramatic evidence of the connection between the cold war and prosperity was evident in the aftermath of the U-2 incident. No proof has ever been published to support hints by a few public figures that the U-2 plane had been deliberately sent over the Soviet Union by the military in order to wreck the Summit conference. But the U-2 incident did cause the collapse of the Summit. At one point in the planning for summit meetings there were hopes in some quarters and fears in others that President Eisenhower and Premier Khrushchev might reach some agreements about Berlin, Germany, and other issues that would give disarmament negotiations a real boost. When the summit conference collapsed, the *New York Times* of May 22, 1960 reported a big stock market gain. "Traders decided that the 'cold war' was due to heat up considerably in the coming months . . . and that this would mean a step-up in the nation's defense program." The *Times* added, "The upshot was the most exciting week for the stock market in many months, certainly this year so far."

Conversely there was a sharp drop in the market in September, 1959 after Premier Khrushchev had proposed total disarmament. The financial journal *Barron's* reported that Mr.

Khrushchev's mere "presence" in this country "was painfully felt by investors in aircraft and other defense issues."

The military control over the economy is possible because of the cold war but it is also possible because of the myth that military spending means prosperity. Fundamental to this myth is the idea that many persons, in the words of the *New York Times* of April 29, 1962, "are sharing in benefits that have spilled over into civilian life from the defense industry."

Actually, the American economy is being injured by military spending. The program of huge sums of military aid to other countries and the large amounts expended in pay and maintenance of American troops overseas has increased the drain on American gold reserves. A second injury is what Professor Seymour Harris of Harvard calls "underspending" for years "under the pressure of cold war costs . . . in such vital areas as education, urban renewal, housing, power, pollution, irrigation, conservation, flood control, navigation, forestation, airport improvement, highways, hospitals and health services and social security."

This underspending has been encouraged by the big business group that profits from the cold war. In November, 1957 *Fortune* magazine summarized this line by asserting that the economy "can stand the load of any defense effort required to hold the power of Soviet Russia in check. It cannot, however, indefinitely stand the erosion of creeping socialism and the ceaseless extension of government activities into additional economic fields." At another point in the same article Henry Luce, the publisher of *Time, Life,* and *Fortune,* urged Congress to "begin a massive pruning of non-defense outlays all along the line."

Luce and similar spokesmen never acknowledge that everyone in the armed forces is now involved in socialized medicine, housing, and other forms of socialism, whereas civilians in the lower income brackets cannot afford decent housing or adequate medical care. Nor do they publicize the fact that military control of our economy involves subsidizing defense industry. Only when President Kennedy used Pentagon spending to force United States Steel and other steel companies to hold the price line in the spring of 1962 was there any outcry from this group. In practice, however, the United States, as one economist and former Congressman, Byron Johnson, remarked, "now has socialization of risk. We just haven't taken title to what we have paid for." This subsidy of the big military and armaments industries has resulted in heavy taxation and, therefore, in lower real income. In turn this heavy taxation has had an important influence in the very real decrease in the rate of saving and capital formation. At present about 7 per cent annually of gross national product goes into saving, less than half the rate prior to 1900. When there is a relative shortage of savings in a period of increasing demand for capital, the interest rate will increase, as it has been doing in recent years.

Higher interest rates tend to increase prices, thus restricting demand for capital goods and thereby limiting business expansion. It is no wonder that the rate of economic growth in the United States is so small compared with that of some of our competitors.

President Eisenhower aptly summarized the human problem implicit in our huge military budget. On April 19, 1953 he said: "Every gun that is made, every warship launched, every rocket fired signifies, in the final sense, a theft from those who hunger and are not fed, those who are cold and not clothed. We pay for a single fighter plane with a half-million bushels of wheat. We pay for a single destroyer with new homes that could have housed more than 8,000 people."

CHAPTER 10

A PROPAGANDA MACHINE
SECOND TO NONE

The military-industrial complex that rules so much of America today reached its present peak of power partly by riding roughshod over civilian America and partly by an effective public relations program that softened the blow. The Army used every available Madison Avenue publicity technique during the UMT campaign. But only after John Kennedy became President did the American public realize how often high civilian officials had tried and failed to curb military officers in one propaganda approach to the people, their public speaking around the country. In his February 1, 1961 news conference the President announced that leading military figures should not make speeches in conflict with Administration policy and revealed that the Eisenhower administration had made sixty-five efforts to make such a rule stick.

Walter Lippman, more than a week earlier, had summarized the international implications of the problem by calling "the talkativeness of American military men . . . an international scandal. Throughout the world it causes us trouble, it causes great loss of respect and confidence. No other military establishment on earth," he added, "except perhaps in small disorderly countries, thus permits a running commentary on critical affairs by its generals and admirals and the colonels down the line."

The problem of military publicity and propaganda, however, is much bigger and more complex than speeches by top officers. Even if the Kennedy administration is more successful in its coordination of military statements with civilian policy than was President Eisenhower, the major propaganda power of the military will still be with us.

113

If any of the Joint Chiefs of Staff do not like a decision of the President or his civilian Secretary of Defense it is always possible to put him on the spot before Congress and the public. During the first year of the Kennedy Administration the Air Force was assigned a space mission. There was a complaint among the Joint Chiefs that the mission had been granted too hastily. This complaint was leaked to the press and caused a Congressional hearing.

In similar but more overt fashion the Air Force has refused to accept the decision of both Presidents Eisenhower and Kennedy on the development of the B-70, a supersonic bombing plane. On May 16, 1962 General Curtis LeMay, Air Force Chief of Staff, asked the Senate Appropriations Committee for $491,000,-000 to speed development of the bomber. He had lost several appeals to the civilian Secretary of Defense, who, along with the Chiefs of the other branches, had questioned more investment in bombers which were being superseded by missiles. General LeMay, in response to such a decision, told the Senators, "I object to having the term 'bomber man' applied to me. I will use the effective weapon system that will do the job. If that's kiddie cars, I'll use kiddie cars." The "kiddie car" approach is reminiscent of the Army effort to hang onto cavalry units years after the development of tanks. Far more serious is the publicity given to the military. The *New York Times,* for example, devoted three columns on the front page to a picture of the General and the report of his appeal which were distributed throughout the country by the United Press International and the Associated Press respectively.

News stories which serve the vested interest of one or more branches of the armed forces are almost always inspired by the public relations experts employed in the Pentagon. Each branch has its own public relations program in addition to a central agency which serves the Department of Defense. Sometimes the public relations officers simply see to it that their carefully cultivated contacts in the civilian world are present at the right moment for a speech or other public appearance of a high-ranking officer. More often a whole series of techniques are used to present the military line to the people, techniques which are rarely discussed in print because a newspaperman who does may find it difficult in the future to get certain breaks from military public relations.

But in 1959 a few journalists did describe the Army's effort to sell germ and gas warfare to the American people. On August 9, 1959 the *New York Times* reported that "Leading military officials are trying to overcome public horror of chemical, biological and radiological [CBR] warfare." Actually the Army was trying to accomplish two things. It wanted to increase the CBR budget from its level of $40 million a year to $125 million. It also wanted to reverse the policy established in 1943 by President Roosevelt that "we shall under no circumstances resort to the use of such weapons unless they are first used by our enemies . . ." Roosevelt, who had called them "terrible and inhumane weapons" added, "Use of such weapons has been outlawed by the general opinion of civilized mankind."

Brigadier General J. H. Rothschild, in the June, 1959 *Harper's Magazine,* stated the military position in saying that "we must reject once and for all the position stated by President Roosevelt that an enemy can have the first chemical or biological blow wherever and whenever he wishes." Rather, wrote the general, "we must make it clear that we consider these weapons among the normal, usable weapons of war."

In its effort to sell the public on germ and gas warfare, the Army stressed certain themes: Germs and gas do not destroy property; the Soviet Union is prepared to use such warfare; CBR weapons are really humane because they can paralyze or destroy the will without killing. In House hearings, however, a more realistic picture was presented. Daniel Flood asked: "You have various degrees of gases that produce temporary paresis?" Major General William Creasy, the chief of the Army's Chemical Corps, replied: "I would not want to say 'Yes' to that for this reason. While there are varying lethal doses for those G-gases, all of these gases or doses are so small as to be hard to guarantee that any amount is not going to be fatal."

The House Science and Astronautics Committee, following hearings on CBR warfare, issued a report which received virtually no coverage in the press. It had no publicity machine to disseminate its statement that "the Committee cannot bring itself to describe any weapon of war as 'humane' and makes no moral judgment on the possible use of CBR in warfare."

The Army's publicity campaign was described by Walter Schneir in the October 1, 1959 *Reporter* as having several "principal elements." These included speeches by high military officers to selected groups with reporters present to cover the story, articles in magazines written by retired officers who are less accountable than those on active duty, and private briefing of writers and editors by some civilian consultant to the military. This consultant "meets informally with a writer and stresses that the information he gives is 'not attributable.' " In this way he "cannot be held accountable for anything he says and the reader has no way of knowing the source of the story."

Another approach is through Congressional hearings which are closed to the press, but after which . . . "carefully screened material is then released with some fanfare."

Writers who specialize in military affairs or scientific matters are tipped off that formerly secret material "is now available to them for stories." Other writers "are also informed that certain high military officers are now receptive to interviews."

These techniques, said Congressman Robert Kastenmeier (D., Wis.), resulted in the press being "deluged with feature articles and interviews" with scores of groups hearing persuasive speeches. In the December, 1959 *Progressive* Kastenmeier pointed out that "until a few months ago there was rarely a story on CBR in the popular press. But when the Pentagon decided to 'sell' the American public on adopting CBR warfare as a 'normal usable' weapon it let out all the stops in its public relations campaign. . . "

That this type of campaign pays off and continues to pay off is evident from the following statement in the Appropriations Committee Report to the House on the 1963 Defense Department budget: "One area, chemical and biological warfare weapons, has been allocated an approximate increase of four times the amount provided in the current fiscal year."

The propaganda techniques used in the CBR campaign are not the only ones used by the armed forces. There is, for example, a unique approach that virtually guarantees public acceptance of military suggestions. On a national level, after the top policy makers in the Pentagon decide on a policy, orders go out to public relations officers and other officials instructing them on the "line" to be taken with the public. A story is planted with a reporter, columnist or radio commentator. This story prompts questions to the Secretary of Defense or Secretary of the Army, the Navy or Air Force at a press conference which Public Information officers arrange. The Secretary develops the new "line" and gets headlines across the country. Speeches on the new policy or proposal are made by these same Secretaries of military agencies, by generals and other officials, before groups in different parts of the country, insuring still more headlines.

These stories and speeches lead to questions at a White House press conference. The President backs the proposal and more headlines appear. Some Senators and Congressmen use the new "line" in speaking around the country. Throughout the country, meanwhile, public relations officers, colonels and generals use the prepared speeches manufactured in the Pentagon. In this way the unorganized public is faced with a policy which it is difficult if not impossible to oppose.[1]

Public relations techniques are used also for more general purposes. Various programs are utilized, as befits the need. One such program is intended to keep the industrial allies of the military informed so that public opinion may be properly molded in communities throughout the United States. The Industrial College of the Armed Forces has a system of traveling National Security Seminars. Between 1948, when the program was begun, and 1960 a total of 197 seminars had been conducted in about 110 different cities. The schedule for 1960-1961 included such cities as Bethlehem, Pa.; Milwaukee, Wis.; Wichita, Kan., and

Albuquerque, N.M., and others of comparable size or industrial composition. During these programs leaders and the senior officers of the military reserve, who are themselves largely drawn from the business and professional community, are the chief participants.

One seminar description during 1960-1961 was entitled "A Businessman's Briefing on National Security." The briefing and general approach of these seminars, each lasting two weeks, has been summarized by Dr. Roscoe Giffin, who attended one. In nearly every lecture the Chinese-Soviet bloc was described as our implacable enemy bent on world conquest. The United States, on the other hand, "has little responsibility for the current international chaos and our policies are clearly beyond reproach, since our conduct during the cold war years has been a necessary response to Sino-Soviet aggressiveness." That the military could say this after the false war crises they engineered and the pressure they put on Germany and Japan to rearm, as well as numerous other ventures, illustrates a callous disregard for truth as well as a self-righteousness that is highly dangerous to world peace.

Giffin went on to say that the military believed our only possible fault has been in too little military preparation, but "if our national security is not what it ought to be, the primary reason is the budgetary limitations imposed on the military department." Disarmament programs were undercut and discounted. Giffin described the Army's view in these words: "Disarmament is a desirable goal, but given the nature of the enemy, disarmament cannot provide the security the nation requires." [2]

The number of military reserve officers attending these seminars was limited to about 200. Since this was a form of training and active duty they received "points" toward advancement. At the Bethlehem, Pa. Seminar, daily attendance averaged about 400. These included teachers as well as managerial employees of local industries. Giffin reports it as "an interesting commentary on the racial composition of those in positions of military and civilian authority that I did not observe a single Negro participant." [3]

A related program is the Orientation Conference, the purpose of which is to sell the national military establishment and its program once and for all to the important leaders invited to attend. The officer who developed this technique must have known his psychology, for it is extremely difficult for a person not to be friendly to anything military after several days as a guest of the military, with colonels opening and shutting doors for him and various demonstrations, boat rides, plane rides, etc. being put on just for his benefit. In addition, he is given supposedly secret information to which no one else has access and encouraged to go home and sell the military program to people who can be told only part of the story.

There are two types of orientation conference. One is for a specific group, such as ministers or newspapermen. The second type is the Joint Orientation Conference to which leaders from various fields such as labor, industry, and the professions are invited.

The first of a series of Joint Orientation Conferences was held November 8 to 18, 1948, in Washington. In each case the "top industry, labor, press, education, church and professional leaders" received a personal letter of invitation from Secretary of Defense James Forrestal "to the first of a series of ten-day closed door conferences on National Defense."

Since this first Joint Orientation Conference many hundreds of leading Americans have received similar propaganda treatment.

Bennett Cerf described his impressions of the seventh Joint Orientation Conference in an article, "Ten Days with the Armed Forces," which appeared in the July 22, 1950 *Saturday Review of Literature*. At the outset it is obvious that Cerf was completely sold on the conference. He wrote of the invitation, "I consider [it] one of the biggest honors and luckiest breaks of my career." Throughout the article he indicated how impressed he was, with such expressions as, "Our men in the field are absolute tops."

He points out that the Secretary of Defense wanted leading citizens "to see and hear at first hand . . . how the Department of Defense was carrying out its own obligations . . . " and counted "on his guests to spread the good word as loudly and

vehemently as they knew how. It worked like a charm." After
listening to generals, admirals, and civilian department heads
of the military establishment, the group was flown to Fort Benning, Ga. There "a display of our remarkable new recoilless
weapons (and other arms still considered secret) had the audi-
ence gasping." They also saw "the airborne troops begin their
parachute training."

"It was at our next stop, Eglin Air Force Base, Fla., that I
had my unforgettable ride in a jet fighter plane. It all began
over cocktails with Hal Stuart, dashing young Assistant Secretary of the Air Force . . . " After a joke of Stuart's, "I told
Stuart 'If I've got to listen to jokes like that I demand a ride in
a jet plane as retribution.' . . . The next afternoon Capt. Jack
Fallon of the Three Thousand Two Hundredth Fighter Test
Squadron equipped me with a Mae West and a parachute, clapped
a crash helmet over my head, and strapped me into a two seated
F-80 Shooting Star jet plane."

After a harrowing 31-minute flight "over the Gulf of Mexico
at the modest speed of 510 miles an hour," Cerf "made a speech
that sent all the others clamoring for jet rides. The air was full
of petrified VIPs the next day. I must have cost the Air Force
a pretty penny."

Cerf continued: "The next day we boarded the Midway
. . . Planes landed on the carrier deck and took off moments
later, submarines submerged and snorkled, a drone was cata-
pulted from the deck and sunk by amazingly accurate ship fire
and night operations were more spectacular still."

He concluded his article:

I came home revitalized and simply busting to shout from
the housetops this deep-felt conviction; when and if a war
comes with Russia or anybody else this country is blessed with
the basic equipment and leadership to knock hell out of them.
We need more fighter planes and more carriers. We need
more men in the Armed Forces. Our intelligence and propaganda departments need bolstering most of all. The money
already allotted to defense has been on the whole wisely spent.
In light of day to day news developments, increased appropriations are not only a wise investment but an absolute must.

What more could the Defense Department want in return for ten days entertainment? Even if a person attending one of these Orientation Conferences disagreed with military policy, having once accepted the invitation and the "secret information" he could not denounce the military very convincingly. It is an effective technique.

Another approach is through the press. The armed forces encourage their industrial allies to engage in expensive advertising. Under "cost-plus" negotiated contracts, every cost associated with defense can be included in the total cost. This means that all advertising, public relations and entertainment, as well as production costs, are covered by the armed forces in addition to a handsome profit. As a result of a cost-plus-10% arrangement, a corporation can place a series of ads in trade or technical journals for $50,000 and receive $5,000 for itself plus the actual cost of placing the advertising. When newspapers and popular magazines are used, advertising may be deducted as a business expense, which means that perhaps 50 per cent is paid by the government. These various advertisements by military contractors are for products such as missiles which government alone can buy, so their chief advertising value is in the good will of the newspapers and magazines in which they are published.

In addition to this, the armed forces themselves are directly involved in advertising. In 1947 the Army alone was the third largest advertiser in the nation. Given such "business" by the armed forces and their industrial allies, it is not surprising that the newspapers and magazines of the nation tend to cooperate with rather than oppose military policies that keep the cold war going.

At an annual dinner of the Bureau of Advertising of the American Newspaper Publishers Association, Charles E. Wilson, then Defense Mobilization Director, commended the publishers for their cooperation in printing

> . . . millions of words laying down the premise . . . that the free world is in mortal danger . . . If the people were not convinced of that it would be impossible for Congress to vote

the vast sums now being spent to avert that danger . . .
With the support of public opinion as marshalled by the press,
we are off to a good start. But the mobilization job cannot
be completed unless such support is continuous . . . It is
our job — yours and mine — to keep our people convinced
that the only way to keep disaster away from our shores is
to build America's might.[4]

Colonel W. G. Caldwell, Deputy Chief of Military Personnel and Procurement, confirmed this press and magazine cooperation and linked it with advertising. In 1952 he told the Senate
Appropriations Committee: "For the paid advertisement you
might say that we are receiving approximately ten or twenty times
public service or free advertisement, which we probably obtain
by using the paid advertisements." He added: "The magazines
are very cooperative in writing stories . . . The newspapers and
the radio, particularly, give us a great deal of public service space
and time." [5]

The military builds good will among columnists and reporters as well as publishers. They are taken on cruises, flights
to Europe and around the world. A former newspaperman who
had been the recipient of military favors wrote in the Ridgewood,
N. J. *Herald News* of December 15, 1960: "Friends of mine
in the Washington press corps have enjoyed trips to the Far
East — by way of Paris, of course — and Greenland, and indeed
around the world . . ."

Sometimes columnists are included in cruises and flights
with others the military wants to woo. A Berkeley, Calif. *Gazette*
columnist, in a series of articles beginning December 10, 1951,
wrote: "We have always had a great deal of respect for the
men who wear the gold Navy wings . . . To that we now add
awe and admiration. For we have been to Florida and back, a
guest of the U.S. Navy." He pointed out that this was "not
exactly a newspaper cruise but a few of us were invited to ride
along with some of the top educators in the Bay Area and some
VIPs." The Navy made a real friend of this columnist, for he
lauded the Navy and spoke of the "new and valuable knowledge"
the educators and industrialists were able "to carry back to their

various schools and industries . . ." He concluded: "The knowledge imparted will repay the Navy many fold for the comparatively minor expense of the trip."

These trips are not always just to build general good will. There are often specific objectives. On one such occasion when the campaign against discrimination in the armed forces was at its height, the Army took a group of Negro newspaper publishers and editors on a trip to Europe.

While cultivating the press, the military has not neglected television, radio and the movies. Army and Air Force policy, which was set forth in the April 10, 1950 *Radio Daily,* provides that each station supporting Army and Air Force programs will have "an opportunity to obtain a portion of the national or local advertising." Through the Advertising Council which was set up in World War II to marshal the forces of advertising for the war effort, the armed forces have continued in peacetime to get similar support. This "free" advertising, which is wholly or partially deductible in figuring taxes, as well as direct military advertising, is intended not only to help the military recruiting programs but to build prestige and general support for the armed forces.

As early as January, 1948, *Variety,* the voice of American show business, stated that the military is now "Radio's No. 1 music sponsor," playing "a $6,000,000 parlay at cut-rate." This figure is *Variety's* estimate of what the various military shows would cost on a radio time-and-talent basis. The networks and advertising agencies write off their contributions as "public service" except for agency executive expense accounts which the government foots.

Army planning for its extensive public relations program began during World War II. It was in 1942, for example, that the Army bought from Paramount Pictures the largest motion picture studio in the East, built at a cost of $10,000,000. At this Army Signal Corps Photographic Center in Long Island City, New York, civilian actors in Army uniform get a minimum rate of $45 a day. They are assisted by about 150 to 200 real soldiers. Many of the best known films about the Army have been made at the Center.

The Army helps private motion picture firms in order to influence the public. In describing this work on motion pictures, a spokesman for the Defense Department said: "The impression they convey must be a correct one because much of the attitude of the public toward the Army, Navy, and Air Force . . . revolves around these pictures which have a very great influence on the public." He added, "It is stuff that we simply couldn't buy and it is priceless." [6]

The Army's Motion Picture Chief points out that "to qualify for military cooperation" a film depicting an Army subject must be a "picture that will reflect favorably on the Army." The Army advisor appointed to work with the film company must be "forceful enough to insure that his suggestions will be followed." [7]

Every medium that can be used is penetrated and exploited. There are branches of the Pentagon propaganda machine to maintain liaison with national organizations and to arrange special events such as military exhibits at state and county fairs. A Speakers and Public Appearances Branch arranges for armed forces speakers to be invited before certain gatherings to present the military point of view. When an address by a prominent general before a national convention of educators or farmers or labor union members is widely reported in the press, the probability is that this Pentagon branch suggested that he be invited and even wrote his speech. Again and again during the UMT campaign this writer was informed by leaders of national organizations how difficult, if not impossible, it was to turn down the Army when it wanted an opportunity for General Marshall or General Bradley or some other general to speak.

Even the comic strips are used to advantage. *Look* magazine for October, 1947 indicated that much of Joe Palooka's comic strip when he was in uniform was inspired by long conferences at the Pentagon. This was at the height of the UMT campaign when the Army wanted to sell teenagers as well as

parents on the idea that the Army was the place to build men
like Joe Palooka. Even today a number of comic strips con-
sistently or periodically portray military heroes and military
themes favorable to the armed forces or some particular program.

The military public relations program is one of the best
organized groups in the armed forces. It functions not only as
a centralized unit for the entire Department of Defense but also
in each of the three military branches — Army, Navy and Air
Force. It permeates the whole organization. An official Army
directive, for example, states: "Public Information officers will
be appointed to the staff of each installation and to the staffs
of all commanders down to and including the regiment or unit
of equivalent size."

Undoubtedly one reason for the fact that important generals
like Eisenhower and MacArthur were so well known and popular
as to be considered for the presidency was their full-time publicity
men. General MacArthur in 1948 had 135 military and 40
civilian aides assigned to his command in the Far East as publicity
personnel. General Eisenhower, while Chief of Staff, had
similar numbers doing his public relations work. In 1948 the
Chief of Staff had 44 military personnel and 113 civilians working in this capacity.[8]

Other personnel are given propaganda assignments as well.
The September, 1952 *Army Information Digest,* in listing the
six main duties of the chaplain, listed public relations as the
first field. Even the Army Nike teams are publicity-conscious.
In June, 1960 a Nike team brought their weapon to display in
the public square in Ridgewood, N. J. In one news column it
was pointed out: "Incidentally the team brought along its
portable kitchen and served apple pie and coffee to the spectators."
What is this but smart public relations?

The cost of maintaining such an extensive publicity and
propaganda establishment runs into millions of dollars each year.
In 1950 Congress appropriated $9,644,143 for this work. In
1951 the amount was increased to $12,293,576. In 1952

Congress decided that the military request for $15,622,903 should be limited to $10,950,000. For 1953 the military asked for $11,759,702, but Congress, in one of its periodic revolts against some aspect of military spending, decided to limit military propaganda to an appropriation of $5,554,851.

Faced with this cut, the armed forces reduced somewhat its public relations staff, which had been estimated by a Congressional Committee on Reduction of Nonessential Federal Expenditures, at 3,022 civilians and uniformed personnel. Instead of complying with the intent of the Congressional mandate, the armed forces sought ways of avoiding it. The August 3, 1952 *Washington Star* reported that "the reduction in appropriations has brought about a careful screening of all public information activities to determine if some functions should not properly be carried under other labels." One way the intent of Congress was evaded was having officers or soldiers perform public relations as a part-time or "spare time" activity.

After the cutback in the public relations budget the armed forces became much less talkative about their techniques and resources for propaganda, but their molding of public opinion continued.

The issue of military propaganda was first raised seriously in Congress in 1947. After a careful study of Army propaganda for universal military training, a house subcommittee headed by Forest A. Harness described the problem in an extensive report. That report said:

> It has become apparent to your committee that Government propaganda is designed, in most instances, to make the individual believe he is thinking for himself. In reality, Government propaganda distorts facts, with such authority that the person becomes prejudiced or biased in the direction which the Government propagandists wish to lead national thinking. It is the authority and the supposed objectivity of Government which leads people to accept, without question, the words released by Government officials and agencies. Propaganda in its crudest form appeals to emotion only. Government propaganda is frequently only "slanted," but accomplishes the same result. An individual might be wary and critical of material coming from a "special interest group." He knows

such groups have an axe to grind, but he will consider it as gospel truth, if the Government says the identical thing, because he thinks Government officials are impartial.

Your committee, therefore, reports its firm conclusion that, on the basis of the evidence at hand, the War Department, its personnel, and civilian employees have gone beyond the limits of their proper duty of providing factual information to the people and the Congress and have engaged in propaganda supported by taxpayers' money to influence legislation now pending before the Congress.[9]

As a result of this finding by the committee, the Attorney General was officially informed of the Army's consistent violation of the law. The Army nevertheless persisted in its illegal propaganda and the Truman Administration took no steps to enforce the law.

In 1948 the Senate Committee on Post Office and Civil Service conducted public hearings on the Army's use of the mails for propaganda. As a result of this investigation the Army made a concession to the Committee and discontinued the mailing to civilians of one magazine which had been a matter of discussion in the hearings.

The military has asserted its right to propagandize civilians against the expressed will of Congress. No President or Secretary of Defense has been able to stop it except temporarily and then only at a few specific points in the interests of coordinating military policy with State Department policy. "There is little doubt," wrote a distinguished scientist, Harrison Brown, in 1960, "that the armed services exert more control over Congress than that body exerts over the Defense Department." [10]

The executive director of a White House commission that reported on U.S. publicity activities wrote in 1961: "And through its links with a battalion of national organizations, the Defense Department has a built-in system of communication with the American people unequalled in scale by anything available to other Federal agencies." [11]

In general the public is unaware that it is being deliberately propagandized by the military. Although Congressmen know what is happening, few take any steps either to expose or oppose the steady militarization of the American mind. In high places there seems to be a willingness to let the military-industrial complex continue to exercise power. James Forrestal, when he was Secretary of Defense, encouraged this attitude. In speaking to the first class of the Armed Forces Information School he told the graduating publicity specialists they would have to overcome traditional American suspicion of militarism and make each citizen and community feel a responsibility to the military. "It is difficult," he said, "because our democracy and our country are founded upon an underlying suspicion of armies and of the force that they reflect and represent." [12]

So well have the military publicists done their job in the years since Forrestal's exhortation that there is no longer an underlying suspicion of armies. Instead those who insist on maintaining civil supremacy or in curbing military power are themselves put on the defensive in our society. Today, for the most part, the American people acquiesce in military demands. Except for those minorities who protest nuclear weapons tests and the nuclear arms race the people are strangely silent. The economic activity of the Pentagon and the military public relations experts have succeeded in establishing a new climate in America.

CHAPTER 11

THE ARMY VERSUS THE RESERVES

One of the continuing civil-military problems is the Army's relationship to the National Guard and the Reserves. The record of Army relations with the Reserves in the postwar period is a revealing one. During the days when the Army was building its military-industrial alliance, the reserves were thought of as fitting into the industrial as well as the military pattern. The April 2, 1947 *New York World Telegram* said, "The War Department wants to convert a large part of the so-called organized reserve from paper army status into genuine marching and drilling units established among factory employees throughout the country." This program, known as the Army's Affiliation Program, envisioned 2,500 units in various industries and business firms throughout the nation.

The Army's Affiliation Program was intended to make static the employer-employee relationship by having the employers function as officers and the employees as subordinates or enlisted men. The Army felt that in the event of an emergency, the members of these units would be doing exactly the same kind of work they were then doing under the same bosses and with the same associates. The only difference is that they would be in the Army. The commanding officer of the unit was to be jointly chosen by the Army and the sponsoring industry.

Although the Army did organize a number of reserve units in industry, the reserve program in the postwar period was largely left up in the air because General Marshall and his colleagues wanted to wait until Congress adopted universal military training. Brigadier General E. A. Evans, the Executive Director of the Reserve Officers Association, complained to the Senate Armed

129

Services Committee April 1, 1948 that "nowhere do we hear of the possibility of doing something to maintain, revitalize, keep intact our Reserve which we have at the present time. A 2,400,-000 Reserve is no small-sized Army and Navy." General Evans testified before the House Armed Services Committee on April 22, 1948 that the Army had done "very little" to help the Reserves and had done "nothing" in its obligation to furnish equipment.

The May, 1947 *Reserve Officer* charged that the attitude of the Regular Army toward the Reserves is "anything but encouraging to the civilian soldier." It illustrated its complaint by referring to the proposal of the Army to transfer $30,000,000 from the Reserve budget to the Regular Army. Secretary of War Robert Patterson in a reply printed in the June 19, 1947 *New York Times* admitted the transfer of funds and added that the War Department had also transferred to the Regular Army $53,000,000 from the National Guard appropriation.

In 1949 the Reserve Officers Association was complaining that only three months after members in 2,800 units began receiving drill pay "the Army suddenly claims that it has run out of funds . . . This is the kind of irresponsible lack of consideration that has marked the relationship of the Army to its reserves for many years."

When the Korean War began the Army's previous downgrading of the Reserves was clearly evident. A House Armed Services subcommittee in July, 1951 reported:

> We have the unpleasant picture of some reservists being left behind who should have been called first, some being called first who should have been called last, many being called who, because of the national interest, should never have been called, and still others attempting to volunteer for active duty and not being accepted.

The Army responded to criticism of its handling of the Reserve program by insisting that only a compulsory reserve program built upon universal military training could provide an efficient reserve system.

When the Army finally got its way with the passage of a

compulsory reserve program in the Reserve Forces Act of 1955, nothing happened to alter the Army's basic attitude toward the Reserves.

One new reason for traditional Army downgrading of the Reserves and National Guard is found in the new technology of warfare. The original assumption that underlay the whole reserve program was the idea that the United States should be prepared for a large general mobilization on the pattern of the two World Wars. Yet the now general acceptance of nuclear weapons in tactical as well as strategic warfare has altered this. Walter Millis, the military historian, has pointed out how this assumption is being questioned today:

> If we ever mobilized the thirty-seven infantry and armored divisions envisaged by the 1955 Reserve Act it seems most unlikely that we could transport or supply them over railways, through ports, and across beaches smoldering and radioactive from the nuclear fires. The ground soldier is thought of today principally as an instrument for limited or "brush-fire" wars; as such, he is scarcely any longer a ground soldier, but must be air-transportable, which limits his numbers severely. Military men now pretty generally believe that any major war will have to be fought to the end with whatever was ready at the beginning — and that means combat ready . . . Even if we should again be required to mobilize great masses of man-power, comparable to the 15,000,000 raised in 1941 45, most of them would have to be trained to complex technical skills not usually acquirable from the kind of training one gets in boot camp or in National Guard and reserve divisions.[1]

In support of this concept of a highly mobile force, Major Thomas J. McDonald wrote in the August, 1957 *Army:* "But such a force cannot be built around UMT. We will need long term regulars receiving adequate inducements to offset a rigorous training program."

It is also significant that Regular Army units are being trained in the use of tactical atomic weapons. John Graham, an attorney and veteran, reported in 1958 that

. . . the reserve units were not equipped with atomic weapons, nor was there any plan to do so; their present members were totally unfamiliar with the use of, and defenses against, such weapons; the six-months men were receiving no instruction in atomic weapons during their active duty training . . . In the event of hostilities the Regular Army units equipped with tactical atomic weapons would be committed. Even assuming that it was possible to mobilize the reserve, there could be no place for it on the atomic war ground.[2]

Originally the Army had wanted UMT in order to put everyone in the Reserves. Later when the Army began to doubt the usefulness of the reserves, it found serious obstacles in its effort to reduce or eliminate certain reserve programs. Many Congressmen had a vested interest in the National Guard because the Guard performs state as well as federal functions. The State governors and the various state political machines were supporters of the Guard. It would, therefore, be difficult to destroy or rationalize reducing the reserves without having to face a similar proposal for the Guard. Congress, for this reason, had written into the Military Appropriations Act for 1959 a mandatory minimum strength for the Army reserves. President Eisenhower, reflecting the Army point of view, indicated in his budget message to Congress on January 19, 1959 that he was opposed to Congressional efforts to determine the minimum strength of the reserves. Calling this an "unprecedented departure from past policy," he added, it "is entirely inconsistent with a policy of promptly adjusting our military forces and concepts to rapidly changing world conditions and revolutionary advances in science and technology."

The President's statement that there was no need to maintain a mandatory minimum number of reserves should have led Congress to eliminate the compulsory reserve and the six-month program. But the Army had no intention of giving up compulsion even though it was easily possible to get all the volunteers needed for the size reserve for which the Army was willing to pay. The military position was perhaps best summarized by a Deputy Assistant Secretary of Defense, Stephen Jackson, in a statement to a Senate subcommittee on veterans' affairs: "The military obligation is the normal life for young men today and requires no special reward." [3]

While insisting on compulsion and on the idea that everyone belongs in principle to the military, the armed forces nevertheless act as if the reserve obligation is relatively unimportant. A further indication is the evidence found by a Senate Preparedness subcommittee in 1959 that there is military politics in the assignment of top reserve officers. The committee contended that higher ranks had been conferred "without reference to the nation's needs, to any known military requirement, or to the capability of the individual." The committee found that reserve commissions were often given as a reward for past service in or to the military rather than on the basis of expectation of future military service. There is "a disturbing trend," said the committee, to "use the reserve component as an instrumentality of some benefit for regular officers who resign their commissions to accept paying jobs with industry." [4]

In October, 1961, 155,000 reservists were called to active duty chiefly as a military show of strength to bolster Administration policy with respect to Berlin. This mobilization produced widespread criticism both from reservists and their representatives in Congress. Senator William Proxmire (D., Wis.) summarized the first complaint in pointing out that the "men have not been given a satisfactory explanation of why they were called." A second complaint dealt with inadequate arrangements, including shortages of housekeeping equipment and military hardware.

The Army admitted when confronted with the evidence that in the assignment of reservists there had been many mistakes. A heavy weapons infantryman had been assigned as a neuropsychiatric specialist and an air defense missile unit commander was assigned as a general duty nurse. In one reserve unit in which an officer and 27 enlisted men had been receiving drill pay the officer and 16 men were unqualified for their military specialties. A report of the General Accounting Office revealed that 448, or 28 per cent, of 1,619 reservists in seventeen selected units had been assigned to duties not related to their military speciality. A second report said that studies covering other sections of the Army showed similar results.[5]

The most serious and persistent criticism, however, was leveled at the call-up of men who had records of extended duty in the past when many reservists with only a few months' service had not been called. The official Army explanation for this criticism was given to a House Armed Services subcommittee in April, 1962. Assistant Secretary of Defense C. P. Runge reported that out of a pool of 54,000 reservists with six months training, only 14,500 had the military skills needed to fill out mobilized reserve units.

The Reserve Forces Act, as we have noted in Chapter 8, provided for compulsory reserve duty for all who enlisted or were drafted. In addition it provided for a six-month enlistment for boys seventeen to eighteen and one-half. Technically these were volunteers, since by enlisting for six months plus seven and one-half years they were able to escape a two-year draft term. Because the program was very unpopular at first the reserve term was by administrative regulation reduced to five and one-half years and expanded so that anyone who had not yet received his induction notice could enlist. Walter Millis has written:

> There was no real military requirement for this particularly useless form of reserve training; it was rather simply a device for insuring that there would be enough military places, active or reserve, to absorb substantially all those reaching military age and thus to maintain the universality of a system which, to be just and to survive, had to be universal in fact.[6]

After Runge, the Pentagon's spokesman, had admitted that six months training had not and could not give men the skills the Army needed, Representative F. Edward Hebert asked "So what is the use of the six months service? Except for them to do the sit ups or calisthenics and wear a uniform and learn how to salute and all the basic training of the military man." In spite of the ineffectiveness of the six-month program, neither the Army nor the House Armed Services Committee made any move to eliminate it. Instead, the Committee on June 18, 1963 proposed that the active duty obligation be increased from six months to eighteen months for those reservists including National Guardsmen who receive training in certain military skills.

One result of the criticism of the 1961 reserve mobilization was a Pentagon decision, announced on April 4, 1962, to reorganize the Army's Reserve and National Guard so as to reduce numbers and increase readiness for combat. The Army felt that of a total of thirty-seven Army National Guard and Reserve divisions eight were in excess of need. A total of 892 company-sized units could be dispensed with, said the Army spokesman, Stephen Ailes.

The proposed reduction was attacked by the President of the National Guard Association, state governors, and members of Congress. Congressmen, who leveled their attacks at civilians in the Pentagon rather than the military, could scarcely have forgotten that three years earlier, when different civilians headed the Pentagon under the Eisenhower administration, the military had wanted the flexibility to make just such a proposal. Moreover, General Warren, Chief of the Army Reserves, had indicated in Congressional hearings, that the Joint Chiefs of Staff had made the decision to recommend cutting the numerical strength of the reserves.[7]

President Eisenhower had summarized the problem in his final Budget Message of January, 1961. Calling for a reduction in the National Guard and the Army reserves approximating the reduction later proposed by the Kennedy administration, he said: "The excess strengths which have been provided by the Congress above my recommendations in the last several years are unnecessarily costing the American people over $80,000,000 annually and have been too long based on other than strictly military needs." [8]

The Reserve problem is a complex one. It is a source of political controversy between the states and the Federal government, if only because the National Guard performs certain state functions while being largely subsidized by the Federal government. Congressmen who on every other military issue back the Pentagon tend for political reasons back home to support the

National Guard when any conflict occurs. For this reason the Kennedy administration and the Army had to bow to Congressional legislation that provided a drill-pay force of 400,000 for the Army National Guard and 300,000 for the Army Reserve, although the Army had planned to cut the Guard and the Reserve to 642,000.

The Reserve problem is also a civil-military one. Although the Army was defeated by Congress in its effort to reduce the overall number in the Guard and the Reserves, it may nevertheless accomplish its purpose. The Army has decided to raise qualifications for entering the Guard and Reserves. An Associated Press dispatch in the September 13, 1962 *Kansas City Star* stated that "one effect of the upgrading will be to make it harder for the Guard and Reserve to maintain the 700,000 total that Congress has decreed."

Another aspect of the Reserve problem is the compulsory-voluntary argument. The Army has been under Prussian influence for so long that it is difficult for most West Point graduates to think in terms other than compulsion. The distinguished engineer and former President of Antioch College, Arthur Morgan, described in the February, 1946 *American Mercury* the origins of this influence, in an article entitled "Conscription and the West Point Mind":

> West Point is Prussian in conception. The revered Captain Thayer who reorganized the Academy in 1817, brought the pattern back with him from Europe, where military institutions rigidly followed the lines of the anti-democratic European governments. Three factors have helped West Point to perpetuate that pattern: the habit of appointing its own graduates to its teaching staff; the admission of immature and impressionable youth, mostly just out of high school; and the system of extreme isolation.

The Prussian system is anti-democratic, not only in its emphasis on compulsion but also in its tendency to look upon citizen soldiers as too civilian in orientation to be trusted.

The conflict in points of view was evident in the 1962 Congressional hearings on the Army's plan to reorganize the

Guard and Reserves. A Pentagon spokesman said, "the Department of Defense is opposed to placing all Reserve participation on a volunteer basis." On the other hand, Maj. Gen. William H. Harrison, Jr., president of the National Guard Association, argued for a voluntary reserve in asserting that "it is a well recognized fact that a volunteer is a happier and better adjusted soldier than one who is compelled to participate."

This position of the Guard is not new. It was held by Guard leaders prior to the adoption of the present compulsory reserve program. Col. Robert F. Cocklin, in the August, 1953 *Combat Forces Journal,* reported that "Most Guard leaders strongly oppose such measures. They want the Guard to remain a voluntary service (despite the time and difficulties in recruiting) and they have not seen a workable method of forcing civilians to attend training sessions against their will."

The Guard, of course, is right. It is impossible for a modern industrial nation like the United States to rely on a compulsory reserve without severe dislocation in emergency and serious interference during peacetime in necessary civilian preparation for emergency. Both Congress and the Pentagon were aware of this problem before the compulsory reserve program was adopted in 1955. The Manpower Resources Committee for National Security reported:

> Since large numbers of men having critical skills are in the Reserves the extent to which Reservists are actually available for military duty is uncertain. On the other hand, civilian research, development and production cannot be considered in a high state of readiness for an emergency if a large fraction of key personnel in these activities are subject to sudden withdrawal for military service.[9]

If the present compulsory reserve is continued and men between the ages of twenty and thirty-five (depending on date of enlistment) are to be almost universally in the Reserves, we would in the event of their full mobilization take such a large cross section of men from industry, agriculture, educational and professional work that, as the Manpower Committee pointed out,

"A disproportionate number of these persons might be withdrawn from industry at a time when industry itself will be meeting emergency requirements."

General Lewis B. Hershey, head of the Selective Service System, has estimated that about one-half of those eligible for military service would be deferred in the national interest.[10] The Pentagon thus would need a workable system for screening out essential men. Its failure to have such a system in the 1961 Berlin mobilization was in part due to the complexities inherent in the compulsory system.

The Army's emphasis on compulsion has been neatly camouflaged in the phrase "equity of military obligation." This is simply a phrase to express the military dogma that "a period of military training for every young man is of intrinsic benefit to the Nation, even if a percentage of those trained cannot qualify. . . ."

But the direct result of all this is a waste of time, money, and men.

CHAPTER 12

THE MILITARY TAKE-OVER
OF FOREIGN POLICY

American foreign policy today is almost totally conditioned by the cold war and almost totally subordinated to military considerations.

This strong military influence has been carefully developed over the years since the middle of World War II. During the war, military officers began to work with the Treasury Department "to coordinate foreign and domestic military purchases." Then a European Advisory Commission, on which both the War and Navy Departments were represented, was created in 1943. In December, 1943, an informal "working security committee" which included military members was created by the State Department. The next step was the creation of an influential policy-making group, the State-War-Navy Coordinating Committee (SWNCC), sometimes referred to as SWANK. Although formed in December, 1944, it was not publicly identified until May, 1946, when Secretary of State Byrnes mentioned it in testimony before the House Foreign Affairs Committee.

This Coordinating Committee, now known as the National Security Council, was authorized by the National Security Act of 1947, the law intended to unify the armed forces. The law provided that the Council shall "advise the President with respect to the integration of domestic, foreign, and military policies relating to the national security . . ." It also provided that the Council "shall be composed of the President; the Secretary of State; the Secretary of Defense; . . . the Secretary of the Army; . . . the Secretary of the Navy; the Secretary of the Air Force; the Chairman of the National Security Resources Board" and certain other officers if the President desires to designate them.

Thus, of the seven permanent members, aside from the President, only one member of the Council headed a strictly non-military agency — the Secretary of State, and for a time he was a General, George C. Marshall. Although not a member by law, the Chairman of the Joint Chiefs of Staff has attended regularly the meetings of the National Security Council.

Subsequently, membership on the National Security Council has been revised by law to eliminate the Secretaries of the Army, Navy and Air Force. The Secretary of Defense and the Director of the Office of Defense Mobilization, however, are by law members of the Council. In addition to these representatives of the "defense" viewpoint and the Chairman of the Joint Chiefs of Staff, two other persons representing agencies allied with the military, the Chairman of the Atomic Energy Commission and the Director of the Central Intelligence Agency, regularly attend council meetings.

Military influence is also brought to bear on the National Security Council through its planning board, which prepares the data for Council decisions. Within the Department of Defense an assistant secretary with a staff of about forty-five senior military officers formulates views on foreign policy matters for and furnishes a representative to the planning board of the National Security Council.

In this and in other ways, the attitudes of the Joint Chiefs of Staff and of the individual services are transmitted, directly or indirectly, to the Council and to the planning staff that prepares papers for its deliberations.

As Blair Bolles, Washington Director of the Foreign Policy Association, wrote in 1948: "Since the Council meets without publicity, the American people cannot challenge its thinking directly. Decisions which it makes are never attributed to it." In this way, foreign policy matters have passed out of the realm of public and Congressional discussion. The ironic thing about this arrangement is that it was adopted as part of the bill which unified the armed forces. The entire debate which raged between 1945 and 1947 was over the issue of whether one or two military agencies might dominate the rest. The question of Military representatives on the National Security Council dominating the civilian State Department never entered the discussion.

Although the National Security Act of 1947 gave Congressional approval to military participation in the formulation of foreign policy, such participation had in fact reached important proportions during the period when the State-War-Navy Coordinating Committee was involved in policy making. For example, one of the earliest efforts of the integrated military-foreign policy Council was the naive proposal for solving the Chinese civil war by "the integration of the armed forces maintained by the Nationalist Government and the Communist Party in China." This integration was to be accomplished by sending to China a "military advisory group of American Army and Navy personnel." [1] This plan was evolved after an effort during 1945 to help the Chinese Central Government with military means to suppress the Communists.[2] The scheme was embodied in a bill which provided that the United States would, with 750 Army and 250 Navy personnel, give military training to the Chinese. Secretary of State Byrnes, in a letter to the Speaker of the House, wrote that "the proposed bill has been prepared in collaboration with the War and Navy Departments and has the full endorsement of General of the Army George C. Marshall." [3]

When President Truman appointed Gen. George Marshall as Secretary of State on January 7, 1947, the military emphasis in foreign policy became even more clearly evident. General Marshall conducted foreign policy like a soldier facing an enemy. The *New York Times* of April 30, 1947 described Marshall's conduct at the Moscow Conference of foreign ministers as follows:

> In the entire six weeks of the Moscow conference, however, Gen. Marshall apparently did not unbend. He was as rigid as the Washington Monument . . . though there were many outstanding questions between the United States and Russia and the United States and Britain, he apparently made no effort to talk out these problems . . .

The *New York Times* called "probably without precedent"

Gen. Marshall's instructions concerning military precautions at a diplomatic conference. The instructions were printed and stated: "It must be assumed that there is no security outside the office and rooms of Spasso House and the Chancery." The newspaper added: "A detachment of United States Army military police, working in shifts, is standing twenty-four hour duty outside Ambassador Walter Bedell Smith's home." The *Times* of March 30, 1947 pointed out that Gen. Marshall slept with a pistol by his bed while in the American embassy at Moscow. Since all of this information was available to the press, it could not have failed to have an impact on Russia and other countries. General Marshall's prestige in this country was so great, however, that few persons challenged the military conduct of foreign policy while he was Secretary of State.

One of the first accusations about military control made by a person with full knowledge of the problem was made by a former Under-Secretary of State, Sumner Welles. In a public address in 1948 he spoke of American foreign policy as being made by "militarists" when it should be made by civilian "diplomats with a long range point of view." [4]

It was not only military planning but civilian acquiescence in it, especially that of President Truman, which made military control over foreign policy possible. In May, 1951, at a Senate hearing Senator Styles Bridges (R., N.H.) asked Gen. Marshall: " . . . when there has been a division between the Defense Department and the Chiefs of Staff . . . and the State Department which advocated or stood for more pacifying methods . . . has not the President generally sided with the State Department views?" General Marshall replied: "I can answer that pretty accurately out of my own knowledge and my experience. I can recall no occasion when Mr. Truman has acted adversely to the Chiefs of Staff and the Secretary of Defense in relation to the State Department." [5]

In those early postwar years, the Pentagon was so clearly desirous of helping shape foreign policy that on August 3, 1949 an Office of Foreign Military Affairs was set up in the Pentagon "to help keep the National Military Establishment in step with the National Security Council, the State Department, and other agencies in the field of 'politico-military affairs.' " [6]

In line with the new postwar trend of military penetration of politics and foreign policy, the U.S. Military Academy at West Point began a new program called "Operation Statesman" in the late 1940's. This program was designed to prepare officers for a role in government and foreign policy. A *New York Times* report of the program said: "For the future officers are preparing for the role they may some day have to assume in earnest — the unique combination of soldier-diplomat born of World War II."

In 1953 the Air Force listed a new position of "international politico-military affairs officer," which is a title now held by "a few dozen senior officers." The Navy and Army have similar classifications. The Air Force describes his duties as follows: "Plans, formulates, coordinates, and implements Air Force aspects of international politico-military policies, advises and briefs commanders and Government officials on international problems affecting the Air Force; and represents the Air Force in international and interdepartmental conferences and negotiations." [7]

The strong role of the military in comparison to that of the State Department in the immediate postwar period is also evident in military educational programs. The National War College has trained not only army officers but also about 18 State Department officers assigned to it each year. State Department students have also been assigned to other War Colleges. But in June, 1954, following the report of the Wriston Committee on State Department personnel the department began a major effort to restore its Foreign Service Institute to a strong position. The State Department recognized the need for its personnel to know what the military agencies of government were planning, but, partly for prestige reasons, it was anxious to build up its own education program.

The military has also established direct relations with the future officers of foreign nations. A foreign liaison office at the Pentagon arranges for visits of foreign officers and cadets to the

United States to inspect military establishments here and to be entertained on a royal scale.

Naval officers have also become involved in foreign affairs. They played a major role in determining the status of the mandated islands of the central Pacific, and conducted the conversations which led to the creation of American bases in Spain.

Bases were not our only goal in Spain, of course. American officers through the economic aid offered in return for bases sought to invigorate the Spanish economy. They also aimed at bringing Spain into NATO. By 1959 the United States had poured more than a billion and a half dollars into Spain and had created valuable military facilities, but had apparently had little constructive effect on the political dictatorship or its limping economy.

One of the most important factors in Pentagon foreign affairs activities is its ability to dispense large amounts of military aid to overseas nations. Turkey is an example. In Turkey in 1948 there were 245 officers and men engaged in giving specialized training to the Turkish Army. The U.S. Army mission to Turkey used the original appropriation of $100 million authorized by Congress, but then announced that it had poured into Turkey close to a billion dollars in additional military aid. This aid, unauthorized by Congress, was managed by drawing upon the vast reserves of arms, munitions, and supplies of the American military establishment, writing it off as surplus goods, and sending it to Turkey. This was done at a time when the Army and Navy were asking Congress for more funds for weapons and equipment.

That this additional aid to Turkey was not the orginal intent of Congress must be obvious not only from the limit in the act placed on military aid to Turkey, but also by the failure of the military-sponsored bill S. 226. This bill had been introduced by Senator Gurney in the Eightieth Congress to authorize the President "notwithstanding the provisions of any other law . . . to sell, lend, or give naval ordnance material to foreign Governments."

The ability of the military to give large amounts of money

and equipment to foreign governments results in tremendous influence in those governments. In many countries of the world American military missions have been in a position to offer more aid than the civilian representatives of the State Department. In the event of subtle or overt conflicts between the military and the civilian points of view the military has had a greater leverage with which to move foreign relations.

From July 1, 1945 through June 30, 1960 the United States military assistance program involved the following money and military missions: Spain $456,600,000, 106 military, seventeen civilians; West Germany $947,700,000, 141 military, twenty-four civilians; France $4,242,800,000, sixty-four military and twenty-six civilians; Iran $457,500,000, 375 military, ten civilians; Thailand $305,700,000, 245 military, two civilians.[8] These samples from a much longer list of countries receiving military aid reveal something of the influence the armed forces can bring to bear on countries around the world.

One result of our extensive military aid is the building, equipping and financing of armies in underdeveloped lands to such an extent that they often become the most powerful force in the life of their countries. Because of this power which we have created and continue to support, the armies either tend to become elite groups who manipulate the civilian rulers, in their countries, or else they tend openly to usurp and establish military dictatorships.

Another result of our big military aid program is that the United States becomes dependent on the military regimes we create. Once created, such seem to American military men to be the only hope of stability and hence the only alternative to the country's going Communist. Since military distatorship tends to strengthen any well-led opposition to such regimes and often brings Communists and non-Communist opponents into a working relation, we have to meet increased demands of the military allies we have created. Likewise if such dictators are threatened with external opposition we seem to have no alternative but to give them further support. The Senate majority leader, Mike Mansfield, acknowledged this problem in June, 1961 when he indicated that the United States realized its aid money was being wasted in Korea but we were in no position to withhold it.

Representative Wayne Hays (D., Ohio), in an exchange with General Lyman Lemnitzer, Chairman of the Joint Chiefs of Staff, before the House Foreign Affairs Committee in 1961, said of Pentagon proposals for renewed military aid: "Your experience in Cuba with Batista should have taught you that you can't build an armed force on a base of quicksand. It was the same in Korea where you built a monster and a 32-year-old captain proclaimed himself a lieutenant general and took over the Government." General Lemnitzer denied the monster analogy, saying that the Korean Army had provided an effective defense against outside aggression.

American military aid also has the effect of stimulating arms competition among other countries that badly need to use their resources for building their standard of living. In 1956 American arms shipments to Pakistan, said Chester Bowles, led India to take $100 million from her second five-year plan for economic development and place it in military orders with the British and French. Similarly, weapons sent to countries in the Near East in the 1950's led to mounting competition for armaments there and in turn led to munitions orders being placed with both Communist and Western powers.

When military aid is given to colonial powers, still other problems arise. Angolans fighting for freedom from Portugal, and Algerians who fought against France, have charged that some of the weapons used against them had been given by the United States to their Portuguese and French allies in NATO.

In August, 1958 during President Eisenhower's term of office a group of eight Senators protested the "overemphasis on military assistance." They asserted that it has contributed to the maintenance of undemocratic regimes, "created a militaristic image of the United States abroad," and "tended to create military hierarchies which . . . may endanger the very . . . individual freedom we seek to safeguard." [9]

President Eisenhower acknowledged the protest and on November 24, 1958 appointed a nine-member committee headed by William H. Draper, Jr. to make an appraisal of military and economic aid. The committee was representative of the military-industrial complex, with two retired Army generals, an admiral, an Army colonel, three former under-secretaries of the Army, and a former Assistant Secretary of Defense. Four of the group were key figures in industry and finance.

The Draper Committee on March 17, 1959 urged an increase in long-term military aid and an immediate increase of $400,000,000 in addition to the $1.6 billion already requested for the next fiscal year. By an amazing coincidence the $400,-000,000 increase was the amount previously trimmed by the Budget Bureau from the original military-State Department request. On November 21, 1959 President Eisenhower created a new post of Chief of Staff in the Pentagon to direct foreign military assistance programs. He appointed General W. R. Palmer to this post and thus carried out another recommendation of the Draper committee.

In our relations with Central and South America there has been a strong military influence for many years. As early as May 19, 1926 Congress authorized military missions to all countries in the Western Hemisphere. On June 4, 1938, it agreed also to authorize the Navy to help train Latin American forces. Since then the Army and Navy have been operating on an important scale in Latin America. In early 1946 there were 17 military missions in thirteen countries and in the year 1946-1947 $408,390 was spent on American military and naval missions to Latin American governments for the training of troops. In the year 1947-1948 the sum for these missions was increased to $1,240,000.

The purpose of the increased use of military missions, according to Army spokesmen before the House Appropriations subcommittee, was to encourage training in our methods and utilization of our equipment by Latin American armies.

In line with this, the Army and Navy began a program of pressure to get the United States to transfer a considerable quantity of equipment to Canada and the Latin American nations.

They were successful in getting President Truman on May 26, 1947 to ask Congress to make arms and military equipment available to the other American states. Despite Army and Navy pressure, civilian elements in the State Department, led by Spruille Braden, opposed the Latin-American arms program on the ground that it would not strengthen their defenses but would strengthen the non-democratic elements in the hemisphere at the expense of the democratic elements.

Dean Acheson, then Under Secretary of State, in a letter to the War and Navy Departments on March 19, 1947, said that encouraging expenditures for armaments in Latin and South American countries would weaken their economies and therefore their political stability. But General Marshall rejected the advice of his State Department Latin American advisers and fell in alongside his old Army associates to support the Truman proposal.

President Truman's message and General Marshall's support were hailed by those nations where the Army had long played a major role in politics. One of the first to endorse the plan was Argentina's Peron government. Many civilian elements in Latin America, however, regarded the arms program with genuine distress. The *Washington Post* editorially opposed the measure on June 28, 1947, saying:

> We conclude that the whole thing is dangerous from beginning to end, and we should rue the day that we inaugurated this arms traffic, set up our military missions as the dominant element in our representation to Latin American countries and elevated the status of Latin American military staffs as the dominant element in those countries.

Although an Arms Standardization bill did not pass, lend-lease military equipment was sent to South American nations as late as 1947 and war surplus was made available at a fraction of the original cost of the material. In addition to this, the State Department sanctioned munitions sales by American firms to Central and South America totalling $54,064,878.63. This was only slightly less than the sum of $55,670,593.23 paid by Europe to United States munitions firms.[10]

In 1947 the United States and Latin American nations

signed a mutual defense treaty known as the Rio Pact. During the Korean War General Marshall, then Secretary of Defense, along with the State Department and General Charles L. Bolte, the chairman of the Inter-American Defense Board, asked for a new program of military aid to Latin America. Congress appropriated $38 million. In 1952 this was expanded to $65 million. Military aid averaged about $65 million annually between 1952 and 1959.

American military policy in Latin America is publicly announced as being for hemisphere defense but in actuality has no genuine military objectives. Instead, as Edward Lieuwen has suggested in *Arms and Politics in Latin America,* it serves four political objectives:

1. Since army officers dominate politics in most Latin American countries, the United States can play a key role by cooperating with their armed forces.

2. The United States needs votes in the United Nations and other support in the cold war. Since Latin American nations have about one-fourth of the voting power in the United Nations, military aid and military missions are sent to Latin America in the hope that the return for assistance will be made in the form of political support.

3. Arms standardization, which has now been largely achieved, serves a political purpose as well as an economic one. If the United States has a practical monopoly in the supply of arms, it eliminates the danger of military aid and hence military missions from other nations.

4. The United States is interested in maintaining internal stability. The army is the power behind nearly every Latin American government or can, if it desires, take over the government. By aiding the army the United States hopes to maintain its position of influence whatever government is in power.

The dangers in such military efforts to control politics in

Latin America are evident. Through military aid we encourage Latin American officer corps toward politics, increasing their power and inflating their ambition to play a decisive political role.

American military missions interpret hemispheric defense in terms of defense against internal subversion. In practice this means that Latin American armies are the judge as to what constitutes subversion. Support of dictators and military strong men as a measure of stability has often resulted in military opposition to genuine democratic movements. Carleton Beals has reported that "U.S. generals, admirals and the Caribbean fleet rushed in at a time when revolt might have toppled the bloodthirsty regime" of General Rafael Trujillo in the Dominican Republic.[11] The Kennedy administration, under the impact of spreading Castroism, reversed the process and helped topple Trujillo. But in Peru, after a military junta took over the government, the Kennedy administration did not stand behind Ambassador James Loeb, who defied the instigators of the military coup. Loeb lost his post.

Among the dictators who were advised and supported by American military missions was the Cuban, Batista. His overthrow, the rise of the Castro regime and the Castro turn toward the Soviet bloc are all part of the background for the present level of increased American military aid to Latin America. In 1961 the Kennedy administration proposed $74,100,000 in military assistance to Latin America, of which $21,000,000 was earmarked for "anti-subversive" equipment. At the same time military plans were stepped up for the training in the Panama Canal Zone of Latin American officers and specialists in anti-guerrilla warfare.

Over the years military aid to Latin America had been given to dictators such as Gen. Rafael Trujillo in the Dominican Republic, Gen. Alfredo Stroessner in Paraguay, and Francis Duvalier in Haiti. But these and other dictators whose military regimes have been strengthened have done nothing to end the poverty and oppression of the people. As a result the United States, now faced with the problem of desperate people planning revolution, is fearful that these revolts will be anti-American and lead to Castro-type programs. The Pentagon wants to pour even more money into Latin America to suppress revolts against regimes created by our military programs over the years. Some Congressmen have raised serious questions about such proposals. Barratt O'Hara (D., Ill.) has called the expanded aid proposals "dangerous." The Pentagon, he said, is asking a "blank check from Congress to maintain governments in power; they can be strong only if cherished in the minds and hearts of the people." [12]

Senator Hubert Humphrey (D., Minn.) has asserted that by emphasizing military aid to the detriment of economic aid the United States is "giving in to the Communists and it is just plain stupid." [13]

The United States in 1961 instituted an economic aid program called the Alliance for Progress, intended to encourage economic development and reform in Latin America. Whether this will be partly or largely nullified by the military program in Central and South American countries is not yet clear.

Military influence over foreign policy is exercised by direct intervention in international relations as well as through military aid and military missions. One illustration of this direct activity was the organization of raids against the Chinese mainland. Beginning in 1950, a series of commando-type raids were launched from Quemoy and the Tachens against the mainland. The raids, which were sometimes mounted in battalion strength, were organized by Western Enterprises, Inc., a cover name for Central Intelligence Agency activities in the area. These attacks (which were continued until 1954) and the policy of Chinese Nationalist participation in the program were decided by the CIA and the Pentagon, not by the White House and the State Department, to say nothing of Congress.[14]

This venture, planned by the military and CIA, resulted in a threat from the Chinese Communists and their shelling of Quemoy in 1954. In that crisis, the cause of which was not revealed to the American people until 1958, Admiral Arthur Radford, chairman of the Joint Chiefs of Staff, favored bombing Red China. He was backed by Air Force Chief of Staff Gen.

Nathan Twining and the Chief of Naval Operations, Admiral Robert Carney. The only dissent in the Joint Chiefs came from Army General Robert Matthew Ridgway. President Eisenhower agreed with Ridgway's point of view, and we retreated from the brink of war to which secret military action had taken us.

Another and perhaps more dangerous illustration of military intrigue is the action in Laos. At the nine-nation Geneva Conference of 1954 which ended the fighting between the French and Communist-led guerrillas in Indo-China, the United States was represented by an observer, Gen. Bedell Smith, then Under Secretary of State. The Geneva agreement among other things provided that Laos would not participate in military alliances nor permit foreign powers to establish military bases "not in conformity with the United Nations Charter." Laos also agreed not to "request foreign aid, whether in war material, in personnel or instructors except for the purpose of effective defense of their territory." All citizens of Laos would be permitted to take their place in the national community and participate in general elections.

President Eisenhower in his news conference of July 21, 1954 said that the United States would not be "bound by the decisions taken" at Geneva, but he added that "the U.S. will not use force to disturb the settlement."

In the three and one-half years following the Geneva agreements, the United States poured $135 million into Laos. Haynes Miller, a former investigator for the International Cooperation Administration, said that "more than five-sixths of the money we have spent has gone to support an Army that is almost entirely unsuited to the sort of fighting it might be called upon to do, whose very size we can estimate only with a forty per cent margin of error, and whose morale is understandably low."

He added: "In order to pay, feed and equip this army, we have flooded a primitive country with money and goods it could not possibly absorb and thereby created a situation in which corruption and fraudulent currency exchanges have flourished openly." [15]

It is no wonder that in the May, 1958 elections the Com-

munists and their allies won a majority of the seats they con-
tested in Laos. A non-Communist Laotian leader was quoted in
an interview in *Lao-Presse* as saying of this aid: "It enriches
a minority outrageously while the mass of the population remains
as poor as ever . . . Laos maintains an army of 30,000 men
including the police force. This army costs us dearly. It takes
men from agriculture and industry. And it could not possibly
defend the country from invasion." [16]

After a Communist front party polled a heavy vote in the
elections, the anti-Communists formed a united front to control
the National Assembly. American advisers put pressure on the
King and other influential Laotians to eliminate certain pro-
Communist cabinet ministers; disarm the Pathet Lao, or rebel
battalions, which under the Geneva agreement were permitted
to keep their arms; to overthrow the neutralist government of
Prince Souvanna Phouma; and to wage a determined anti-Communist campaign. Graham Greene, in the *London Times* of
January 6, 1961, reports that "Prince Souvanna's government
has been undermined by the aid given by the United States to
right wing forces" and refers to "the intrigue of American under-
cover agencies."

As a result of such American pressure, Laos on February
11, 1959 denounced the Geneva agreements and thus "cleared
the way for the United States" reported the February 13, *New
York Times*, "to give Laos stronger backing."

Under the Geneva agreements the only foreign military
personnel permitted in Laos were French. The United States
had been paying for the Laotian army but American military
leaders were unhappy about the French military training given
to that army. United States pressure on France resulted in
French consent to American assistance in training the Laotian
army. The *New York Times* reported on August 1, 1959 that
"the start of hostilities" between Pathet Lao forces and Laotian
troops "coincided with a Paris announcement that Laos had invited [Americans] to work with French military instructors in
training her armed forces . . ." The reason given by the Communists for the start of hostilities was the American intervention

in Laos. The United States Army, Navy and Air units in the Philippines were put on a semi-alert and American planes shuttled arms into Laos.

On August 9, 1960 Captain Kong Le led his second paratroop battalion in an uprising that overthrew the American-sponsored government of Premier Tiao Somsanith. Believing that Laos should not be involved in the cold war, he restored as head of the government Prince Souvanna Phouma. Souvanna's cabinet included the right-wing Gen. Phoumi Nosavan as Vice-Premier. There were "no pro-Communists in the group" and "at least half of the members of that government were right of center," according to the October 10, 1961 *New York Times.* "It is now widely accepted," the *Times* continued, "that Gen. Phoumi Nosavan was persuaded to spurn his post in the government and rebel against it by agents of the Central Intelligence Agency and United States military officers stationed in Laos to train the Laotian army."

Britain, France and even the civilian-staffed American Embassy in Laos held that American support of the right-wing general would result in strong reaction from the Communist bloc. They were right and the military were wrong. Pro-Communist troops began moving and left Gen. Phoumi Nosavan with only about 40 per cent of the country.

Upon the collapse of Gen. Phoumi, top Pentagon officers in Washington decided that American intervention was too difficult logistically. The decision to seek a coalition government in Laos, said *I. F. Stone's Weekly* of May 21, 1962, was made "before Kennedy's inauguration when the Pentagon . . . decided that it didn't want to invervene."

After a cease-fire had been declared, the British, Russian and American representatives agreed on a coalition government to be headed by Prince Souvanna Phouma again. In this coalition the ministries in charge of the army and the police were to be given to neutralists. But Gen. Phoumi refused to agree, apparently in an effort to insure that these posts stayed under his control. The State Department withheld monthly aid payments amounting to almost $4,000,000, for the salary of General

Phoumi's army, as pressure to persuade the general to agree to the coalition. When he agreed to meet in Geneva to discuss the coalition, the aid was resumed in January, 1962. Aid was again suspended in February after General Phoumi resisted efforts to create the coalition.

The French newspaper *Le Monde* on December 17 and 18, 1961, and some British newspapers in May, 1962 as well as *I. F. Stone's Weekly* in the United States reported that the efforts of the United States Ambassador to bring Phoumi into the coalition had been undercut by American military and CIA agents. The *London Times* of May 24, 1962 reported that civilian Washington's pressure upon General Phoumi "to accept the political solution of neutrality, including the suspension since February of the monthly subsidy of $3 million, failed because the [Central Intelligence] agency provided them with some funds from its own capacious budget." It is thought, the *Times* continued, "that the Agency transferred the money from its operations in Siam [Thailand] . . ."

According to the *London Observer* of May 27, 1962, "General Phoumi's closest personal American adviser is a senior CIA officer." He and other CIA representatives in Laos "urge that if necessary the country be partitioned" rather than be governed by a coalition cabinet.

In May, 1962 the armed truce in Laos was broken after Phoumi had built up his troops in Nam Tha in violation of the cease-fire. There were accusations by both sides that the other started the fighting. Phoumi's men were defeated not far from the Thailand border. President Kennedy dispatched 4,000 American troops into Thailand. The Pentagon, said the *New York Times* of May 16, 1962, had recommended sending a force "large enough to make a real impression on the Pathet Lao movement . . ."

As a result of increasing military disillusionment with General Phoumi and continued State Department pressure, a coalition government was finally formed in June, 1962.

The Army has similarly been making policy in South

Vietnam. The United States had a military mission of 685 men
stationed there and was contributing about $300 million a year
to the government. A Special Study Mission of the House Foreign
Affairs Committee reported that at the end of the fiscal year
1961 "the total amount of foreign aid given to this country of
some 14 million people amounted to nearly $2 billion." Diem,
who became president in 1955, "has taken dictatorial control
. . . It is estimated some 30,000 South Vietnamese nationalists
are in concentration camps."

Five paratroop battalions of Diem's own armed forces tried
to overthrow his regime. Several thousand civilian demonstrators
also approached the palace in the November, 1960 attack, but
were driven back. In February, 1962 some South Vietnamese
air force planes bombed and strafed the palace. In asking for
renewed military aid, however, the American Secretary of Defense, Robert McNamara, and the Chairman of the Joint Chiefs
of Staff, Gen. Lyman Lemnitzer, became angry when a member
of the House Foreign Affairs Committee suggested that an oppres-
sive political regime supported by American military aid was at
least partly responsible for the warfare in South Vietnam. "Mr.
McNamara," said the New York Times of June 9, 1961, "shouted
this reply: 'The condition in South Vietnam is due to the flood-
ing of that area with 12,000 Communists from North Vietnam
by all coastal roads." Diem had 170,000 troops trained by the
United States Army.

When the situation became more serious a Presidential
mission proposed to President Kennedy increasing the size of
Diem's armed forces to 200,000 men and expanding American
aid to $400 million a year. In October, 1961 the President sent
his military adviser, Gen. Maxwell Taylor, to South Vietnam to
see what should be done militarily. Less than four months later
the New York Times of February 25, 1962 reported an increase
of American military personnel there to 4,000 men under the
command of Gen. Paul Harkins. The Kansas City Star of March
8, 1962 reported that U.S. Navy craft were patrolling the coast-
line to assist in the interception of Communist boats. By November, 1962 news reports indicated that the United States had

11,000 soldiers, marines and airmen in South Vietnam and since mid-1960 the United States has poured unofficially some two billion dollars worth of military and economic aid into South Vietnam.[17] Three Army helicopter companies were reported in South Vietnam flying troops to battle the guerrillas. Marines have been engaged in ground reconnaissance in the mountains of Central Vietnam and in the same area special forces teams have been "arming and organizing primitive mountain tribes" according to Homer Bigart of the *New York Times*.[18] All of this action, the Pentagon insists, is not war, because the United States soldiers have orders to fire only if fired upon by the enemy. If it were war, presumably Congress would need to be consulted.

The military have been also actively involved in making foreign policy with respect to Berlin. This policy began during World War II when plans were made for dividing Germany into zones of occupation. Since Berlin was to be wholly within the Soviet zone, civilians representing the State Department in the European Advisory Commission wanted guaranteed access to Berlin by land. The military, however, made the actual decision. The Army felt its superiority over the Russian Army and did not believe a signed written agreement was necessary. So the military planners insisted that the problem of access be left for settlement at the military level. This decision by the military has been at the root of all the postwar troubles over Berlin.

At this time Russia apparently had no intention of controlling Berlin, since it rejected an American request that the Soviet Union feed Berlin, a decision that would have put the city under Russian economic control.

The United States was not prepared to press for constructive agreements on social and economic matters in Germany, because the War Department supported the Morgenthau plan of vengeance and harshness against a more moderate line advocated by the State Department. President Roosevelt, apparently as a result of this controversy, issued a directive which forbade any policy settlements over Germany at the end of 1944. Thus when Germany surrendered in May 1945 there was uncertainty among the great powers as to their policy. This failure to solve problems before the postwar break-up of the alliance was another factor in the long continued German problem. Also in the picture was a military decision not to push on to take Berlin. Against Churchill's advice General Eisenhower and his colleagues decided to move south to let the Russians take Berlin.

Military influence on foreign policy has been visible at a number of other points. For example, the military acted on its own without even informing the State Department of important decisions about the Berlin crisis between the United States and Russia in 1948. "The State Department was not informed in advance of the decision of the military authorities to seal off the Western zones to Russian rail traffic in reprisal for the Soviet blockade" and "on more than one occasion recently the Pentagon has made important decisions on operations in Berlin without the knowledge of the Secretary of State . . . decisions that had they been known would have affected State Department policy making." [19] This situation was possible only because the American military commander in Germany, Gen. Lucius D. Clay, "unlike his collateral British and French military chiefs, does not receive orders from the State Department but from the War Department." [20] As James Reston pointed out, "What the War Department does in Germany affects our relations with many countries, but the State Department complains that many times it never knows what goes on there until some aggrieved country sends its Ambassador to complain." [21]

One of the real problems in the Berlin situation was the military control exercised there. Drew Middleton summed it up in a Berlin story in the July 18, 1948 *New York Times* when he said: "There is naturally in a military community a strong sentiment for some show of force . . . The tragedy of the entire situation is that at no time in the last three weeks has anyone here advocated a conference with the Soviet Union over the differences on Germany."

Another report claimed that the State Department staff in Germany "has been bitter at being forced to sit on the sidelines, unable to step in on many occasions when it thought it should."

The same report indicated that the program for turning over administration of Germany to the State Department was stopped by General Clay when the tension with Russia "made it easy to argue necessity for keeping the military control." [22]

In December, 1950 the United States, after considerable pressure, secured an agreement from Western European nations that Germany should eventually join an integrated armed force. After NATO had developed and the rearmament of Germany had begun, Soviet bloc leaders became disturbed not only at the rearmament of their former enemy but at the possibility that Germany might someday be given nuclear weapons.

On October 2, 1957 Adam Rapacki, the Polish Foreign Minister, had proposed in the United Nations establishing a zone of Poland, Czechoslovakia, West and East Germany, from which nuclear weapons would be barred. In early February, 1958 the Soviet Union not only indicated its backing of this proposal but offered to discuss reduction of foreign troops and conventional armaments in the zone. The Soviet Union also agreed in principle to the idea of control and inspection in the zone. The Moscow communique on the Rapacki-Gromyko talks said acceptance of the Rapacki plan would contribute to a solution of other problems.

A number of civilians active in the field of foreign affairs, including George F. Kennan, formerly head of the State Department's Policy Planning Division, favored discussions exploring the possibility of Russian withdrawal from Central Europe if nuclear weapons were barred from Germany and American troops withdrawn from that country. Apparently uninterested in any move that might ease or end the cold war, American military leaders opposed any discussion of the Rapacki plan on the ground that it could lead to a United States military withdrawal from Europe and the disintegration of NATO.

The military were not the only ones desirous of rearming West Germany. Their industrial allies, desirous of increased profits, began to pour huge amounts of American capital into West Germany in order to revive the German armaments industry.

There was also commercial rivalry for alliances with German corporations.

The Russians began using divided Berlin, well inside Communist territory, as a means of forcing a solution to the whole German problem. They wanted the United States to recognize East Germany and her existing boundaries in return for a Berlin settlement, and they wanted to eliminate the U.S. base in Berlin.

When the Russian demands for a Berlin settlement had produced a crisis in 1959, the Pentagon recommended a military approach — partial mobilization of reserves and equipment. The suggestion was rejected and President Eisenhower in a significant exercise of civil power moved instead to hold discussions with Premier Khrushchev. These discussions led to plans for a summit meeting, which failed because of the shooting down of an American U-2 plane over the heart of Russia just before the meeting was to take place. The decision to send the plane over Russia prior to the Summit was made by military and CIA officers overseas rather than by civilian government leaders. There is no evidence that the military intended that the plane be shot down. There was simply no effort made to avoid an incident from sending the plane over Russia, as there had been when General Nathan F. Twining visited Russia from June 23 to July 1, 1956. During that time U-2 flights over the Soviet Union were suspended.[23]

After the abortive summit meeting and the emotions that flared on both sides there was little chance of further negotiations. There was also some evidence that Soviet leaders felt the military rather than President Eisenhower were in control.

After waiting until President Kennedy had been in office about six months, the Russians tried again to get the Berlin and German problems settled on their terms. The Pentagon took advantage of the opportunity by suggesting declaration of a limited emergency, call-up of troops in Germany and other steps.[24]

The *New York Times* of July 12, 1961 reported that Deputy Secretary of Defense Gilpatric said that the President had received many proposals for dealing with the Berlin situation, including various ones from the Pentagon.

These proposals, he said, were narrowed down to certain

specific possible courses of action at a week-end conference of
the President, Secretary of State Dean Rusk, Mr. McNamara
[Secretary of Defense] and General Maxwell D. Taylor, the
White House military representative. The Pentagon's assignment now, Mr. Gilpatric continued, is for the Joint Chiefs and
the service secretaries to determine whether the existing force
structure would permit adoption of favored plans; and what
new demands, particularly in defense appropriations, must be
made upon Congress.

There were indications that the Berlin crisis had an artificial
tone in its military side. John Hightower in the July 14, 1961
Kansas City Star, writing from Washington about possible ways
a war might start, said that

. . . one of the big problems which American military planners face is that they do not know how such a conflict would
start and they find it difficult to know what to plan for. So do
the policymakers from President Kennedy down who may find
themselves at some point late this year or early next year
taking a strong stand on what appears to be one of the minor
issues of the long Berlin controversy.

At a news conference on October 11, 1961 President Kennedy reported that, "since January we have added more than
$6,000,000 to the national defense budget which is more than
14 per cent increase over the previous budget." Later that
month the *United States News* described the "powerful and growing support to business all across the country," as a result of the
step-up in arms orders. "Whole industries as well as local communities, are beginning to benefit from the military build-up."

Although the military have effectively dominated American
foreign policy with respect to Laos, Vietnam and Berlin, probably
the most successful effort of the military and the closely related
Atomic Energy Commission has been the prevention of disarmament and a treaty banning nuclear weapons tests.

Ever since World War II the United States followed a
policy of advocating disarmament and participation in disarmament negotiations, for the purpose of propaganda. In 1954 the
United States endorsed a British-French program for partial

disarmament which called for reduction of troops. In 1955 Britain and France added a complete prohibition of the use of nuclear weapons as well as their elimination. The United States endorsed these and other aspects of the joint proposal. To the surprise of everyone, after persistent efforts to get Soviet agreement, the Russians on May 10, 1955 accepted the main proposals and also agreed to international inspection. The British delegate welcomed this Russian move and noted "that the proposals have now been largely, and in some cases, entirely adopted by the Soviet Union and made into its own proposals." [25]

The Pentagon was shocked. No one had expected the Russians to agree to our proposals. The thought of cutting back American armed forces to 1.5 million men was too much. We had originally made this proposal because it was the size of our armed forces prior to the Korean War. But the American people had accepted a much larger strength and commitments around the world had been increased. There were other arguments against disarmament, including the idea advanced years before that no one could be sure of detecting secret nuclear weapon stockpiles.

The Pentagon agitated against disarmament and was successful. In September, 1955 the United States withdrew its support of the disarmament proposal. Instead, American military leaders urged a program of aerial photography over the Soviet Union and the United States so as to prevent surprise attack. This "open skies" proposal was the military alternative to disarmament because it involved no reduction in budget or manpower. The proposal originated among a group of Air Force officers. From them the idea went to the Joint Chiefs of Staff and then to the President. Before it was finally presented at Geneva, General Alfred Gruenther and Admiral Arthur Radford reviewed it and did the final editing. At Geneva the Soviet Union turned the proposal down and continued to press for other measures.

In the meantime President Eisenhower announced that he had appointed Harold Stassen as a Special Assistant with cabinet rank to work on disarmament policy. In the course of some negotiations Stassen angered Secretary of State John Foster

Dulles, who felt Stassen should not have discussed a proposal with the Russians until it had been cleared in advance with our European allies. Admiral Arthur Radford, Chairman of the Joint Chiefs of Staff, who opposed any agreement with the Soviet Union, and Chairman Lewis Strauss of the Atomic Energy Commission also opposed Stassen.

Stassen's proposal, with which President Eisenhower agreed, was that a ten-months' suspension of nuclear tests should be offered to the Soviet Union as a bargaining point. The proposal pushed Edward Teller, Willard Libby, and others in the Pentagon and Atomic Energy Commission into the anti-Stassen camp. The tactic of those who opposed Stassen was "to agree with the President that Stassen should try to negotiate an agreement, but to undercut it by making the conditions as tough as possible." [26]

Stassen, after trying to negotiate, finally resigned under pressure in February, 1958. Even the budget allocation for his work reflected the Pentagon's opposition. In fiscal 1956 $550,000 was spent by Stassen's Special Disarmament staff. In fiscal 1957 the amount was $530,000. But for fiscal 1958 only $375,000 was allocated for his work.

From this point on the Pentagon and its friends had to be represented in disarmament planning. President Eisenhower on February 27, 1958 set up a four-man "brain trust" to advise the government on future disarmament policy. These included General Alfred M. Gruenther, former Commander in Chief of NATO forces in Europe; General Walter Bedell Smith, Eisenhower's former Chief of Staff; John J. McCloy, a former Assistant Secretary of War; and Robert A. Lovett, who had served five years as an Assistant Secretary of War and also had worked closely with General George Marshall.

After Premier Khrushchev proposed total disarmament to the United Nations General Assembly in September, 1959, the United States continued to oppose disarmament while appearing to favor it. In an article in the October 15, 1959 *Foreign Policy Bulletin*, William R. Frye, a staff correspondent for the *Christian Science Monitor*, wrote: "The West has devised a counter strategy which may work. The first element in it is to be sedulously constructive in all its public response — to avoid the appearance of negativism." The second element in it was a proposal for "a world police force under the United Nations, free of the veto, with power to keep the peace," a plan the Russians and some Americans were known to be against. Frye concluded: "The fact that a proposal is impractical, however, does not necessarily rob it of its political value. As a device to make the adversary say No, it can be of very great value . . . "

President Eisenhower appointed in July, 1959 a disarmament study group headed by Charles H. Coolidge. Coolidge was a Boston lawyer who also served as chairman of the board of trustees of the Mitre Corporation, a corporation established in 1958 to supervise electronic research projects for the Air Force.[27] When the Coolidge Committee reported its recommendations, Marquis Childs on January 19, 1960 wrote: "It will be combed over by the Departments of State and Defense and eventually will go to the National Security Council for a final policy determination." Speaking of the content of the report, Childs added: "But it is already fairly evident that the first step is too timid. In deference to powerful forces in the Pentagon and the Atomic Energy Commission the Coolidge Report is said to avoid almost entirely the challenge of nuclear disarmament."

After disarmament negotiations opened in Geneva in 1960, the *New York Times* repeatedly referred to the "propaganda" objective of the talks. On April 6 the *Times* reported, "The West rejected today Premier Khrushchev's proposal for complete disarmament as the basis for any disarmament compromise."

When President Kennedy took office the foes of disarmament seemed to have the upper hand. Kennedy appointed Paul H. Nitze as Assistant Secretary of Defense for International Affairs. This, said the December 26, 1960 *New York Times,* indicates that Kennedy expects the Pentagon to play a direct role in disarmament planning. Nitze's position was summarized in these words: "If we can see any possibility of working out reciprocal actions with the Russians whereby mutual deterrence can be made substantially more secure, we should continue to strive for that goal."

On January 26, 1961 the *New York Times* reported that the Kennedy administration appears to be focusing its attention on arms control measures rather than disarmament.

President Kennedy temporarily seemed to move toward a disarmament position when in September, 1961 he challenged the Soviet Union to "a peace race . . . until general and complete disarmament has been achieved." He announced a new Arms Control and Disarmament Agency which had been created by a reluctant Congress over the opposition of those in Congress who generally speak for the military.

The Disarmament Agency director appointed by President Kennedy was William C. Foster, who had previously held high posts in the Defense Department and foreign aid programs. The *Washington Newsletter* of the Friends Committee on National Legislation in April, 1962 reported that "Among the other top officials there are many from the Defense Department and the Atomic Energy Commission and too few from the universities, law and other occupations." Foster himself has urged measures that are not calculated to result in disarmament agreements, such as resumption of nuclear tests in the atmosphere and additional inspection for test preparations over and above the international inspection system previously proposed in the Geneva talks.

Kennedy himself has not subsequently given any real leadership for disarmament. The problem he faces and has not so far as is known tried to solve was summarized by Senator Joseph S. Clark (D., Pa.) in an address at Swarthmore College:

> Inside the Government of the United States . . . a contest is being waged for the minds of men in power. On one side of this contest are the men who see no end to the arms race. . . . They think of disarmament purely as propaganda and cite the failure of past disarmament talks. They see no future for the United Nations. All too often they have a vested interest in a continuing arms race as members of the entrenched military-industrial complex. They have many strong allies in Congress.[28]

The group in government to which Senator Clark referred was able not only to prevent an agreement banning nuclear weapons tests but also to secure resumption of such tests. The Atomic Energy Commission or individuals connected with it often led the pro-military attack. This is quite understandable: AEC personnel and the military are closely involved in each other's work. For example, the bombs of the Strategic Air Command are in the Atomic Energy Commission budget.[29] There is collaboration on nuclear tests, and for more than ten crucial years Brig. Gen. Kenneth Fields was a key figure in the AEC, serving as its general manager from 1955 to 1958.

In September, 1957 the United States exploded a small 1.7 kiloton nuclear bomb underground in Nevada. Atomic Energy Commission officials and scientists, notably Edward Teller, who were opposed to ending nuclear tests, authorized or permitted a public statement in March, 1958 that "the earth movement was so slight that it could be detected on extremely sensitive seismological instruments. The earth waves were recorded at seismological stations at Los Angeles, about 250 miles air line from the shot mesa. This was the maximum distance at which the shock was recorded." [30]

This statement was made less than a week after Harold Stassen reported that the same nuclear shot had been detected by every seismic instrument within 1,000 miles.[31] The statement tended to discredit Mr. Stassen as well as the whole proposal to ban weapons testing. James Reston in the March 12, 1958 *New York Times* revealed that those in the government "who oppose any test ban agreement with Moscow" have "contended on the basis of this evidence" that the Soviet offer to permit detecting instruments on its territory was "meaningless." Reston also revealed that some scientists who questioned the AEC statement went to Hubert Humphrey, the Chairman of the Senate Foreign Relations Committee's subcommittee on disarmament. Humphrey, who discovered that the United States Coast and Geodetic Survey stations all over the United States and Alaska had detected the tests, said of the AEC statement: "It gives the impression that scientific facts are being used by someone to prove a political point — a dangerous concept to perpetuate in our efforts to work out effective arms control agreements."[32]

Edward Teller a day later admitted that he had known previous to the Humphrey investigation that the underground blast had been detected more than 2,000 miles away, though he did not correct the false impression.[33]

The first significant effort to interfere with an agreement to ban nuclear tests occurred after a conference of scientific experts from Communist and Western countries in August, 1958 in Geneva agreed to recommend an effective control system and after a conference of diplomats had met to negotiate a test-ban treaty.

On January 5, 1959 President Eisenhower released a statement claiming that new scientific data showed it was more difficult to detect underground tests than the Geneva scientists had thought. Eisenhower's statement was based on Pentagon-AEC tests in Nevada which did not confirm the technical findings at Geneva. But later investigation by the Senate Disarmament subcommittee revealed that the instruments used for the tests were not only inferior to those recommended at Geneva but not even as good as those operated by the United States Coast and Geodetic Survey.

Senator Humphrey on February 19, 1959 concluded from this investigation "that technical problems are not the main obstacle to an agreement on the stopping of nuclear weapons tests. The main problem is political."

Edward Teller also asserted that it was possible to muffle underground tests if they were conducted in large underground chambers. Many scientists disputed his contention but were unable to prove him wrong without a test. But long after Teller and others had successfully interfered with treaty negotiations a test called Project Gnome proved Teller wrong. In a *Saturday Evening Post* article on April 14, 1962, a group of eight top scientists not only attacked Teller's articles "as a signal example of factual error and emotionalism," but also exposed the fallacy in Teller's underground muffling theory. They wrote:

> Dr. Teller has repeatedly attempted to "prove" that the Russians could easily conceal underground nuclear tests. A couple of months ago a remarkable experiment, Gnome, was

conducted by a laboratory recently headed by Dr. Teller. A small 5 kiloton shot — one fourth the size of the Hiroshima bomb — was fired deep in a bed of salt, material supposed to muffle and conceal underground bomb tests. Contrary to predictions, this salt-bed shot was picked up and identified as an underground explosion as far away as Finland and Japan. Based on published reports one would estimate the muffling factor to be at least 10 times smaller than the factor quoted by Teller in his articles.

The Pentagon-AEC effort to prevent a treaty with the Russians was successful through the device of persuading the President to exclude underground tests from the treaty. The Russians had indicated that only a treaty banning all tests would be acceptable to them.

The real purpose of this exclusion was stated by James H. Douglas, a Deputy Secretary of Defense who, in the words of the March 21, 1960 *New York Times,* "made it clear that as far as he was concerned the reason for excluding small blasts was not merely that they could not be detected but that the United States wanted to carry on tests of its smaller 'cleaner' weapons."

Harold Stassen also wrote, "We are insisting upon an impossible amount of inspection in the Geneva negotiations." He summarized the situation in these words:

Russia has agreed to the installation of inspection posts with scientific instruments and competent United Nations inspectors within Russian territory in July, 1957. In July 1958 and 1959 able scientists from both sides worked out the inspection arrangements.

Then the United States began to put on more and more extreme requirements for inspection. These extreme conditions were urged by those inside our government who are opposed to any agreement whatsoever.[34]

As a result of military and AEC efforts, test-ban treaty discussions got nowhere. President Eisenhower, under pressure from these elements and angry at what he thought was mere Soviet intransigence, announced on December 29, 1959 that the United States considered itself free to resume tests at any time but would give notice if it did so. This formal ending of the voluntary test moratorium of October 31, 1958 may have been one factor in the Russian decision to prepare to resume its tests. There were undoubtedly other reasons for the actual Soviet testing, which began on September 1, 1961.

The Russian tests, conducted in the midst of the Berlin crisis, made possible renewed military demands for further American tests, even though pressure for American testing had been evident well before the Russians broke the moratorium. The *New York Times* of June 13, 1961 reported that pressure on President Kennedy to resume tests was coming from those "Democrats who in the past have been generally skeptical about a test ban agreement," and also from the military and pro-military civilians who do not even want to discuss disarmament.

The pressure continued to mount in spite of opposition from civilian scientists. Dr. Hans Bethe, who had served as President Eisenhower's scientific adviser, and Dr. Jerome Wiesner, President Kennedy's scientific adviser, were reported as opposing renewal of American tests. Bethe in a speech January 5, 1962 at Cornell University said: "The value of tests has been grossly exaggerated. We already know so much about atomic weapons that there is very little more to learn. We have weapons of all sizes for all reasonable military purposes."

President Kennedy, in announcing resumption of nuclear tests on March 2, 1962, indicated that if the Russians signed a treaty before tests began we would not test. But the Soviet position had changed from one of permitting on-the-spot inspection to one of insisting that all inspection should be by instruments.

The United States and the Soviet Union were in agreement that atmospheric tests could be detected without on-site inspection and the real issue was whether underground tests could be detected by instruments. The Russians asserted they could, whereas American military and AEC leaders said they could not. This was the basis for American insistence on strict on-spot inspection requirements.

Two British government scientists came to Washington in March, 1962 to persuade the Kennedy administration that it could safely reduce its requirements for a test inspection agreement. They brought evidence that the British had detected all the tests in the underground series the United States had conducted in Nevada and New Mexico.[35]

The British Prime Minister also talked of possible modification of Western inspection proposals, according to a report in the March 9, 1962 *Kansas City Star*. "But," added the same report, "[Secretary of State] Rusk said inspection requirements would have to be tightened." In practical political language this meant that the United States was prepared to favor an ideal test ban treaty and to blame the enemy for not getting one.

The British were not the only ones who claimed that it was possible to detect underground tests. Earl Voss, the State Department correspondent of *The Washington Star*, reported on March 11, 1962: "One key scientist advising the American government reports that every one of the Nevada-New Mexico shots, even those below one kiloton, have produced warning signals which almost certainly would have been picked up by a test-ban inspection system." But this information was "leaked out only in eyedropper proportions [to be] noted only by a few careful readers. . . "[36]

Actually the United States could have accepted a Russian treaty proposal banning all tests on the assumption that there are ample ways of detecting violation without on-the-spot inspection. Two American companies, Raytheon and Allied Research Associates, according to *Aviation Week* of July 17, 1961, claimed that underground tests can be identified by radio waves. This was supported by Sheridan D. Speeth, a full-time consultant for the Bell Telephone Laboratories working under Defense Department contract, who wrote in September 1961 in a magazine article:

> The major problem for the scientists engaged in the design of a monitor system for the enforcement of a test ban treaty is that of discriminating underground explosions from natural earthquakes . . . A series of experiments conducted last summer indicates that one can train listeners to distinguish the seismographs of earthquakes from those of underground explosions simply by their sound. Listeners were successful in separating one class of events from the other in over 90 per cent of the cases presented, although the explosions studied

were smaller than the "nominal yield" bomb discussed at
Geneva. The events were monitored from as far as 4,000
kilometers.

Speeth went on to state that efforts to modify or alter the shock
waves and confuse the seismograph "produce a strong low frequency radio wave . . . " He added, "Therefore the more you
try to cheat the seismic detectors the easier you would make it
for the radio detectors." [37]

The American argument that there might be occasions when
one nation would dispute the interpretation of another's detection
instruments was — and is — valid. This was a basis for American demands for some on-site detection. But it is also true that if
there were only one such questionable interpretation of an underground seismic event it would not jeopardize any nation's security
if in fact it were an underground test. If there were a whole
series of such disputed detection interpretations, it would undoubtedly be evident on Swedish, Japanese and other instruments.
There were thus two possibilities: One was to establish a neutral
commission to arrive at a final decision whether any nation was
violating the test ban. The other was to recognize that any test
ban is a self-enforcing agreement. By this we mean that if there
is substantial evidence that one power is violating it others are
legally entitled to denounce that portion of the agreement and
resume comparable tests if the power allegedly in violation does
not permit adequate investigation.

The United States had never proposed such an alternative.

A Russian thesis about underground tests was that they were
difficult, time consuming, expensive, and not fruitful enough to
use dependably. On March 3, 1962 Secretary of Defense Mc-
Namara, in a statement intended to justify resuming atmospheric
tests, in effect confirmed the position held by Russian and civilian
American scientists. He said:

> Even if the United States limited itself to an underground test
> program the United States technical growth would not provide
> an acceptable rate of development in weapons systems con-
> sidered so necessary for the national security . . . The De-
> partment of Defense in conjunction with the Atomic Energy

Commission made every effort to examine the feasibility of
accomplishing the necessary development and system analysis
objectives without resorting to an atmospheric test program.
However, since the actual high altitude physical environ-
ment cannot be duplicated below ground, it was recognized
that on the basis of technical developments in nuclear weapon-
ry, the United States under the present conditions had no
alternative but to proceed with an atmosphere test program.

The nuclear testing in the atmosphere had no important
opposition within the government that was prepared publicly to
differ with the military. Even the Arms Control and Disarmament Agency was used to make a propaganda statement in support
of the Teller thesis on the difficulty of detecting underground
tests.[38]

Civilian scientists who have tried to assist the Disarmament
Agency have been frustrated by the pervading military influence.
A Harvard professor, L. D. Leet, who is an earthquake seismolo-
gist, has asserted that the Berkner panel report which insisted
that the United States raise its inspection demands just when
treaty plans had been settled, was simply dead wrong. "They had
data so insufficient that they shouldn't have made any claims,"
Leet said. Leet pointed out that the Berkner panel excluded
professional seismologists, using instead "seismic prospect seismologists," electronic engineers who use a fraction of the know-
how of earthquake seismology.

"At his own expense" reported the *Harvard Crimson* of
March 24, 1962,

> Leet made two trips to Washington in an effort to complain.
> One official of the Disarmament and Arms Control Agency
> listened patiently to him and finally asked, "If your theories
> prove correct does it mean that we'll need more or less inspec-
> tion in the Soviet Union?" When Leet answered "less," the
> official told him don't call us we'll call you. He has never been
> called. He went to the Defense Department and was given a
> similar hearing.

Leet, who "had no political axe to grind," said the Harvard newspaper, insists the Russian seismologists "were right" in rejecting
the U.S. position on underground detection.

In a cold war such as exists between the Soviet Union and the United States few people are prepared to insist even on an isolated matter that an enemy proposal may be more scientifically accurate or politically feasible than the position of their own military establishment. Yet the national interest of the United States and the welfare of people everywhere sometimes demands precisely such judgments. This does not mean, however, that an opposing nation is acting as a moral unit. There is no reason to believe that the Soviet Union will act on the basis of morality or integrity. Great powers act from their own national interest or that of parties or pressure groups within them. Communist interests have frequently conflicted with the best interests of the Soviet people as well as of people in other countries.

The real foreign policy problem facing the United States is not whether an occasional Russian proposal happens to coincide with our own national interest but whether the vested interest of the Pentagon is willy-nilly to be identified with that of the United States and western civilization.

Time will reveal how seriously the military has jeopardized American and world security by efforts to intervene in problems of foreign affairs and prevent disarmament agreements, including a nuclear test ban treaty.

Any summary of how the military achieved such tremendous power over American foreign policy would reveal at least five factors.

The first is that the sheer size and power of the military establishment plus the prestige of leading it have given to the Joint Chiefs of Staff authority which few if any in government can overcome.

The second factor is the penetration of civilian government by military officers. One State Department official was quoted in the September 11, 1962 *Look* as saying: "There are so many military men at so many meetings around so many tables in Washington that they have an effect. Even if they say nothing, they have an effect — in what the others don't say because they are there." He added, "They don't have to connive or plot. They just permeate." [39] Military men in the Atomic Energy Commission, in the Central Intelligence Agency, in the Arms Control and Disarmament Agency, and various other government posts are able to influence policy long before the National Security Council, on which they also function, has to make a decision.

The third factor is the presence of armed forces and their officers in many countries in the world. They are able to dispense aid, talk to foreign government leaders, and collaborate with foreign military leaders.

A fourth factor, the molding of public opinion, is accomplished through a steady stream of articles, broadcasts, speeches and news releases. These, wrote Waldemar A. Nielsen, the executive director of a White House Commission on U.S. Information activities, "stress that our national security fundamentally — almost exclusively — depends on military strength, not upon the possibility of negotiation." Nielsen also pointed out that "Defense officials, civilian and in uniform, make several times as many speeches and write several times as many articles bearing on foreign policy as officials in the Department of State." He added, "because of the preponderance of military statements on international issues, the question must be asked whether a systematic bias is not being introduced by this branch of government into the stream of American public opinion." [40]

One result of this systematic bias is the absence of Congressional debate on almost every matter affecting military spending, military intervention overseas, resumption of nuclear weapons tests, or any other issue on which the professional officers have taken a clear position. This fifth factor, the absence of Congressional opposition, has been sold to Congress and the people by a clever slogan: "bi-partisan foreign policy." "Total conformity has become so prized an ingredient in political life," wrote the editor of *The Progressive* in June, 1962, "that we no longer have our little bands of wilful men to speak out on the floor so the country might hear the other side. There is often not even a single voice of dissent on issues that are warmly and continuously debated in the other democracies of the world." He then indicated that there are no debates because of the fear of being "falsly labeled as 'soft on Communism.' " The one sure way of being acceptable in terms

of "true blue patriotism" during the emotionalism of the cold war
and the continued military talk of enemies is to be for anything
the military favors.

There are, of course, other things that encourage the bi-
partisan foreign policy. To some degree fear plays a role in these
and to some degree secrecy and lack of information are involved.
The average Congressman is almost as handicapped as citizens
who know only what they read in the newspapers. In describing
this problem Jack Raymond, a military writer for the *New York
Times*, wrote on February 7, 1960 that "High officials made the
rounds of Congressional committees and created entirely different
impressions with the same set of facts." According to Raymond,
the reasons for such activity "include differing interpretations of
intelligence, service politics, national politics and the fact that
most military testimony is given in secret."

Congressmen whose access to military information is only
through word of mouth reports from those who heard secret
testimony are in a difficult position authoritatively to oppose military foreign policy. Few Congressmen are prepared to risk their
careers in such opposition. They would have to oppose not only
the military but also those colleagues in the House and Senate
who by virtue of long service on Armed Services Committees have
come to be the Congressional spokesmen for the military point
of view.

The armed forces carefully cultivate key members of
Congress. This is done by various favors such as establishing
military posts in the state or district the Congressman represents.
There is also careful personal cultivation by top generals and their
legislative representatives. It is generally acknowledged that the
Pentagon has the most active lobby in Washington. It actually
has offices in advantageous locations in both the Senate and House
Office Buildings. In 1962 there were 55 military officers steadily
working out of these offices with members of Congress. For this
work about $2,500,000 is annually spent by the Defense Depart-
ment .

Paul Appleby, a former Assistant Director of the Budget
Bureau, has pointed out that "A member of a committee gets

special attention from a department dealt with by this committee
. . . .;" he even "develops a vested interest in it and its program
because the prestige which his specialized knowledge gives him
links him with the department." [41]

It is therefore very rare that anyone opposes the policies of
the military. They are almost inevitably backed by their spokesmen in Congress. And if Congress does not oppose them, who
can?

CHAPTER 13

MILITARISM AND THE POLITICAL FAR RIGHT

One of the most dangerous results of the alliance between the military and industry is the growth of a large right-wing extremist movement in the United States. Most of the groups that make up the right wing receive heavy financial support from industry and substantial organizational support from professional military officers.

The most publicized organization of the radical right is the John Birch Society. Robert Welch, the founder of the John Birch Society, wrote Tristram Coffin, has "had a crush on the military since attending the United States Naval Academy for two years." [1] Not only does Welch run the Birch society as a general might direct his troops, but he relies heavily on military men for advice and assistance in promoting his work. Among the key leaders of the John Birch Society are a score of retired colonels, generals and admirals and one former Marine sergeant, Matthew McKeon, who was court-martialed for taking his trainees on a training march that resulted in death for many. Still others not listed as leaders are members. Among these is General Edwin Walker, who distributed John Birch Society literature in his division and who was reprimanded by the Army only after unfavorable publicity about his efforts to influence the voting of his troops forced the Army's hand.

Another right-wing group is the Christian Anti-Communism Crusade, led by an Australian physician, Fred C. Schwarz, which uses General Albert C. Wedemeyer in its forums. More frequently, however, the armed forces invite Schwarz to speak at seminars and conferences which officers on active military duty set up for civilians in various communities throughout the nation. Schwarz, who uses as one of his favorite lecture topics "Why Millionaires, College Professors and Ministers Become Communists," has lectured at the National War College, at the Eighth Naval District Headquarters in New Orleans, at the U.S. Naval Air Station in Glenview, Ill., and at many other places under military sponsorship throughout the nation. "For several weeks following an appearance at the Glenview naval air station," wrote Coffin, "Fred Schwartz was given office space at the base, where he tape-recorded a statement criticizing the Democratic candidate for Congress" from that district. "It was used extensively in the 1960 election campaigns."

One industrialist backer of Schwarz is Patrick Frawley, Jr., President of the Schick Safety Razor Company and chairman of the board of the Technicolor Corporation. Frawley, who is also chairman of the Southern California School of Anti-Communism, a subsidiary of Schwarz's Crusade, sent copies of Schwarz's book, *You Can Trust the Communists (to be Communists)*, to ministers in the Midwest.

Billy James Hargis' Christian Crusade employs General C. A. Willoughby, former aide to General Douglas MacArthur as an "intelligence expert." One dramatic Hargis tie with the military was revealed following the publication on January 4, 1960 of the *Air Force Manual* which attacked the National Council of Churches, the Revised Standard Version of the Bible, and distinguished clergymen. According to the February 26, 1960 *Daily Oklahoman*, Hargis, who lived in Tulsa, "prepared part of the material in the currently disputed Air Force manuals . . . " Hargis, who holds fundamentalist religious convictions and who has a degree from an unaccredited college and theological seminary known as a degree mill, let his own religious prejudice against a new translation of the Bible and the National Council of Churches be the basis for alleging a connection between them and Communism. So completely did Air Force personnel rely on Hargis that his attack became an official Air Force attack without anyone ever investigating the charges.

The Air Force was subsequently forced to retract the charges made in the 1960 Air Force Manual.

Another right-wing group has its headquarters at Harding College in Arkansas. According to an article in *The American Federationist* for May, 1962, Dr. George S. Benson, the President of Harding, "turned his down-at-the-heels campus in Searcy, Arkansas into a college with a six million dollar endowment" as a result of gifts from industrialists. Harding College's National Education Program is an extreme right-wing effort to sell the American people on the danger of internal communism and, through films such as *Communism on the Map*, to equate democratic socialism in Norway, Sweden, England and other countries with Communism. The National Education Program is similar in composition to the military-industrial elite, since it is run by a retired Army officer, Brig. Gen. William P. Campbell and a former General Electric executive, Howard W. Bennett. The National Education Program, which claims to be non-profit and therefore is free from taxation, has been able to get its films depicting the internal danger from Communists at work in labor and the civilian government, accepted as a regular part of the public school curriculum in Louisiana, parts of California and elsewhere.

In spite of its "educational" nature and its tax-free status the Harding College group is involved in politics in an effort to eliminate from Congress those who do not fit the right-wing pattern. At an Army-sponsored conference at Fort Smith, Arkansas, for example, Dr. Ganus of Harding College made the statement: "Your Representative (James W. Trimble) in this area has voted 89 per cent of the time to aid and abet the Communist Party." [2]

Another influential right-wing group with military ties is the Manion Forum, founded by a former dean of Notre Dame's College of Law. The Manion Forum includes a weekly radio program of a network of over 200 stations in 41 states as well as a monthly newsletter. Manion, who is on the John Birch Society Council, features interviews and talks by leading right-wing people including military and retired military men like Admiral Ben Moreell and General Bonner Fellers.

These extremist groups are among the better-known right-wing organizations because they function openly and are frequently publicized. They are by no means the only or even the major channels by which the military-industrial complex seeks to change the thinking and practices of the American people. Four largely unpublicized and interlocking groups provide the strategy, propaganda and personnel for the right-wing program of the military-industrial complex.

The first of these groups is the American Security Council, which describes itself as "a not-for-profit corporation which was organized by industry as a national, centrally-located research and information center on subversive activities."

The American Security Council has three basic functions. It is designed to be a liaison group for industry with active and retired military leaders. *Time* magazine, on December 4, 1961, said in a discussion of "the Military Right": "Many of these retired military men have joined the American Security Council, a quiet-spoken but rigidly doctrinaire organization." A brochure of the Council published in 1961 states "a major function of the ASC Washington Bureau is to maintain close liaison with the legislative and executive branches of government and the armed forces."

The American Security Council also maintains a huge filing system and hires ex-F.B.I. men to check on various individuals throughout the country. Richard Dudman of the *St. Louis Post-Dispatch* reported on August 13, 1961 that the Council was "set up in 1955 to operate a loyalty-security blacklist where employers could check their employees and applicants for employment for reported leftist connections." Austin C. Wehrwein in the July 10, 1958 *New York Times* stated that the ASC also assists "member companies in checking on 'questionable' organizations asking for support or money." In addition it makes "material from the files and books available to certain member company executives and to outsiders, such as journalists that the Council feels it can trust."

The ASC files, which include the names of about one million Americans, were compiled, wrote Richard Dudman, from those of Harry Jung, publisher of a right-wing newspaper in World War II known as *The American Vigilante* and from the files of certain other corporations and investigating groups.

The third function of the American Security Council is propaganda. It publishes a newsletter which "provides internal security information" and a *Washington Report*. "During 1960," said a Council brochure, "the Council distributed over 100 copies of the movie 'Operation Abolition' to its member companies . . . It was shown by ASC member companies to their employees and by their employees to hundreds of community groups, high schools, and churches in forty-eight of the fifty states."

Operation Abolition is a film made from film footage of California television stations which the House Un-American Activities Committee subpoenaed and turned over to a commercial film company in Washington. The original film footage, which was distorted by rearranging the sequence and by inaccurate narration, was sold at $100 a print for a tremendous profit. Although the chairman and staff of the House Un-American Activities Committee have admitted that the film contains distortions and inaccuracies, it was made a part of an official report of the Committee. The students shown in the film were neither organized nor led by Communists in their protests about the Committee methods, but *Operation Abolition* tries to link students with the Communists subpoenaed by the Committee for its hearings. The film serves right-wing purposes by making it seem as if such political action by American students cannot have a validity of its own but must be Communist-inspired and by identifying as Communist all attempts to abolish the House Un-American Activities.

The key figure in the American Security Council's speakers' bureau is Admiral Chester Ward, who was listed in the 1961 ASC brochure as Director of Education. Ward, in speaking to a Christian Anti-Communism Crusade meeting in California, called for the dismissal of civilian government officials "who do not have confidence in America." According to the August 29, 1961 *Los Angeles Times* he included in such a list Adlai Stevenson, Ambassador to the United Nations; William Fulbright, chairman of the Senate Foreign Relations Committee; George Kennan, then Ambassador to Yugoslavia; and three White House advisers. Admiral Ward, according to the same newspaper, said "they and other policy makers in Washington have brought defeat to the defenders of freedom over the last fifteen years . . . "

Admiral Ward made similar remarks in Pittsburgh at a conference sponsored by the Chamber of Commerce with "the assistance and support given us by Lt. Gen. Ridgely Gaither, Commanding General, 2d U.S. Army, and his staff, and Maj. Gen. Ralph C. Cooper, Commanding General 21st U.S. Army Corps and his staff . . . " At this military-industrial conference attended by 300 businessmen, military reservists and, according to the *Pittsburgh Press* of April 14, 1961, "by invitation — city, county and parochial school children," Admiral Ward indicted civilian leaders when he "said he fears a national sellout of freedom in order to buy peace." Specifically, in the words of the Pittsburgh Press, "Admiral Ward's speech developed the themes . . . that negotiations with the Russians for disarmament are in fact appeasement."

The American Security Council is interlocked not only with industry and the armed forces but with three other right-wing groups, the Institute for American Strategy and the Foreign Policy Research Institute, both of which received financial support from the third, the Richardson Foundation, set up by Sid W. Richardson, Texas oil millionaire. Frank R. Barnett, who is a key figure on the American Security Council, is also Director of Research for the Richardson Foundation. Barnett is also research director of the Institute for American Strategy, and is a key figure in the Foreign Policy Research Institute. Barnett, said an article in the March, 1961 *Bulletin of the Atomic Scientists,* has been associated with a militant approach to the Communist threat since 1951 "when he proposed a foreign legion for refugees from communism . . . "

Barnett, according to the same article, "has now become a frequent lecturer to the National War College, the Industrial College of the Armed Forces, the Army and Naval War Colleges, and to the national conventions of the American Medical Association, the National Association of Manufacturers, and the Reserve Officers Association."

The Institute for American Strategy uses as its chief program the work of the Foreign Policy Research Institute, which is directed by a Viennese, Robert Strausz-Hupé. Closely associated with Strausz-Hupé at his Institute is "Colonel William Kintner, an active Army Officer assigned to the Plans Division, Office of the Assistant Chief of Staff for Military Operations but attached to the Foreign Policy Research Institute for duty." [3] Kintner, along with Admiral Ward, was a speaker at the Pittsburgh Chamber of Commerce-Army Conference in April, 1961. The *Pittsburgh Press* on April 14 reported that "The chief of long-range planning for the U.S. Army, Col. William R. Kintner, advocated an integrated national strategy based on military power to turn back Communism and extend the frontiers of freedom."

The interlocking directorate of the American Security Council, the military, and the Institute for Strategy can be further illustrated. Dan A. Sullivan, executive director of the Institute for American Strategy, is on the Industry Relations Committee of the American Security Council. Among those on the ASC's National Strategy Committee are Lt. Gen. Edward M. Almond (Ret.), a key figure in the John Birch Society in the South and in For America, an extreme right-wing group. For America is led by Brig. Gen. Bonner Fellers; among its objectives is the abolition of the income tax and the development of "overwhelming air power." Others on the Committee are Adm. Ben Morrell (Ret.), chairman of the board of trustees of Americans for Constitutional Action, another right-wing organization; Adm. Arthur W. Radford (Ret.); Adm. Felix B. Stump (Ret.), and Gen. A. C. Wedemeyer (Ret.).

The Institute for American Strategy grew out of the National Military-Industrial Conference held in Chicago in 1955 which, said the March, 1961 *Bulletin of the Atomic Scientists,* "brought together leaders of industry and government and enjoyed the sponsorship of some of the largest corporations in the country," as well as that of "various branches of the armed forces . . ."

The industrialists and representatives of the armed forces who formed the National Military Industrial Conference in 1955 continued it each year thereafter. They decided formally in 1958 "to continue it on an annual basis and to broaden its scope to include all matters affecting the security of the United States." Thus it moved into the domestic political field. "At the same time plans were also made to develop a permanent year-round program to awaken the public to the 'all encompassing nature of the Soviet Communist challenge.' The Institute for American Strategy was established to carry out this objective." [4]

By an amazing "coincidence" it was also in 1958 that President Eisenhower accepted a similar recommendation of the National Security Council, an official government agency on which the Chairman of the Joint Chiefs of Staff generally sits along with the Secretaries of Defense and State and others. That, recommendation gave the green light to professional military officers to educate and propagandize their troops and the American people on the cold war and related political issues.

As soon as the top officers of the armed forces had been freed to engage in obviously political propaganda, the Institute for American Strategy moved into the picture. The story of what happened was revealed in a letter from the Army to Senator Joseph S. Clark which was inserted in the August 2, 1961 *Congressional Record*. Beginning in 1959, he reported, "a two-week long Defense Strategy Seminar has been held annually . . . at the National War College." These

. . . seminars, authorized by the Joint Chiefs of Staff, were sponsored by the Institute for American Strategy and the Reserve Officers Association and funded by the Richardson Foundation. The curriculum for 1959 was prepared by the Foreign Policy Research Institute . . . ; the 1960 curriculum was a combined effort of this group and the National War College.

The letter tried to assure Senator Clark "that it is not official Army policy to propagandize and organize its reservists to oppose the policies and personnel of the Administration." Yet that is

precisely what the Army was doing, because the viewpoint of the
Army generals and their right-wing speakers was very different
from the Administration's on both internal and external estimates
of the problems facing the United States.

In another paragraph of the same letter the Army said:

> The purpose of the seminar [is] to disseminate to Reserve
> Component officers, who are also leaders in their civilian en-
> deavors, information on the current world environment, the
> cold war and Communist stratagems. A primary aim is to
> encourage these leaders to organize and to conduct local sem-
> inars and other activities to alert the public to the menace of
> the cold war.

Very little is actually known about the intrigue of the
military-industrial group in persuading civilians on the National
Security Council to turn the propagandizing of civilians over to
the military. General Barksdale Hamlett, vice-chief of staff for
the Army, told a Senate Committee that the Richardson Foundation suggested the holding of the first seminar at the National
War College which became the forerunner of a whole series.[5]

Who sold the program to the National Security Council
seems still to be a secret. This "cold war policy paper of the National Security Council," wrote a *New York Times* reporter on
June 18, 1961, is "still classified" as top-secret along with the
actual military directives "as to the particular tools and approaches
to be employed in this effort . . . But commanding officers were
supplied "[by the military propaganda staff] with literature and
speech material and were required to report regularly on their
cold-war activities."

In practice this military invasion of a traditionally civilian
sphere has involved military officers in extreme right-wing
political indoctrination. The June 18, 1961 *New York Times*
report indicated that "A number of officers of high and middle
rank are indoctrinating their commands and the civilian population near their bases with political theories resembling those of
the John Birch Society." The *Times* reporter, Cabell Phillips,
added, "They are also holding up to criticism and ridicule some
official policies of the U.S. Government."

This military group wants war with the Communist bloc as well as the silencing of Americans whom they think of as opponents of their policy. In Chicago in September, 1959, Adm. Arthur W. Radford, former chairman of the Joint Chiefs of Staff, called for "total victory over the Communist system — not stalemate." This theme has dominated the strategy seminars "that have been held throughout the country . . . in New York, Cleveland, New Orleans, and Wilmington; in California, Massachusetts, Texas and Washington, D.C." The Institute for American Strategy has been "the chief force behind these meetings of businessmen, teachers, servicemen and church leaders . . . " [6]

So powerful is this military group that their civilian superiors are for the most part afraid to discipline them. Cabell Phillips reported that "Civilian chiefs in the Pentagon find themselves in a delicate position with respect to this sort of activity in the higher uniformed echelons. They are disturbed by the right-wing views displayed by many of these officers." But they fear if they move against them they will be "tagged, as one of them put it, as being against anti-Communism." He added that a civilian official had told him, "These fellows . . . change the target to looking for spies under the bed or in the PTA" and thus "divert that much energy and support away from the main objective of the 'cold war.' " Nevertheless, if "General X wants to make a speech about Communism in the schools or play footsie with the Birch Society people," the official explained, "we can't discipline him [unless] he gets 'way off base like General Walker did . . . "

As a result of the continued military propaganda program directed at civilians, Senator William Fulbright (D., Ark.) sent a memorandum to Secretary of Defense McNamara, protesting this whole propaganda effort. He called attention to the apparent liaison between certain right-wing extremist groups and military spokesmen. Pointing to specific seminars and programs that had been held around the country under military sponsorship, he wrote:

> . . . running through all of them is a central theme that the primary, if not exclusive danger to this country is internal

Communist infiltration. Past and current international difficulties are often attributed to this or ascribed to "softness,"
"sellouts," "appeasements" etc. Radical right-wing speakers
dominate the programs.

Fulbright indicated that the view of the Communist menace
was distorted by over-simplification which identified Communism
with socialism and socialism with social legislation of the kind
the Kennedy Administration was supporting.

Referring to the right-wing programs aimed at discrediting
"foreign aid, cultural exchanges, disarmament negotiations and
other international programs as extremely wasteful if not actually
subversive," Fulbright said: "There are many indications that the
philosophy of the programs is representative of a substantial element of military thought and has great appeal to the military
mind."

The Fulbright protest was long overdue. The military had
been "educating" the public with distorted presentations ever
since the closing year of World War II. What disturbed Fulbright
was the apparent civilian governmental approval of these activities by the Eisenhower Administration. The military, he said, do
not have "the necessarily broad background to relate the various
aspects of the cold war effort, one to another."

The second and apparently more provoking aspect of military propaganda was its connection with right-wing extremism.
Given the context of Communist activity in Cuba and Laos and
other disturbing events, Fulbright noted that

The radicalism of the right can be expected to have great
mass appeal during such periods. It offers the simple solution,
easily understood, scourging of the devils within the body
politic, or in the extreme lashing out at the enemy.
If the military is infected with this virus of right-wing
radicalism, the danger is worthy of attention. If it believes
the public is, the danger is enhanced. If, by the process of the
military educating the public, fevers of both groups are raised,
the danger is great indeed.

It is no wonder that Senator Strom Thurmond (D., S.C.)
became the chief Congressional critic of the Fulbright memoran-

dum as well as the chief supporter of Gen. Edwin A. Walker. Thurmond, who is a Major General in the Army Reserves, was supported by Senator Barry Goldwater, another Reserves General, in charging that military leaders were being muzzled as a result of the Fulbright memorandum. In the public hearings before the Senate Preparedness Subcommittee which resulted from Thurmond's charges, there was a division of opinion among top military officers. Lieut. Gen. Arthur G. Trudeau, Army Chief of Research and Development, in general disliked civilian interference with the content of speeches by military men especially on the part of the State Department. "There are probably more people, more officers in the U.S. Army who have advanced degrees in international relations or closely related degrees than there may be even in the State Department," he claimed. After referring to "the error of judgment of these people or of the position or attitude they take," he declared "I will not accept the criticism that the military man is not prepared by education to have a competence in this field." [7]

On the other hand, the chairman of the Joint Chiefs of Staff, Gen. Lyman Lemnitzer, endorsed the review and clearance of military speeches but justified military involvement in civilian policy-making. Lemnitzer's endorsing of review of speeches does not alter the right-wing orientation of the Joint Chiefs. Lemnitzer had months earlier sent a letter to General Edwin Walker commending him for his famous right-wing voting list which subsequently led to his being reprimanded.

General Hamlett, the Army's Vice Chief of Staff, pointed out in the Senate Hearings that the Army planned to continue the seminars which the Fulbright memorandum called into question, because the Army feels it is necessary "to keep the American public fully alert to the ever present threat of Communism." [8]

While the net impact of the hearing was one of approval of civilian officials reviewing speeches of military officers, there was no evidence that the military would abstain from meddling in politics or would abandon an extreme right-wing position. In fact, civilian officials have at certain points bowed to the military.

For example, on January 9, 1962 the Secretary of Defense, Robert MacNamara, announced the appointment of an advisory committee to study the question of the military seminars and the indoctrination of troops. He appointed as consultants to this committee Frank Barnett of the Richardson Foundation, the Institute for American Strategy, and the American Security Council; and Colonel Kintner of the Foreign Policy Research Institute, both of whom were deeply involved in launching the pattern of military seminars. Kintner, now retired from the Army, wrote an article for the May, 1962 *Reader's Digest* entitled "The Insidious Campaign to Silence the Anti-Communists" wherein he implies that critics of the right-wing extremists, like Senator Fulbright, are really serving the Kremlin.

In addition to these consultants the Defense Department has promoted to the civilian position of Director for Armed Forces Information and Education John C. Broger, a radio executive who was brought to the Pentagon by Admiral Radford, whose right-wing views are well known. Broger, according to the August 13, 1961 *St. Louis Post-Dispatch*, started in the armed forces a "program of militant liberty" and has made hundreds of lectures. In addition, he has shown the film *Operation Abolition* to a number of groups and feels "it doesn't go far enough." Under Broger's leadership a pamphlet entitled "Soviet Treaty Violations" is being distributed in the armed forces. This pamphlet, which lists the broken agreements of the Soviet Union but does not discuss the broken agreements of other great powers, is apparently intended to get across the idea that it is unwise to negotiate with the Soviet Union. All great powers, unfortunately, make and break or keep agreements on the basis of their national interest.[9]

The decision that military officers should in effect serve as political interpreters of national and world events was an outgrowth of a mood of despair and frustration about the United States position in the conflict with the Communist bloc. At least three illustrations of this frustration have contributed to the military effort to educate civilians. The first of these is the widespread conviction among professional military men that the civilian leaders of the United States and the American people themselves are either losing their nerve or under the influence of ideas or groups that are pro-Communist. This has led to the accusation that civilian leaders have adopted a "no-win" policy. One high-ranking Army officer, Col. John E. Dwan II, a member of the faculty of the Army War College, wrote in the April, 1962 *Army:*

> There exists in the military services today a definite mood of frustration and dissatisfaction about how the United States is doing in the cold war. In my opinion a number of mature, professional officers appear convinced that the United States is losing the cold war to the Communist enemy and that inadequate steps are being taken to reverse the trend. . . . Accompanying this pessimistic point of view is usually the clear implication that solutions are obvious if our people and their leaders only had the courage to act or were not somehow unwittingly under insidious influences of the enemy and his accomplices.

Colonel Dwan believes these attitudes "are sincerely held by responsible officers in . . . appreciable number . . . "

Undoubtedly the number one reason that the National Security Council decided to authorize military officers to engage in political education was this strong feeling among officers of the necessity of educating civilians to their point of view. The civilian and military representatives of the Pentagon in the National Security Council and the General then serving as President could not have been ignorant of what Colonel Dwan called these "deep-rooted frustrations on the part of responsible military officers " . . . [which] have aroused violent passions and intemperate action in more than one nation of the world in the recent past."

A second factor in the decision was the sense of panic in Washington in 1958 when a series of incidents seemed to indicate mounting international problems for the United States. Some of these included mobs antagonistic to Vice President Richard Nixon while he was on a tour of South America, President Eisenhower's sending of Marines to Lebanon after the Kassim revolution in Iraq which was incorrectly diagnosed as Communist, and Communist Chinese artillery attacks on Quemoy and Matsu.

These and other mounting tensions worried President Eisenhower and his top military and civilian leaders. Cabell Phillips, in describing this anxiety in the June 18, 1961 *New York Times,* said these officials felt the cold war "must be fought with a concentration of all the resources of the Government and with the full understanding and support of the civilian population." The President agreed that the military should play a major role in molding the attitudes of civilians as well as those of the ordinary enlisted man already in the armed forces.

A third factor in the final decision to let the military educate civilians was an Army study of American prisoners of war in Korea and the particular interpretation of that study which right-wing officers spread widely among military men and civilian groups. The major role in this propaganda about the study was played by Lieut. Col. William F. Mayer, the only medical officer who served on the Japan Joint Intelligence Processing Board, which made the original study and reported to Army authorities.

Mayer, who holds right-wing views, has been described by the *Chicago Tribune* of March 19, 1962 as believing that "the Government of the United States is brainwashing the populace in advance of any contest with the enemy." The *Tribune* added, "When, as it has in recent years, the Government is forever emphasizing and advancing the goals of the 'welfare state,' said Colonel Mayer, it is robbing the people of personal responsibility, of initiative, of the will to resist and stand on their own feet."

Colonel Mayer, in testimony before the Senate Preparedness Subcommittee in March, 1962 asserted that after the study of prisoners of war had been finished "the report was suppressed" because "someone decided that the American public was not ready to hear the things that the report had to say." Actually there has been some feeling among certain Army officers that Mayer and presumably the report overstressed the negative features of prisoner-of-war conduct and did not give a balanced and therefore accurate picture. Mayer, who seems to have had a major hand in shaping the report, was disturbed that it had not been made public. He began a one-man campaign to educate civilians as well as military commanders who had not seen the report. In so doing he made the following generalizations:

1.   "In more than one out of three cases, [Korean war prisoners] admitted openly that . . . they had done something . . . that the Communists had bade them do" such as signing peace petitions, "writing letters home to their parents and friends asking that they form peace committees" and in other ways lending "support to the Communist cause . . ."

2.   Having once entered the prisoner-of-war camps, "never did a single man escape successfully and return to our hands." Yet in other wars Americans have organized and engaged in successful escapes.

3.   Americans "were not equipped to face a Communist enemy . . . in any intellectual or ideological sense." [10]

The point of view of those who felt that Mayer's interpretation was too negative or inaccurate was summarized in the Senate Preparedness Committee Hearings by Brig. Gen. S. L. A. Marshall. He took issue with Mayer's analysis at four points:

1.   "More Americans were decorated for courageous and steadfast conduct in the Korean [prisoner-of-war] camps than ever were investigated under suspicion that they criminally had disgraced the uniform."

2.   Although some Americans had collaborated with the enemy, this was because the captors, instead of following traditional precepts, used captives for political purposes. The Army had not prepared its men for this possibility.

3.   The fact that no one escaped from prison camps was not due to any failure to try. The camps were "a terrible distance and those were awful miles. . . . There was almost no chance of a man getting through but still men tried . . ."

4.   There is no reason to feel that the schools, churches, and homes of America are not doing their job. "I cannot agree that we are in a moral decline," he said. "I don't think there is any marked change in our people." [11]

In spite of Mayer's exaggeration and his blanket indict-
ments, he was encouraged by certain high Army officers to spread
his views. He delivered his message "to all medical personnel
in the Far East Command" and "toured Japan talking to intelligence personnel." He returned to the United States and spoke
"to all major military installations throughout the 4th Army" and
to prominent civilians who, by directive of Gen. I. D. White,
were invited by local commanders to attend the Army meetings.
He went to Hollywood to help in making a movie of his study and
views. He testified that his superiors had made it possible for him
to be away speaking. "They have bent over backward to adjust
my schedule for a meeting that seemed especially important."

Mayer's indictment of American institutions and his insistence on the idea that American youth were soft and unable to
stand up to the Communists has become widely known and
accepted. The idea that American institutions had failed in their
duty and that there had been a terrible breakdown in the morale
of American prisoners of war has almost become a national myth.
Public officials as well as right-wing speakers have advanced
these interpretations. J. Edgar Hoover, for example, has written:
"The behavior of these prisoners of war was less an individual
failure than it was an indictment of our entire society . . . "[12]

When the conviction grew that we were entering a crucial
phase of the cold war, that we were losing, and that civilian
institutions were in large part the reason for our inability to stand
up to the Communists, it was but a short step to the conclusion
that the military ought to step into the breach with a program to
educate civilians.

The reason for criticizing the American prisoner of war in
Korea for "fraternizing" with his captors instead of acting steadily
with enmity toward them was essentially the same reason advanced against co-existence. Many military men are unhappy
that the United States government has decided to recognize the
existence of Communist nations as a fact of history instead of
trying to crush them. Colonel Dwan wrote: "There appears to
be a general feeling among some military professionals that the
United States objectives in the cold war, because they do not

apparently include the destruction of the Soviet system, are in-conclusively defined, and this creates a mood of dissatisfaction and anxiety."

This mood of "them or us," with no meeting ground or possibility of negotiation, is a result of a military habit of analysis to which some civilians as well as military men subscribe. Colonel Dwan feels not only that this is an over-simplified analysis of a highly complex world situation but recognizes that "military pro-fessionals quite naturally conceive of conflict situations in terms of a two-sided context. This is the pattern of the war game, and the pattern within which thought is so effectively applied to problems at Benning, Knox, Sill, and Leavenworth." [13]

The frustration of military and civilian right wingers is by no means confined to the international scene. Most right-wing criticism is in fact directed to internal American problems. They oppose the income tax, social security, labor unions, Supreme Court decisions against segregation and all the social legislation adopted since 1930. Their domestic criticism is linked to their criticism of foreign policy in that all the things they dislike any-where are, they are convinced, caused by the Communist enemy or by people who are subverted or duped by that enemy or else are soft on Communism. Since many of these people are funda-mentalist Protestants or Roman Catholics accustomed to explain-ing evil as the work of the devil, it is easy to accept a military oversimplification that evil is the work of the enemy rather than the result of honest mistakes or personal or group egotism.

"Project Alert" held in Los Angeles in late 1961, illustrates something of this mood. Mitchell Paige, a retired Marine Colonel, asserted that Chief Justice Earl Warren was "guilty of sabotage in the first degree." The Colonel added, "It is my personal opinion that he should be hanged." General Orvil Anderson demanded that "initiative he restored to the military." Admiral Chester Ward urged doubling the military budget. Colonel Paige praised the John Birch Society for doing "an out-standing job to awaken the people to the Communist agents in this country." [14]

As a result of the green light given to military officers by the National Security Council and the President in 1958, top military officers planned or promoted a series of "Project Alerts" as well as public seminars dominated by right-wing extremist speakers. They made speeches to civilian groups about the dangers of internal communism which included criticism of State Department personnel, schools and churches, and circulated to schools and libraries copies of lectures made at the military-sponsored alerts and seminars.

A typical seminar was sponsored in Glenview, Ill. by Naval officers. In August, 1960 officially franked Navy envelopes were sent to civilians in the vicinity with an invitation to attend the program, "The United States Naval Air Station, Glenview, Illinois, presents Education for American Security." The program, which lasted from August 29 to September 9, included Lt. Col. Mayer, who gave his views on American prisoners of war in Korea; E. Merrill Root, a right-wing professor who is author of the fantastic *Brainwashing in the High Schools;* Professor Gerhardt Niemeyer of Notre Dame; Herbert "I Led Three Lives" Philbrick; Richard Arens, a staff member of the House Committee on Un-American Activities; and Dr. Fred Schwartz, who was the central figure in the seminar, listed by the Navy program as "Host and Moderator."

The commanding officer of the station opened the conference, giving an address of welcome. Other naval officers served as lecturers. During the conference, according to an article of October 4, 1961 in *The Christian Century,* America's leading Protestant magazine, participants "heard recommendations for armed intervention in Cuba, for resumption of U-2 flights over Russia and of nuclear testing, for expulsion of Communist nations from the U.N., for the breaking off of diplomatic relations with Russia, for the fomenting of student riots during Khrushchev's pending visit to the U.N., for ending of aid to underdeveloped nations, and for a halt to the bringing of African students to this country, since they only 'return as Marxists'."

Speakers also attacked school textbooks, public libraries, naive ministers, the American Friends Service Committee, the

National Committee for a Sane Nuclear Policy, and lauded Barry
Goldwater, J. B. Mathews, George Sokolsky, Daniel Poling, and
conservative religion. *The Christian Century* in an editorial on
September 14, 1960 said: "It seems pertinent to ask why the
facilities of our government or of any branch of it are put at
the disposal of an organization which turns Americans against
Americans and against their institutions."

A similar conference was held April 14 to 15, 1961 in
Little Rock, Arkansas under the leadership of Major General
William C. Bullock. A reserve officer was placed on active duty
in order to promote the conference, and the Arkansas National
Guard as well as Reserve units were used to encourage attend-
ance. Among the speakers were Dr. George S. Benson and Dr.
Clifton L. Ganus, Jr. of Harding College.

In his Memorandum to the Secretary of Defense on the
propaganda activities of military personnel, Senator J. William
Fulbright listed eleven instances of military projects that promoted
right-wing political programs. Since one of these instances
referred to three conferences and another referred to "233 talks
to civilian groups on the danger of internal Communism" by a
Naval officer who was commander of the Sands Point Naval
Air Station, much more is involved than the formal listing of
eleven illustrations.

Since the Fulbright memorandum and the public controversy
about right-wing extremism, the military have given formal
obedience to civilian directives that speeches must be cleared
in advance. But in various ways professional officers continue
their partisan right-wing political activity. On April 19, 1962
Maj. Arch E. Roberts, in addressing a Daughters of the American
Revolution meeting in Washington, attacked the mayor of Los
Angeles for what he called a "Communist background" and an
Assistant Secretary of State for having "leftist leanings." The
major's proposed speech was vetoed by Army censors, but the
Army nevertheless gave him clearance to speak to the D.A.R.
Among the reasons the Army gave for refusing to clear the
proposed speech was that it would have been susceptible to the

interpretation that former General Walker's troop education program is or was under official attack. In other words, the Army has not really committed itself against the Walker right-wing political indoctrination of troops.

The Army's willingness to let Major Roberts speak and his clear violation of civilian directives resulted in extensive unfavorable publicity. As a result, Roberts was suspended pending an investigation. Ironically, the most that happens to right-wing officers like Roberts and General Walker is a verbal discipline or at most transfer to another command, but a private, Bernie G. Owens, who in 1962 while off duty and out of uniform protested the recall and continued duty of reservists, was court-martialled, convicted and sentenced to the stockade.

It is even more ironic that the Armed Forces, which exist for the defense of the country, may actually contribute to undermining it. By the very assumption that the military know better than civilians how to run internal as well as foreign affairs, the military have entered politics. In turn this leads to a riddling of the military with different political opinions and thus affects its discipline. If it is to avoid conflicting political opinion and hence political cliques, it would have to require a political conformity which would rightfully render it suspect among freedom-loving civilians.

Even if military men in some cases have superior education or seem more intelligent than their civilian counterparts, the military context in which they function is likely to betray them and render them less able than civilians to see the total problem confronting the nation. All too often military men become so preoccupied with the intentions and capabilities of their major enemy that they view "the current world," in Colonel Dwan's words, "as a two-sided game between reds and blues" and hence oversimplify the problem. "Such a vision is entirely consistent with professional military experience in conflict situations," Dwan adds, "and as such it is understandable; but it is not a wholly accurate description of an incredibly complicated world of infinitely diverse and dynamic forces, some of which basically have nothing to do with the East-West conflict." [15]

As a result of this overconcentration on the enemy, right-wing officers seem "to insist that U.S. cold war objectives toward the Soviet Union be shaped by enemy intentions — and what is even more startling, that our ultimate objective be a mirror image of his. The result in effect is to let the enemy determine the ultimate character of one's own strategy."

Military men are men of action who must always guard against or be guarded against rushing into action or commitments to act without full consideration of other factors. In large part the Communists took Eastern Europe because the American General Staff rejected British civilian advice during World War II and refused to open the second front in the Balkans. And in large part the Army caused the Berlin problem by refusing at the end of World War II to insist on guaranteed land access to the city, as the State Department had urged. But if evidence is needed of deficiency in military wisdom, we have only to consider the questionable alliance of military officers with the fanatical right-wing extremists of our society today, many of whom, like paranoids, see the Communist hand guiding every American action with which they disagree.

CHAPTER 14

RELIGION AND THE MILITARY

One of the military targets is the church. Churches and synagogues became a military target not only because they represent an influential section of American public opinion but also because they blocked Army ambitions at a crucial stage in the military drive for power. During the Army campaign for universal military training, the churches and religious organizations of America were almost solidly opposed to peacetime conscription for every teen-age boy. Moreover, they were vocal.

Cardinal Cushing of Boston (then Archbishop), in a major address entitled "Third Choice, Americanism," denied the military contention that "we must make a choice between two evil ideas — Communism and militarism." The Cardinal said that the armed forces "make no effort to conceal their entry into the field of youth training as frank competitors with the traditional American agencies for the formation of the young: the Church, the School, and the Home." He referred to "authoritative Army circles as asserting that the Army is the *only* organization equipped to develop personality, character, and manhood in our boys — and as boasting that under Universal Military Training the Army will be better able to do this because it will have control of the boy 24 hours a day, 7 days a week."

A Quaker scholar, Howard Brinton, asserted that "Christianity throughout its history has had but one serious rival for the supreme loyalty of its adherents — the State." He pointed out that the clearest point where the authoritarian state might begin in America was through military control, beginning with universal conscription:

The drillmaster will teach to every young man at his most

199

impressionable age, absolute, unquestioning obedience to human command, even though such command leads to actions wholly contrary to the teachings of home, of school, of church. If the Christian churches do not take against peacetime conscription a stand strong enough to defeat it, Christianity will be even more reduced than now to spiritual vassalage to nationalism." [1]

Other religious groups were similarly concerned. Without a doubt the church opposition to UMT and to other manifestations of militarism was vigorous and determined. As a result the Army felt it had to soften or alter the attitudes of church leaders. Accordingly it began to work on the churches at national, regional and local levels.

At the national level, as we have seen, the Army established a model UMT camp at Fort Knox, Kentucky, where highly disciplined volunteers maintained a public front of no profanity, no drinking of alchoholic beverages, no sexual relations, and also kept church attendance records near the top. In addition to effective Army publicizing of this showcase unit, clergymen were invited and in some cases flown in Army planes to see this "character building unit." The unit's emphasis on religion was strikingly set forth by Chaplain Murphy in the March 8, 1947 camp newspaper. "In the UMT you are much more than a body to be bayoneted or bulleted. You are more than organized flesh to be set in the wake of some rolling barrage. You are more than an animated sandbag. You are first, last and always a religious animal; and UMT will not let you forget it."

A report distributed by the Chief of Chaplains' office dated March 24, 1947 contained testimonials from parents and ministers who had been taken in by the publicity and the staged morality at Fort Knox. The following are samples: "UMT affords teen-agers the best religious program I've ever seen either in or outside the Church." And "I thank God each day for the UMT program . . ." "I think it is one of the greatest things the Government can do for teen-agers." "So many boys have no religious training or discipline at home. In this program they can get both."

The chaplains of the Fort Knox unit contributed to this mood by statements to the public press. One chaplain was quoted in the *New York Post* of April 16, 1947 as saying, "I know of no similar situation where so much can be done spiritually in so short a time for our youth." The other unit chaplain was described as feeling "that ethics and morals are so neglected nowadays that UMT is needed as a rescue agency."

Careful investigation of the claims made for Fort Knox revealed that Negroes were excluded from the unit and an experimental platoon of boys of low intelligence rating, whom the General in charge called "the morons," were segregated into a labor detachment. Neither of these could be called a religious approach to persons of other races or persons with different abilities. In addition, investigation disclosed that members of the UMT unit who did not swear in camp when visitors or Army officers were present made up for it in the men's room at the service club. Nor did the men abstain from drinking liquor or from promiscuous relations when on weekend leave in Louisville." [2]

The chaplains were the chief publicity agents, although a staff of thirteen public relations men attached to the model UMT unit publicized the unit. A report issued May 12, 1947 by Col. Patrick J. Ryan, acting Chief of Chaplains, revealed the extent to which the Army uses the military clergy to indoctrinate the civilian clergy. The Report stated:

Upon the advice of the Legislative and Liaison Division, the Office Chief of Chaplains sent representatives from each of the Army areas and the Air Defense Commands to the Experimental Unit for UMT at Fort Knox, Kentucky 26-28 April 1947. The purpose of this meeting was to orientate the chaplains on the aims of UMT so that they may be properly prepared to represent this program to ministerial and denominational conventions as they take place in the United States this year.

The publicity on the Fort Knox unit was so favorable that the whole Army began to emphasize its "character guidance" role and the spiritual uplift features of military training. A

Chicago Tribune story on November 29, 1948 was headlined;
"Chaplain Plays Bigger Role in the New Army." According to
the story, "The chaplains interview every recruit." In addition,
"they describe the virtues of chastity and male continence before
the doctors explain prophylaxis to the troops." The chaplains
"hold eight classroom sessions devoted to morals and citizenship."

After this new program had been tested, the Army and
Navy began to describe it to church groups. One such effort
was made to the National Laymen's Committee of the National
Council of Churches in April, 1953. Another one was held at
the U.S. Naval Training Center, Great Lakes, Illinois on May
27, 1952 with 400 clergymen as invited guests. Two ministers
who were present said; "The entire character guidance program
seems to be geared to making better persons in order to make
better fighters. 'Men with good morals are better fighting men,'
Rear Admiral Francis F. Olds told us bluntly." The clergymen,
after citing similar quotations from other officers, concluded that
"The concern throughout is for utilitarian ends rather than for
the heart-searching which religion demands."

The two ministers reported that 'The program apparently
assumes that character can be changed through lectures. Tests
are given before and after the character guidance lectures and
it has been figured out scientifically that the men have 8 to 10
per cent more character after they have listened to the lectures." [3]

One of the questions by which character was determined
was worded: "Should every able bodied man be required to take
military or naval training?" At the beginning of military training the results were: No, 323 or 45.4 per cent; Yes, 389 or
54.6 per cent. After eight lectures eight weeks later the results
revealed: No, 121, or 18.5 per cent; Yes, 533, or 81.5 per cent.
On the basis of this shift to military values it was assumed that
more character had developed. [4]

Another national program to influence the churches is the
"Orientation Conference for Religious Leaders" held in the Pentagon, similar to those held for other groups which were described
in chapter 10. In such conferences top generals and admirals as
well as top civilian officials present the need for religious support

of the cold war and preparation for a hot one. John R. Wilkinson, a California clergyman, described one of them in an article, "Three Days at the Pentagon," which *The Christian Century* published on March 12, 1952. He reported a heavy emphasis on military training which "should and must become a part of the normal growing up process of every American boy." One officer said that "every American girl should be given a term of compulsory military training and service." A chaplain justified breaking the commandment "Thou Shalt not kill' with the comment: "When the killing is upon orders of others . . . it is homicide [as distinguished from murder] and does not violate the commandment." He added, "As far as the idea of brotherhood is concerned, that is a carry-over from Stoic philosophy and has no place in New Testament teaching."

The editorial columns of the same issue of *The Christian Century* described the Pentagon technique at these conferences. Those attending "have been dazzled with big names and puffed up with assurances that they were being entrusted with secrets so profound that only the selectest of the select could share them."

Religious leaders are cultivated not only to enlist their support of military conscription but also to soften or eliminate their opposition to mass extermination of human beings. The Strategic Air Force, which is assigned the role of massive retaliation, invited a group of important religious leaders to attend a briefing at its headquarters near Omaha, Nebraska, April 30 — May 1, 1962. The letter of invitation signed by Maj. Gen. James H. Walsh offered transportation by military plane from New York and Chicago. "Military transportation will be provided for all who desire it." The invitation was justified on the ground that our national defense "must be based on an informed leadership. We believe that this leadership must necessarily include representatives of the various religious denominations who lead the spiritual forces of the nation."

Although the armed forces have relied heavily on orientation conferences and special outings as a means of influencing

national and regional church leaders, the chief program designed
to win church support involves the military chaplaincy. In the
popular mind the military chaplain is the representative of the
church in the armed forces. In practice, however, he is the
military representative in the churches.

A good illustration of the Army line taken by chaplains in
sermons in civilian churches was given in a *Religious News
Service* report of June 2, 1952:

> In spite of what a lot of mothers seem to think there's noth-
> ing in military service that makes a man go wrong, according
> to a Lutheran minister with 28 years experience as a military
> chaplain. "On the contrary," insisted the Rev. Gynther
> Storaasli, Washington, former chief of United States Air Force
> chaplains and former commandant of the Army Chaplains'
> School, "everything about the armed forces tends to strengthen
> a man's character . . . When a man 'goes wrong' in the
> service, it can be blamed only on a 'lack' of moral training
> in the home — it's as simple as that."

If parents could be reassured during a period of widespread
conscription that the Army was a character-building agency
and only boys with poor home training went wrong, parental
objections to the draft could be muted or eliminated.

One military chaplain, Martin Siegel, writing in the August
8, 1962 *Christian Century*, points out that the chaplaincy is
increasingly an ingrown military institution. "In recent years
a substantial number of line officers and enlisted men have left
the service for a short time, taken the requisite religious training
(often not too rigorous) and immediately returned to the military
as chaplains." Even when they come from civilian life, "Many
military chaplains spend their entire professional career within
the military and as a consequence lose contact with their own
religious tradition." Siegel points out that the chaplain

> . . . sooner or later . . . begins to think of himself in terms
> of his relative rank rather than his religious vocation . . .
> He will not oppose the commanding officer who writes effici-
> ency or fitness reports on him; one bad report could severely
> damage his career. Professionally he becomes more a man of
> the military than a man of religion.

One indication that the chaplain is chiefly a representative of the military is his public relations work for the armed forces. The September 1952 *Army Information Digest* lists six duties of the chaplain, the first one listed being "public relations." This term, public relations, is defined as "any planned program or procedure which will elicit public understanding and good will." A Navy chaplain who headed the Navy's Ecclesiastical Relations Branch wrote; "The Navy chaplain is expected to cultivate good relations with church leaders near his ship or station." [5] An Air Force chaplain, Martin Scharleman, described the chaplain's public relations role at Sampson Air Force Base as developing "Close liaison with community welfare organizations, home hospitality programs, outings both on and off the base, visits by ministerial associations, women's societies, and a superior choral group. One chaplain from our section devotes himself exclusively to this work, serving as the executive secretary of the Community Services Council." [6]

An Air Force brochure published in 1953 made the claim that Air Force chaplains in one year spoke 107,280 times to civilian groups with a total attendance of 4,002,180. In addition to such speaking, advantage is taken of radio and TV opportunities. Chaplain Patrick A. Killeen of the Marine Corps on a Mother's Day radio program during the Korean War effectively used religion in the service of the military. In an effort to reassure mothers about the dangers of death and about foul language, failure to attend Mass, adultery and other forms of immorality, the chaplain concluded that "A Marine will develop a deep respect for authority that shows itself in willing obedience." After implying a connection between obedience to Marine officers and obedience to God, Chaplain Killeen asserted "Be proud of your son, today, because if he is a good Marine you can be sure he will be a good son and a good Catholic." [7]

Another function of the chaplain is to spread the military version of religion in civilian churches. An indication of this is the military effort to get churches to observe Armed Forces Day. Such observance is requested by letters from Naval district, Army Corps and Air Force headquarters chaplains. Such letters ask that a prayer composed in the Pentagon be used in all churches, that chaplains and reserve chaplains "assist in your Armed Forces Day worship observance" and some years have included a "Statement of Principles" which tries to show a connection between national armaments and the will of God.

A letter dated April 15, 1954, for example, began:

> Reverend and Dear Sir:
> Again, as in other years, the Armed Forces Chaplains Board, Department of Defense, has prepared a prayer . . . We are inclosing a copy of that prayer together with other pertinent material, in the hope that you may find it helpful in the observance of Armed Forces Day, Sunday, 16 May, 1954.

One enclosure spoke of "fighting and dying on the battle field locked in mortal combat with the forces of Anti-God who speak so glibly of 'peace.' " Although this military statement disclaimed any intention of believing that "the destinies of this Nation alone . . . are inseparably bound together with the divine purpose in history," the context clearly assumed that we are God's people and our enemies are God's enemies. The statement asserted that "the United States of America claims GOD as the SOURCE of all power." It continued with this sentence: "Confronted as our Nation is today by an enemy which has proved that both in teaching and practice he is anti-God . . . our peace-loving Nation has no other choice but to remain strong and prepared for any eventuality."

The Armed Forces Day prayer distributed in 1952 "humbly" proclaimed that our national armaments defended God's place in the human soul: "We humbly beseech Thy blessing, Heavenly Father, upon the arms of our nation on land, on sea and in the air, as we man the ramparts of the free world in defense of home, country, and Thy rightful place in the human soul."

Another military venture into the field of religion was the effort to force church colleges to introduce R.O.T.C. units into their curricula. This effort was begun during World War II and intensified during the Korean War.

The small colleges in the United States which are largely church-related could scarcely exist if most or all of their male students were drafted. During the years when the armed forces wanted to expand their R.O.T.C. program by introducing units into colleges that heretofore had not included military training, Selective Service was drafting students and potential students but deferring those who were enrolled in the R.O.T.C. The military therefore had a decisive voice when it came to college enrollments. It could decide which colleges would have military units; it could decide also which students should be deferred.

In 1945 the report of the President of DePauw University, a church college, referred to "a formal application on the part of DePauw for one of these new [Navy] units." The president spoke of the discontinuance of the wartime Navy program and "the all-time low" in "student enrollments." He added: "The lean year of which I have frequently spoken is now coming up."

Another church college president, Arthur Fleming of Ohio Wesleyan, proposed during the peacetime years following World War II that R.O.T.C. be instituted because of the Selective Service now "in existence." Boys not in R.O.T.C. could be drafted while in college but those who "attend a college or university that has an R.O.T.C. unit" can enroll in that unit and "their college work will not be interrupted." [8]

An article in *The Christian Century* entitled "Manpower and the Colleges" summarized the problem on March 28, 1951 by pointing out that "comparatively few of the church colleges" have R.O.T.C. units but "schools with R.O.T.C. will have the advantage in securing enrollments." The author, Dr. John O. Gross of the Methodist Board of Education, indicated that "While charges will be made that the introduction of an R.O.T.C. unit on the campus of a church college is a 'sell-out,' most schools offered units will nevertheless accept them because the exigencies in which they are caught leave no satisfactory alternative." Gross concluded that "however much heat may be generated in church circles over the Christian implications of the R.O.T.C., the need of the institutions and their survival are the main question."

Still another approach to the churches is through the Office of Civil Defense. A former Army chaplain, Fred Kern, is employed by the Office of Civil Defense Mobilization to promote civil defense in the churches. Ministers have been invited to several days at the Battle Creek headquarters. One such session held in May, 1959 attended by 90 ministers included among its lecturers Lt. Col. McAllen of the Military Police Corps and Col. W. F. Heimlich, a Pentagon officer on special assignment to O.C.D.M. A clergyman, Dr. Carl Soule, who was present, reported that a great deal of time was spent on indoctrination against Communism, with Dr. Fred Schwartz of the Christian Anti-Communist Crusade, and the House Un-American Activities Committee being quoted as authorities. There was a mood of inevitability of war, and of the impossibility and inadvisability of negotiation with the enemy. Dr. Soule reported that "At the beginning of the course each member was asked to stand, raise his right hand, and repeat a loyalty oath which had been placed on his desk. He was then asked to sign it and return it to those in charge." Dr. Soule referred to the "overtones of fatalism, of national and religious self-righteousness, of existential distrust (amounting to mental illness) of any proposals of reconciliation or disarmament coming from communist nations . . . " [9]

In general the Pentagon has been much more subtle in propagandizing the churches and in trying to use them for military purposes than it has in working with any other group. Yet this subtlety does not minimize the serious military effort directed at the churches. And occasionally the armed forces are far from subtle. For example, the Army sent a paid military lobbyist, Margaret Bannister, to the annual meeting of the United Council of Church Women in Milwaukee in November, 1948 in an effort to sell the church women on UMT. The *Presbyterian Tribune* of June 14, 1947 reported that former Army and Navy chaplains had tried to tell the Presbyterian General Assembly "that the question of military conscription was one which the Church Assembly 'had no right to discuss.' " Such heavyhanded efforts have fortunately done more to harm the military cause than to help it.

The Pentagon has faced real difficulties in winning the churches, partly because of the disillusionment felt by the churchmen at being "taken in," by the military mood of World War I, so aptly described in Ray Abrams' book *Preachers Present Arms* (New York: Round Table Press, 1933). Another factor in keeping the churches from capitulating to the military is the committed pacifist minority within the churches, ever vigilant as to military encroachments. Another factor is the orientation of the church toward the "Prince of Peace," who chose unarmed love rather than armed violence as the key to His Kingdom.

There are nevertheless strong voices raised in the churches in behalf of military demands or goals. Billy Graham, a Protestant evangelist, was lauded in the *Congressional Record* for telling 40,000 persons at a Sunday worship gathering in Washington, D. C., "We must maintain strong military power for defense at any cost." [10] Cardinal Spellman of the Roman Catholic Church has demonstrated his support of military goals such as universal military training on more than one occasion, sometimes even comparing military activity with the actions and will of God. During the Korean War, after General Matthew Ridgway was quoted in the February 7, 1951 *New York Herald Tribune* as saying that our "aim is to kill Chinese rather than to capture ground in the current action," and after this project was referred to as "Operation Killer," Cardinal Spellman said: "And I dare hope that all at home, inspired by our boys' heroic giving of themselves for us, may better understand the true meaning of Christmas and more strongly unite to keep God's peace and the freedoms that he bequeathed us!" He went on to refer to "this sublime sacrifice of mothers' sons in emulation of that first Mother's Son who suffered and died . . . " (*New York Times,* December 23, 1951). This comparison of the suffering on the cross of a "Prince of Peace" with those who were sent to Korea to kill their enemies is evidence that the military mood is not confined to the Pentagon.

Arthur Compton, a Christian who helped develop the atom bomb and who advised the President to use it on Hiroshima, asserted, "I think that not only did God condone our act in dropping the bombs, but that it was only with His help and inspiration that the job was done in time." [11]

How much of this militarism in religion is a result of the confusion of modern nationalism with the age-old concept of a tribal God and how much is a result of Pentagon propaganda is difficult to tell. It is clear, however, that the military has its allies in religion as well as in industry. These allies are flown to Korea and other parts of the world to conduct religious services, are given wide publicity in the press, are received by commanding generals, invited to review troops, serve on Presidential Commissions dealing with the armed forces, and in other ways are honored or feted.

Yet in spite of powerful allies among laymen, clergymen, bishops and cardinals, the churches of the United States have been freer from military commitments and vested interests than any other major organized group in American life.

CHAPTER 15

MILITARY INFLUENCE IN EDUCATION

A statement attributed to Gen. Maxwell D. Taylor that the Army intended "to put the best heads of America in the brass hats of tomorrow" [1] summed up one of the Army's postwar purposes with respect to educational institutions. When World War II ended, the armed forces began a program to enlist the best minds of the nation for military purposes. In so doing it was able to build on three earlier developments in American history.

Military influence in education began during the Civil War when Congress in 1862 passed the Morill Act appropriating tracts of public land for use by the states. The money from the sale of the land was to be used for the establishment of colleges where, among other subjects, military tactics would be taught. This was the first development. The second was during World War I, when Congress authorized the War Department to establish Reserve Officers Training Corps units in schools and colleges. Thereafter the land grant colleges yielded to military pressure and, although not required by law, made military training compulsory for all first and second year students.

The third development took place during World War II when the armed forces turned to the colleges both for research and for student training programs. Almost as soon as the war started "colleges and universities . . . were put on notice that 'every classroom must be a citadel' and that every able-bodied male student should be definitely preparing himself for military service." [2]

A University of Chicago release revealed that "at the peak of its war activity approximately three fourths of the staff and the facilities of the University . . . were required for the war program." [3] Many other universities reported comparable activity, in training programs such as the V-12 plan or in research, or in both.

In the postwar period the financial returns as well as the prestige of doing research for the Army and Navy have been big factors in university decisions to continue accepting military contracts. Then too, it has been much easier for the Army or Navy to continue or renew contracts with schools which had become dependent on them for money and which had become accustomed to the relationship with military departments of government.

In 1947, out of a research budget of $280,000,000 the Army earmarked $70,000,000 for fundamental studies in colleges.[4] In 1948 - 1949 the Office of Naval Research spent approximately $20,000,000 on about 500 projects in colleges and universities.[5] These projects were carried on in more than 150 educational institutions by roughly 2,400 graduate students and 2,000 scientists.[6]

"This program has enabled the Navy to retain the interest of scientists in the Navy," a naval spokesman said in explaining the program to a Congressional committee. He added that the program also "has pioneered in the establishment of cordial relationships between scientists and the federal government." [7]

In 1949, the estimated expenditure by the Military Establishment on research in universities was $53,000,000. In addition the Atomic Energy Commission had a research program in the colleges which cost $81,400,000.

Benjamin Fine, the *New York Times* authority on education, said that altogether the Government spent about "$160,000,000 in 1949 for research to be conducted on the nation's campuses," most of it in technical, scientific and military fields. He added, "This sum has almost doubled in two years and may even go higher within the next year or two." [8]

Over the ensuing years, the Pentagon continued to support research in the universities until by the mid-1950's the rate of support was about $300 million, of which about $30 million was for research involving graduate students.[9] In 1959 almost 20 per cent of the operating income of the nation's universities came from such Federal research funds.[10]

Certain universities received substantial sums. For example, a Great Lakes area state university, in addition to ROTC and NROTC, reported sixty-two research contracts, largely scientific, with an income of $6,099,159, and Veterans' Administration benefits to students of $4,456,700.[11] Columbia University received more than a million dollars annually under contracts and grants from the Atomic Energy Commission and the National Military Establishment.[12] The California Institute of Technology estimated that it had contracts at the rate of about $4,000,000 a year.[13] In 1962 the Defense Department spent $80.513 million at the Massachusetts Institute of Technology.[14]

Programs of such magnitude have important implications for every institution of higher learning. In the first place, as Dr. Hollis P. Allen of the Graduate School of Education, Claremont College, and a member of the Hoover Commission's task force on education, observed, these programs are administered by noneducational federal agencies interested in the promotion of their own points of view.[15] As such, the "preponderance of this research is far removed from the traditional educational and cultural objectives of American colleges and universities." [16]

Dr. Paul H. Kirkpatrick, a physicist at Stanford University, in commenting on this program, said, "Because the military favors such projects as may be of value in warfare, the direction of research in general is being changed." [17] The emphasis thus swings from projects of use and value to the people of the country generally to those which will be useful to a specific group and in a specific situation.

There is also the serious problem of secrecy. The chairman of the Board of Trustees of the University of Chicago, in an address, "Are We Afraid of Freedom?" said on April 11, 1949: "The University of Chicago is engaged in secret projects of vital importance to national defense. The university is under surveillance of professional investigators, agents of the FBI, and of the military intelligence units."

The entire concept of secrecy imposes a serious curb on free academic discussion. Dr. Kenneth S. Pitzer, director of the research division of the Atomic Energy Commission, pointed out, "if adequate security measures are taken I think it detracts from the tone of the University." He added that even the smaller projects build up walls within the otherwise open academic atmosphere.[18]

An illustration of what secrecy means is seen in the reaction of the military to a questionnaire the Federation of American Scientists sent to universities in an effort to discover procedures used in investigating the loyalties of employees. The Research and Development Board of the military establishment sent out a memorandum in comment on the questionnaire:

> There are in existence today a large number of organizations whose objective is to gather such information and later use it as material for propaganda and "smear" programs in an attempt to discredit the United States form of government. It is therefore requested that if any questionnaire of this type or any other *questioning the methods of the United States Government* are received in the future, they be referred to this office for appraisal before any answer is given.[19] [Italics mine.]

Still another problem for universities engaged in military research is the uncertainty of military short-term contracts. There is always the danger that the military, because of a cut in appropriations or a shift in emphasis or for some arbitrary reason, will not renew a university research program. Dr. Vannevar Bush, wartime Director of the Office of Scientific Research and Development, said in December, 1951:

> Many universities are carrying the bulk of their research and the salaries of their graduate faculties on Government funds . . . Dependence on variable and uncertain yearly Government appropriations increases the danger of control and could put our universities into very serious financial organizational difficulties.[20]

This danger tends to make administrators and even some scientific faculties very responsive to military demands. Dr. Philip Morrison summarized the problem in these words: "We cannot tie science to the military and hope to see it used for peace, no matter how ingeniously we write the contracts nor how circumspect the men of good will remain." [21]

The military in turn encourages research that has purely military utility. When Congressman Harry R. Sheppard suggested in March, 1949 that it might be advisable to lessen military controls over university research "in order to effectuate more rapidity and happier minds," Colonel Finks replied: "We lean a little bit more toward keeping them tight." When pressed for a reason, he said: "Primarily because we want to be sure this research work gives us end items that will be used by a field army sometime in the near future." [22]

Many of these problems were at the root of the controversy that led the Army in May, 1961 to sever its research contract with the Johns Hopkins University. For more than twelve years the Army's Operations Research Office was at Johns Hopkins. Dr. Ellis A. Johnson, head of that office, had indicated, according to the May 28, 1961 *New York Times*, that "present Army leaders had sought to maintain 'strict control in detail' over the research efforts of the Operations Research Office, whereas he believed that once given an assignment the researchers must do 'a complete and honest job.'" The Army had responded to University protests by withholding payments to Johns Hopkins. Contrary to original contract, reported the *New York Times*, the Army "had been paying the research group on a month by month basis and had paid no fee for a period of seven months." Since the average annual fee paid by the Army to the University had been $4,500,000, "this was said to have worked a considerable hardship on the University." A staff of 450 persons had worked in the Research office.

When the Army announced this severance of relationship it stated that it was setting up a new independent non-profit organization to do research similar to the Rand Corporation, which does work for the Air Force. One reason military agencies establish such independent corporations is that top-flight scientists can be attracted by the high salaries they pay, whereas scientists working directly for the government must accept the government's lower salary scale.

The Army indicated that it would call the new agency the Research Analysis Corporation. It would be headed by General Omar Bradley, former Army Chief of Staff and now chairman of the board of the Bulova Watch Co. Other prospective members mentioned were for the most part leaders of industry.[23]

On November 19, 1961 the *New York Times* announced that the Federal Government "will spend $9,400,000,000 on research and development [in 1962], thus providing more than 60 per cent of all the support for research in the nation." Ten per cent of this, or about $940 million, was to go to universities and non-profit corporations; 70 per cent was to go to industry and the rest to government laboratories.

There were approximately 1,400,000 scientists and engineers in the United States in 1961. Of these, 400,000 were doing research and development, 280,000 of them working directly in defense or space agencies. This means that only 120,000 research scientists and engineers were available for private commercial and industrial purposes. One result of this largely defense-oriented research is that the rate of patented inventions in the United States has not increased in ten years.[24]

Secretary of Commerce Luther Hodges in an address to a conference of the U.S. Chamber of Commerce in 1963 expressed concern about defense activity taking money and trained men that civilian industry needs for research and development. "Of the total effort, overwhelmingly oriented to defense, relatively little," he said, "is directed to the creation of new consumer products, or to improve machines to make the products or to improve processes to use in the machines." After referring to countries not so militarily involved he indicated that "the speed with which other nations adapt scientific advance to practical use often exceeds ours which explains, in part, why they are able to compete against us today in both price and quality." [25]

It is increasingly clear that the heavy percentage of military research has robbed the American civilian economy; and the heavy taxation for and preoccupation with military matters has robbed the nation of proper support for education and research of a nonmilitary nature.

The ability of the Defense Department to pay high salaries through various military-financed research corporations and the ability of defense industries to do the same has siphoned scientists from universities into defense projects. Yet even the professors who stay in educational institutions often use valuable time for such work. The *New York Times* of November 19, 1961 reported that "the eminent university scientists who are not supplementing their professorial salaries by serving as consultants to industrial research concerns and the non-profit corporations are few in number."

When scientists serve as advisors to government agencies or in non-profit defense corporations they often learn which lines of research will pay off in terms of new weapons or equipment. As a result they are frequently invited to serve as consultants to industries or as members of boards of directors of investment funds, so that these groups may get advance information. This was illustrated in 1961 when an official of a large investment firm phoned a major defense contractor to ask "if a certain scientist who had been advising the Air Force was close to a top Air Force general." When asked the reason for his question he readily admitted that his company "desired to hire the scientist as a consultant in the hope that he could provide guidance on Air Force research contracts." [26]

In turn this means that a limited number of scientists serve a group of universities, investment funds and industries as well as the government. The result, said the *New York Times,* is the creation of "an interlocking directorate" which knows in advance about research projects and weapons development and can use this information for the benefit of its university or industry. [27]

This conflict of interest, which apparently has not disturbed the military branches of government, has led to a Congressional investigation. The House Appropriations Committee criticized the Defense Department for assigning too much of its research management and work to such non-profit groups and in 1962 actually cut $5 million off the $166 million requested by the Air Force for such corporations. [28]

World War II gave impetus to militarism in education, not only by way of research but also through the expansion of direct military training programs. Many colleges received military money through increased enrollments caused by military training programs on campus during the war. If there were another war, the colleges therefore reasoned, those with R.O.T.C. would have a better chance of survival; likewise, if there were to be peacetime conscription some colleges might qualify through R.O.T.C. for military training on the campus as an alternative to military training in an Army camp. Thus student enrollments, they thought, would be insured.

Some colleges have R.O.T.C. because a college president or board likes things military and sees no reason for not making a parade ground of the campus. Other colleges want the prestige that military training gives them in the minds of superficial patriotic organizations as well as with the government. And some schools benefit financially by the erection of buildings by the military or through the providing of equipment from military budgets. The subsidy given to students is in itself an inducement to the colleges. Thus the Reserve Officers Training Corps program has a variety of appeals to a college or university.

In the final analysis, the decision as to whether R.O.T.C. is to be compulsory is made by the college. The college is free to choose whether it will accept the Army's suggestion of compulsion or agree to an elective course only.

In 1960 there were 248 colleges and universities with Army R.O.T.C. programs which enrolled a total of 155,871 cadets. R.O.T.C. was compulsory in about 154 of these institutions. The Air Force had R.O.T.C. programs in 175 colleges with a total enrollment between 92,000 and 110,000. In about half of these colleges the program was compulsory. The Navy, whose program is based entirely upon voluntary enrollment, had 10,295 students in 52 colleges.[29]

For years there has been opposition to military training on college campuses, most of it directed against the compulsory feature. This opposition prior to World War II was led by pacifist and near-pacifist groups such as the Committee on Militarism in

Education. Today it comes chiefly from students or faculty members in isolated college communities. Yet this opposition is substantial and has led to the abandonment of compulsion at the Massachusetts Institute of Technology, the University of Wisconsin, Cornell University, Rutgers and Bucknell, among others.

Much of the criticism of R.O.T.C. has been produced by the authoritarian attitudes of R.O.T.C. officers. At Columbia University in 1962 a group of 177 professors who had protested the government's civil defense shelter program were described by a Naval Reserve Captain as "unwittingly lining up with Russian propaganda." There were immediate faculty protests accusing the captain of "resorting to the smear technique used by those who cannot argue from a position of intellectual strength." [30]

At the University of Massachusetts the student senate decided to hold a campus referendum on compulsory R.O.T.C. After a young instructor wrote a letter against it, Col. James R. Weaver, the Army's R.O.T.C. commander, retorted: "I know officially that two years ago a definite Communist program was initiated on the west coast, the two primary tenets of which were to strive to eliminate loyalty oaths in any form and to get R.O.T.C. off the campus." The strategy, he said, was to eliminate R.O.T.C. "as a requirement and then follow with total removal." In spite of this smear technique, similar to the one used at Columbia University, the students voted two to one against compulsory R.O.T.C.[31]

Within the Pentagon itself there have been serious second thoughts in recent years about compulsion and the purpose of R.O.T.C. Modern technology and military requirements have changed the nature of R.O.T.C. from its original conception. As recently as 1955, when Congress and the President were still thinking in terms of a large citizens' army and had abandoned Universal Military Training only because of public opposition, R.O.T.C. was considered a method for training reserve officers to lead the large reserve forces that would be mobilized in emergency.

Today, however, the Pentagon believes that defense depends

upon military forces currently in service rather than those in a reserve which would take weeks and months to mobilize. This is one factor that has led to the concept of a permanently large peacetime military establishment. It has also led the Armed Forces to require more career officers than the Military, Naval, and Air Force Academies can produce.

One-third of the Army's active duty officers are from R.O.T.C. An annual average of more than 12,500 second lieutenants come from R.O.T.C. The Air Force R.O.T.C. accounts for about 3,500 to 4,000 second lieutenants annually in contrast to some 500 from the Air Force Academy. Naval R.O.T.C. provides about 2,200 new ensigns out of a total annual ensign need of about 6,300 each year.[32]

"Despite earlier pressures the Army and Air Force R.O.T.C. students had not been required to enter active duty upon graduation." [33] Now all three branches require a period of active duty after graduation. In other words, R.O.T.C. is now looked upon as a means of supplying career officers for the regular forces and only partly as a reserve officer program. R.O.T.C. is actually producing more officers for the Regular Army than is West Point. But since R.O.T.C. produces more potential officers than the berths the Army has available, the surplus are given "six month tours of active duty for training" instead of longer term assignments.

In the fiscal year 1959 out of a total new officer group of 9,347, R.O.T.C. provided 5,400 for two years or longer of active duty. The surplus of 7,000 had only six months' active duty.[34]

The Air Force, faced with the fact that R.O.T.C.-trained officers left the Air Force as soon as they could finish their short term service, began a few years ago to require agreement to serve for five years after graduation. "For many young men, the decision to join A.F.R.O.T.C. now involves a decision as to whether or not to make the Air Force a life career." [35] It now has a retention rate of about 65 to 70 per cent for long term or career officers coming out of the R.O.T.C. program.[36]

With this development a new rationale for compulsory military training has entered the picture. By requiring all males at a given college to take military training during their first two years, the Army and Air Force have a larger manpower pool from which to select students for the last two years of advanced training. Since this advanced program is voluntary, persuasion is still required to get the "selected" students. Compulsory R.O.T.C., in other words, gives the military a chance at each boy over a two-year period and the opportunity to pick the "best of the lot." In the case of the Air Force, for example, the first year's enrollment normally averages between 60,000 and 65,000 men, but after compulsion is ended the number dwindles to between 4,200 and 4,700 by the fourth year.[37]

An examination of the statistics suggests that compulsion may not be, even from the military point of view, the best method for recruiting. In 1957 there were 4,759 male graduates commissioned out of the 34,153 graduates who spend their first two years in compulsory training at the 49 institutions which had Army and Air Force R.O.T.C. By contrast, the 22 colleges which offered voluntary Army and Air Force R.O.T.C. commissioned 2,076 out of 15,437 male graduates. The voluntary colleges commissioned 13.5 per cent of their male graduates in contrast to 13.9 per cent of the male graduates from schools where R.O.T.C. was compulsory.[38]

The figures are even more revealing in terms of the present-day purpose of R.O.T.C. Six per cent of the officers from the compulsory schools entered the Regular Army or Air Force, whereas 6.7 per cent of the officers from the voluntary R.O.T.C. schools went into the Regular Army or Air Force.

But the military pressures for the compulsory approach are ideological and designed to indoctrinate the nation's educated leadership with military values. Army leaders say this in other words. Secretary of the Army Wilbur M. Brucker has said that

. . . it would be a serious mistake to regard the R.O.T.C. program merely as one designed to produce a specific number of officers. More importantly, the R.O.T.C. program serves to inculcate and develop in the student ideals of patriotism, sacrifice, and service to our country which can come in no other way.[39]

Another military spokesman has asserted that "the Army's 'firm position' favoring compulsory R.O.T.C. . . . . is predicated on the great good derived from such training in terms of motivation for the duties and responsibilities of American citizenship no matter what profession·the student is preparing for." [40]

Other Pentagon leaders are not prepared to encourage compulsion. The Navy has a completely voluntary program and the Air Force is ready, if the colleges are, to accept a voluntary one by 1965. Charles C. Finucane, Assistant Secretary of Defense for Manpower, in a letter to the American Council on Education dated February 15, 1960, stated that "Compulsory basic R.O.T.C. is not needed to meet quality standards nor is it needed to produce the number of officers required." He indicated that the "Department of Defense policy is to leave the decision [about compulsion] entirely up to the educational authorities concerned." He pointed out that with the "expected doubling of college enrollments during the next decade" there will be 178,000 Army R.O.T.C. graduates "in excess of requirements." [41]

The new policy will not necessarily result in the abandonment of compulsory R.O.T.C. There are college educators who themselves have been indoctrinated in military values. Some believe, said Charles Finucane, that "the compulsory policy makes a significant contribution towards orderly conduct for the entire study body . . . " [42] Others may see financial values in the picture. Hanson Baldwin reported that the annual cost to the Army of producing about 12,500 second lieutenants each year is $20,000,000. [43]

The colleges will increasingly have to face the problems that arise from the new purpose of R.O.T.C. When R.O.T.C. was intended chiefly "to produce reserve officers, the element of competition with other professions and vocations was minimal. A student did not look upon his military service as excluding his chosen field . . . If more professional officers are to be recruited, however, military service will itself be the chosen field." [44] This means that many students enter an essentially civilian college in order to train for a military career, just as other students enter in order to become scientists, engineers or teachers. But the military departments in the colleges are in reality intruders, without the same reasons and standards that motivate the faculties who assist students to be engineers or teachers.

Professors Lyons and Masland in their book *Education and Military Leadership* question whether R.O.T.C. courses "are of collegiate standard at all." They point out that there is centralized control over military teachers from the military hierarchy, with courses of instruction prescribed by that hierarchy at the same time that the military seek academic status for officer teachers and academic credits for their courses. "The R.O.T.C. units thus resemble foreign embassies within otherwise sovereign territories."

One indication of the problem was revealed when Ohio State University assisted the Army by organizing a two-week course in military history for officers who were to serve as R.O.T.C. instructors and who were slated to teach that subject. An analysis of the officers attending the course in 1957 showed that "of 131 officers, 17 had never taken a college course in history, 71 had had from one to three college history courses 'of one sort or another,' and 37 had taken four or more courses. Except in a small number of cases, moreover, the officers indicated little prior interest in reading and owning books in military history."

After a similar course for Air Force R.O.T.C. officers the Ohio State staff conducting the program reported that it continued to hold "to its original view that the average A.F.R.O.T.C. instructor in non-military courses is seriously lacking in the minimum content knowledge for teaching these courses . . . " [45]

In spite of these deficiences the Armed Forces have wanted credit given to students for R.O.T.C. work. The American Society for Engineering Education, in evaluating this problem of college credits, has recommended that "no substitution of R.O.T.C. credit should be allowed for engineering courses or for those in the humanities and social studies" but if an institution does allow a substitution for humanities and social studies it "should not exceed one-quarter of the total credit allotted to this area." The same Society noted the poor quality of instruction in R.O.T.C. classes, the fact that R.O.T.C. "classes are seldom conducted in an atmosphere encouraging the free exchange of ideas" and that "the rigid control exercised by military authority over subject matter and examinations is out of the hands of the academic faculty." [46]

In January, 1963 Secretary of Defense McNamara proposed a drastic reorganization of R.O.T.C. which would permit military departments to offer an elective two-year program of twelve to fourteen semester hours plus twelve weeks of summer camp training at Army or Air Force bases. If the plan is successful, he said, it "would gradually replace the four-year program on a school-by-school basis in all except military colleges." [47]

The proposal to reduce R.O.T.C. requirements to two years by no means constitutes a military withdrawal from the college campus. It is designed to improve the military program for using the colleges for career training and to cut expenses. As such it will keep on the campus all the military shortcomings inherent in a program of indoctrination instead of free inquiry. It will undoubtedly continue to distort the meaning of peace by claiming that the threat of retaliation is the foundation of peace. It will also undoubtedly continue to pervert the study of history and international relations by magnifying the role of war and military power.

Secretary McNamara also proposed the abandonment of the present Junior R.O.T.C. program offered in nearly 300 high schools and the institution of a national defense cadet corps in its place. The *Kansas City Times* of January 31, 1963 in reporting this said "There were indications the plan would run into opposition in Congress."

The Army's strong belief in compulsion undoubtedly was communicated to military-minded Congressmen. So also were the wishes of those school officials who have a vested interest in R.O.T.C. In Kansas City, for example, seven high schools use two officers and ten enlisted men for training 917 cadets. Uniforms and equipment are provided at government expense as well. Superintendent of Schools James Hazlett was reported as saying that if the Army drops this program the school district will have to hire teachers to replace the military men. James H. Parker III, chairman of the military affairs committee of the

Kansas City Chamber of Commerce said: "We feel it is a very desirable program. A lot of this economy stuff by the federal government appears to hit in the wrong places. High school R.O.T.C. isn't a terribly expensive program to maintain." [48] Secretary of Defense McNamara had listed the yearly cost of high school R.O.T.C. at six million dollars.[49]

Less than two months later, on March 6, 1963, the Pentagon dropped its proposal to eliminate high school R.O.T.C. in order to avoid "a budding battle with Congress." Military-minded Congressmen, chiefly F. Edward Hebert, Carl Vinson and William G. Bray (R., Ind.) of the House Armed Services Committee not only opposed ending R.O.T.C. but insisted on its expansion in the high schools. Bray is a high ranking officer in the Indiana National Guard. Hebert said the Pentagon effort to drop junior R.O.T.C. "was prompted by a misguided sense of economy." Hebert has introduced a bill to continue the junior R.O.T.C. program in the high schools now offering it, and to authorize expansion to up to 2,000 units.

It is ironic that Congressmen who are economy-minded on matters of education, medical care and other welfare programs should insist on an officer training program that does not and cannot produce officers. The armed forces do not give officer status to high school boys but insist on college graduation as a prerequisite.

From the Pentagon's point of view abandonment of high school R.O.T.C. was not intended as an abandonment of military training, for these boys, with few exceptions would be caught later in the draft. Moreover, other military programs that are less expensive than R.O.T.C. have moved into the schools.

A group of 41 Michigan high school teachers and principals were taken on a guided tour of Army, Navy, and Air Force installations in 1955 in order to prepare them for their military role in the schools. Everywhere they went in their 4,000 miles of travel in three Air Force planes, they "heard pleas for help in preparing youths for the transition to military life." They were escorted on their tour by Maj. Lewis M. Robinson, sales training officer within the plans and program section.[50] The tour was

co-sponsored by the Department of Defense and the Michigan
Secondary School Association.

A textbook which was mailed to every high school principal
in the nation, according to the November 4, 1955 *U.S. News
and World Report,* is used in the schools along with films and
other Pentagon resources. The textbook emphasizes that "the
ideal of international cooperation must be guarded by military
power of individual nations like ours until safety by some international means becomes a reality." A boy or girl goes into the
Army therefore "to guard the progress being made toward peace
and justice for the world." Students are told at the end of Part
II: "You see, then, that you are fulfilling a purpose as great
and magnificent as man can conceive in serving in the Armed
Forces of the United States during the period when mighty
efforts are being made to bring about order in the world." Thus
American nationalism and militarism are rationalized.

There is an underlying assumption in this textbook that
Army advice to students to "stay in school" is needed to help
education, and that a major function of education is to make
better soldiers.

Advice to students on their life plans includes the following: "Since military service will in some way affect those plans,
it would be helpful for you to select courses for your remaining
time in high school that will help to qualify you for the branch
of service which you wish to enter."

What this means for each locality can be seen from the
following excerpts from a report on the pilot program published
by the Michigan Secondary School Association:

> . . . "the outline of our course followed the text (named
> above); however, we supplemented this with all available
> material we could get from the services plus our own resource
> people. We had recruiting officers from all branches of the
> service; a returned serviceman who had been a prisoner of war
> in World War II; one of our recent graduates who had vol-
> unteered for the draft; a graduate of our 1950 class who started
> to college, quit, and now is back in college."

In addition to films and pamphlets, Marysville used charts,
posters, and library books. They had speakers representing the

Air Force, Army, Coast Guard, Marine Corps, Navy, Selective Service, American Legion, Veterans of Foreign Wars, and National Guard. Chaplains, servicemen home on leave, and former servicemen also spoke to Marysville students. Lansing Eastern had speakers from the armed forces, reserve units, and R.O.T.C. . . . "Army reserve personnel," said Lansing Eastern, "have made use of our general information booth in the central foyer to answer questions during the noon hour. This practice may be expanded."

In 1957-1958 the Department of the Army issued to secondary school principals, teachers and counsellors a booklet entitled *Military Guidance in Secondary Schools*. This encouraged school assemblies for the armed forces. "Such an assembly could be sponsored by the cadet corps, if there is one in the school, or may be developed in cooperation with local veterans organizations." The booklet urges the organization of a Future Military Service Club along the lines of a Future Farmers of America. It suggests ways the teacher can use classroom periods for military indoctrination.

Another military effort to penetrate the public schools is the Pentagon's effort to steer retired military officers into teaching. Too many military men are being retired after twenty years of service to be absorbed adequately in defense industry. The evidence of the increased pace of such retirement is seen in the increase in total retirement pay of $43,441,494 in 1937 to $692,922,000 in 1960. By 1972 an estimated $2 billion will be paid annually to retired military men.[51]

The Army announcement of the teach-in-retirement program indicated that major commanders will be asked to cooperate "in publicizing the national teacher shortage and the opportunities in the educational field" for officers about to be retired. The Army announcement also said

Army men who have baccalaureate degrees and special competency in at least one core subject (science, physics, mathematics, history, language) can offer our high schools and colleges the crystallized lessons of almost a full lifetime of teaching and being taught; the seasoned understanding of young people; and a rich resource of contacts with other peoples of the world.

The Army apparently does not understand that teaching in the schools is different from Army indoctrination. The Secretary of the Army instead asserted that "education is national defense . . . the nation's schools are as assuredly action agents of national security as are the military services." [52]

In the colleges and schools many other tactics are being used by the armed forces. In 1948 for example the Air Force inaugurated a program of giving Reserve Officers on college faculties "inactive duty training credit" for serving as "unofficial liaison officers." The duties of such officers are "To present the Air Force point of view to their colleagues in faculty meeting should the occasion warrant such action;" to write about the Air Force in college and local newspapers, and in other ways to stimulate interest in the Air Force.[53]

There have been large pressures on schools and colleges to thus forward America's military program. Yet in spite of the military effort to use the nation's schools and colleges for military purposes, most educational institutions have shown a remarkable ability to maintain educational techniques and academic freedom. They have succumbed, however, to financial inducements that have brought military activities and values on to the campus and into the academic program.

CHAPTER 16

THE DRAFT IS NOT NEEDED

A bill extending the peacetime draft was introduced in the House and Senate early in 1963. In 1959, a four-year draft extension passed in the House and Senate with only 23 dissenting votes. In 1963 the draft was extended another four years with only three dissenting votes in the House. One Senator, absent during the voting, asked to be recorded against it. It would be only reasonable to assume that legislation vitally affecting the lives of so many millions of young citizens, and reaffirming a drastic departure from the traditional American aversion to peacetime conscription, could pass Congress by such an overwhelming vote only if it were of critical necessity to the military security of the nation. But a careful examination of the background and purpose of the peacetime draft reveals no such compelling necessity.

The record, instead, produces inescapable evidence that the inception and perpetuation of the peacetime draft can be laid at the feet of Army officers who are adamant advocates of conscription. The officers who determine Army policy do not want a system of inducements and persuasion so characteristic of civilian America; they prefer compulsion.

As we have seen, however, both the Navy and the Air Force prefer volunteers. They prefer the voluntary method not only because they want willing rather than unwilling sailors and airmen but also because they prefer longer term enlistments.

Lieutenant General Emmett O'Donnell, head of Air Force Personnel when the draft was renewed in 1955, said, "We have got to have four-year men. If we were forced to the two-year draft it would be the end of the Air Force." He indicated that the Air Force could use only long-term enlistees because of the extensive training required to master the highly complex technology of modern military weapons.

More recently, Air Force Maj. Gen. Harold R. Maddux argued against renewing the draft in 1959 because "it is impossible to provide the required state of instant readiness with men who don't want to be in the armed forces."

That these are not isolated expressions of opinion is seen from an article in the December, 1953 *Air Force Magazine* in which Brig. Gen. Bonner Fellers stated that "ever since Gen. George C. Marshall became Army Chief of Staff in September, 1939, our defense policy has been strongly influenced by ground officers who advocated compulsory universal service. The Navy and Air Force, however, have gone along most reluctantly. In fact, were they free to express themselves, the Navy and Air Force would actively oppose" such compulsory training.

It might be easy to explain this conflict in the Defense Department by saying that the Navy and Air Force need skilled men, whereas the Army needs large numbers of relatively unskilled riflemen. But this is not the case. The Defense Advisory Committee on Professional and Technical Compensation, headed by Ralph J. Cordiner, president of General Electric, indicated in its May, 1957 report that all of the armed forces are using machinery that "is becoming ever more fantastically complex." This, said the Cordiner Report, means that "we must move forward from a concern with numbers to a deeper concern for quality and for retention of skilled personnel for an extended period of productive service."

Or it might be easy to explain the Army position by saying that the Army is less attractive to potential volunteers than the Navy or Air Force. But a Youth Research Institute poll of high-school boys published in the December 4, 1958, *Des Moines Tribune* suggested the contrary. Seventy-four per cent of high-school boys thought the draft should be discontinued and 32 per cent said they might make a career of the armed forces if the pay scale were similar to that of industry. Thirty-one per cent chose the Army as the best branch for active service, 23 per cent the

Navy, 12 per cent the Marines, and 10 per cent the Air Force.

The Army's policy of peacetime conscription is an inheritance of eighteenth- and nineteenth-century Europe. This policy, as Professor John K. Galbraith of Harvard has observed, is based on two obsolete assumptions. The first of these, that manpower must be obtained cheaply, is based on the pre-nuclear assumption that mass armies are needed but that governments are too poor to pay adequately for manpower. The second obsolete assumption is that "the physical hazards of military service should be distributed equally among all members of the community."

Today the United States is capable of paying an adequate amount to those in the armed forces, Galbraith points out. He also indicates that peacetime service "is not more dangerous than ordinary civilian existence. Indeed," he adds, "it is by no means certain now that in the event of war service in the armed forces would involve much more risk of death than residence in Manhattan." [1]

In practice the Army has used these obsolete assumptions to maintain the caste assumptions that are at the very heart of the military system. For example, Americans, many of whom are already underprivileged economically, are, as a result of the draft, set back even further in economic competition with others of their generation. In some cases they are deprived of further education.

Young Americans who want to go to college are not treated equally. Those who must work to earn money before they can go to college are drafted, whereas the young men whose parents can afford higher education are deferred. Those who are drafted are forced into separation from home and family during the years when they ought to have every aid and understanding to make the transition to families of their own. Yet those who marry young are often separated from their mates because of the inadequate pay and living conditions in the armed forces. Those who can afford to have children at an early age are deferred, whereas those who cannot are penalized further by having to wait added years after leaving the armed forces because they have received the extremely low pay of about $100 a month.

Professor Galbraith asserted that "the draft survives principally as a device by which we use compulsion to get young men to serve at less than the market rate of pay. We shift the cost of military service from the well-to-do taxpayer, who benefits by lower taxes, to the impecunious young draftee." [2]

This discrimination against a minority cannot be disguised by the word "Universal" in the title of the law.

A study of "Social Stratification and Combat Survival" which appeared in the December 1955 *Social Forces* revealed that "the number of Detroiters who died, were captured, or were reported missing in Korea, varied directly with the relative economic or racial standing of the city areas from which the men stemmed."

Casualty rates among non-white groups "were almost 50 per cent greater than white rates." The casualty rate "in areas where home values average more than $15,000 was approximately one-fourth the rate in areas where home values average less than $4,000."

The authors of this study indicated that "These findings have obvious implications for the argument that universal military training would democratically insure equal sacrifices by all social groups . . . " [3]

Any compulsory program is bound to be discriminatory and unequal which puts some men in the ranks and others in officer status via college R.O.T.C. or which puts the poor at an economic disadvantage in preparing for marriage and family responsibility.

Conscription is also actually more expensive than a voluntary system of well-paid men. Moreover, it has demonstrated that it cannot accomplish the end for which it was adopted. The purpose for which it was adopted was to supply the armed forces with manpower that could be trained to meet the needs of those forces. The Cordiner Report stated:

The modern military manpower problem, reduced to its simplest terms, is one of quality rather than quantity. It is not merely a matter of the total number of people on hand, but is much more a matter of the level of competence, skill and experience of those people.

The military services are not able, at the present time and

under the present circumstances, to keep and challenge and develop the kinds of people needed for the period of time necessary for those people to make an effective contribution to the operation of the force.

The Report went on to point out that of the 2,500,000-man planned enlisted strength, 305,000 have been inducted by the draft and "another 1,200,000 men are serving their first terms of voluntary enlistment." Of this overall first-term group, 75 per cent leave the armed forces as soon as their initial service period is over. Moreover, 97 out of every 100 draftees leave the army as soon as their two-year term ends. Since, as Ralph Cordiner has pointed out, the advance in "modern war technology makes it almost impossible to train a specialist in two years," the men are being discharged about the time they are becoming trained and hence useful.

This points up two further problems. First, Cordiner said, after talking to hundreds of enlisted men, "I found antagonism and bitterness over the draft. They were checking off the days until they got out. We must devote 25 per cent of our military effort to training men who don't stay. The trainers are discouraged. They resemble the poor teacher whose every class flunks."

Second, the accident rate is so high, as a result of inexperienced men manning intricate weapons or equipment, that the armed forces estimate that close to $5 billion worth of equipment is not now operable.

The Cordiner Report estimated, on the basis of figures submitted by the armed forces, that an armed force paid as adequately as other government and civilian workers would result in sufficient voluntary re-enlistments to permit a reduction in the size of the armed forces, especially in training and transportation personnel, as well as "a 10 per cent cutback in maintenance technicians" and reductions at other points. The total saving in material and maintenance, said the Report, would go from about $5.5 billion in 1960 to about $6.5 billion in 1962.

We might assume that with such experience the armed forces would prefer a voluntary system, but in fact conscription permits the military to dodge responsibility in many areas, including the necessary changes in their own way of doing things. Instead of adopting policies which would attract young men into the armed forces, compulsion has become an easy answer. Prior to June 1950, "approximately 60 per cent of the enlisted members of the armed forces were re-enlisting," said the Cordiner Report. "The force consisted of approximately 1,500,000 men — predominantly volunteers." During that period men were not being drafted. By 1954, and while the draft was being used, the re-enlistment rate had fallen to 18 per cent.

Aside from the pay scale there are other problems which the military and Congress have been able to dodge because of conscription. The Cordiner Report spoke of "deplorable conditions under which military people are forced to live . . . " It added:

> In and around almost every military base can be found sprawling trailer camps and families jammed into "splinter cities" which are five year mobilization barracks stretched years beyond their original life expectancy. Divided families with inevitable inroads into the very heart of the moral fiber of the people involved; injury to the pride, dignity and personal standards of the individual; these are the elements of this tragedy.

But this is only part of the problem. The psychological attitude that the draft will provide men in spite of poor leadership, exploitation, and abuses is an integral part of compulsion itself. Dr. Eli Ginzberg, director of staff studies for the National Manpower Council, has said: "The trouble with the system is that there is a tendency for the defense management to seek the remedy for its errors by the simple method of calling up more manpower." [4]

The committees in Congress which are responsible for legislation affecting the armed forces have become so responsive to the professional officer group that in the 1958 legislation providing for an increase in pay for the armed forces, the monthly increase for a general or admiral was $424 over his previous pay, for a colonel $148, and a major $58. A private first-class, earning less than $100 a month previously, during his first two years of service received an increase of only $3 a month — hardly an inducement to volunteer. Congress and the Pentagon have thus pursued a policy of granting large increases to officers, who are not drafted, and have kept the pay of the enlisted men so low as to make it necessary to draft them.

A further problem arising from the Army's preference for compulsion is reflected in the leadership, discipline and morale of the armed forces. Many college students enter R.O.T.C. in order to escape being enlisted men. One Pentagon official quoted in the May 27, 1958 *Look* estimated that "80 per cent of our officers below the rank of general are draft-motivated." He pointed out that this attitude had also invaded the military and naval academies. He then asked, "What kind of leaders will we have when hundreds of boys at the academies are there, not because they want to be officers but because they don't want to be enlisted men?"

This officer attitude communicates itself to the men. But there is also resentment on the part of the enlisted men who volunteer in order to avoid being drafted. The Secretary of the Navy in May 1958 stated: "Over a long period the increasing disciplinary problems in the Naval Establishment, especially A.W.O.L. rates and the brig population, have been a matter of grave concern to me. The A.W.O.L. rate rose 30 per cent in 1957 over 1956 and courts martial continue at the rate of 1,000 a week. The human and financial losses . . . cannot be afforded."

John Graham has pointed out that "uncertainties about the draft make it impossible for young men to plan ahead and as a result discourage them from getting the advance training in the sciences or professions that the country is needing increasingly." [5]

Those who enter R.O.T.C. as an alternative to the draft in order to stay in college or postpone induction must later serve on active duty. "Like all other forms of military service," wrote Walter Millis, "the reserve officer's active duty period represents a burdensome interruption in his professional training, one so burdensome that the intended professional education may never be resumed." [6]

M. H. Trytten, director of Scientific Personnel, National Academy of Science, after surveying the impact of military training and service on the training of scientists, pointed out that the average age of the young specialists who developed radar during World War II was less than twenty-six. He said:

> I can quite well imagine that had these young men each been required to spend a year or more in military training or service many of them would not have achieved the level of experience which made their employment on these projects possible. Others again could possibly have been deflected from the area of training which they had entered upon, and finally, all of them would have been at least one year less advanced, which at that age is a considerable factor. It would seem to me highly reasonable to suggest that the ultra-important radar developments in World War II would at least have been delayed and in many cases might not have succeeded had this been the case.[7]

A few colleges and universities have in recent years abandoned compulsory R.O.T.C. either because such military courses are not on a par with academic standards or because it forces boys to omit some needed academic courses or for other reasons. But in practice compulsion still exists, if taking R.O.T.C. is the only way to escape the low wages and often menial life of the drafted man who may have to function as a servant to an officer or his family or clean buildings and grounds or engage in other "made" work. A House Armed Services subcommittee in July, 1959 received complaints of military personnel who functioned as servants. One retired sergeant, Joseph Bagwell, told of an assignment to the home of Maj. Gen. James R. Pierce. His household duties and those of two other sergeants included "cooking, answering telephones, baby-sitting for the daughter's children," together with "such duties as cleaning ladies' lingerie and various other details that most men just don't do." These duties, which also included care of the dog, often meant long hours ranging from 6 A. M. to 8 P. M.[8] Although one Congressman received nearly 500 similar complaints, the more typical problem is routine non-military cleaning or detail work to keep the men busy.

When a draft board takes boys to serve at low pay for the

convenience of other citizens, forces them to serve against their will for two years plus reserve duty, it is a serious matter for the persons involved. For most of them it means postponing or interrupting college or marriage plans or their first job. The very fact that they must be compelled to serve in a society in which others may work at jobs of their own choice makes it an interruption rather than a job. It is also an abrupt severance of home and family relationships that in our society are more gradually relinquished in the late teens and early twenties.

Congressman Roman C. Pucinski (D, Ill.), in an address on the floor of the House on February 5, 1959, revealed the impact of the draft on teen-agers. As a newspaper writer he completed, just before entering Congress, a survey in Chicago on teen-age gangs and juvenile delinquency. He pointed to the fact that every boy has to register for the draft. Hundreds of thousands "are forced to live in a shadow of constant doubt as to their future" when actually only a percentage are ultimately drafted.

> This uncertainty . . . makes it virtually impossible for them to plan their future in an orderly manner. The most tragic aspect of this situation is that many young men who graduate from high school and who do not or cannot because of economic reasons, go to college, find it impossible to get decent employment because the first thing they are asked by a potential employer is what is his draft status. The moment a youngster admits that he is eligible for the draft he is either given the lowest type of employment or, as is the case in many instances, flatly denied employment.

The Congressman added that "thousands of youngsters . . . because of the cumbersome mechanics of the draft are involuntarily plunged into this pool of teen-age idleness."

The resentment of youths about to be drafted, followed by the tediousness of useless work which so many experience, and the loss of personal freedom, leave their mark. Even the "six-months-plus" program causes resentment. A veteran of the Reserve Forces Act of 1955 described his eight weeks in radio-telephone school. Writing in *The Nation*, May 10, 1958, he said, "I was to learn nothing more than how to turn a radio on and how to shut one off, turn it on, shut off, on, off. It required simulation, dedication and no skill." He added, "I couldn't help sharing the guilt of my superiors for having let me get away with all this, and as I used to sit and look about my classroom at the many B.A.'s and M.A.'s and LL.B.'s who were turning on and shutting off their radios or as I looked through the window at the even greater number who were policing the area outside I couldn't stop myself from thinking what a waste of talent it all was." [9]

In Great Britain military conscription has been abolished as a result of the recommendations of a government committee appointed "to examine the factors bearing on the willingness of men and women to serve in the armed forces and to make recommendations." That committee suggested better housing, married quarters, a shorter working day with more intensive employment, the ending of mounting formal guard on camp gates, kit inspections and pay parades. It deplored some indications of the caste idea which the *Manchester Guardian* described as

. . . expressions of a basic attitude, carried over from an age in which the officer was a country gentleman, intent on cultivating certain social virtues in himself and his fellow officers. That attitude will change as the officer structure of the Army is changed, and as technical efficiency comes to be regarded as the prime requirement. The most valuable recruits for the armed forces will be men and women who would do well in comparable employment in civilian life and who will therefore expect comparable standards of efficiency and treatment.[10]

In the United States three important suggestions have been made that would result in an adequate volunteer establishment. The first is the proposal that a living wage, on a par with that of other government workers, be paid to first-term enlisted men and that adequate increases be provided to solve the re-enlistment problem.

The second is that Congress provide for decent housing and other decent community standards in places where military personnel must live.

The third is to change the Army idea that every cook, book-keeper and warehouse employee must be physically qualified for and given combat training. No more than 20 per cent of the army are combat troops. The rest are supply or support personnel.

Two examples indicate that the size of the army could be cut drastically if it were concerned about efficiency. The first is "Project Native Son," which the Air Force put into practice about ten years ago, utilizing civilians of the country where the Air Force maintains bases. The Air Force describes this plan as essentially a replacement of a military man by an indigenous civilian. "We would save military personnel in support-type activities . . . [making] an airman available for a new combat unit [rather than for some less-skilled chore]." It also reduced requirements for military housing and supplies, thus saving money. In 1954 the Air Material Command found it could be reduced by using 14,000 civilian personnel. "In fiscal 1955 the total will reach 31,000 foreign nationals and we will relieve thereby 43,000 military personnel." [11]

If this can be done with foreign nationals an even larger program could be undertaken by employing American civilians in the continental United States.

A second example is the Seabee. Representative Thomas B. Curtis, in a speech before the Seabee Veterans Convention in St. Louis in 1954, said:

When we examine . . . the work performed by men in uniform for the military establishment, we will find that at least 80 per cent (and some even estimate higher) is not fighting nor will it ever be fighting. It has to do with supplies, transportation, warehousing, maintenance, overhaul, book-keeping, housing, feeding, overhead. Nor am I referring to the borderline cases, such as field or front-line maintenance, or front-line feeding, etc. Obviously any work on the front lines will involve the need for military discipline.

Now if 80 per cent of the men in uniform are never going to be engaged in fighting . . . what in heaven's name are we talking about training 100 per cent to fight? If indeed an analysis of the job requirements of these 80 per cent re-veals, as it does, that the skills required are essentially civilian skills as were the skills needed in the Seabees, then we had best follow the Seabees formula in our personnel practices as it relates to the 80 per cent.

The Seabee formula was to take men of all ages and physical conditions from civilian life and use their civilian skills without putting them through basic military training or into uniform or under the military code.

Representative Curtis added:

> The men in the Seabees were put into jobs they already knew. The guiding light of the personnel system was to utilize civilian skills. . . . The military knows full well that they need civilian skills. What they have not yet learned is that the civilian enterprise is better equipped to train men in these skills than the military and incidentally at one-tenth the cost, because we don't have to provide room, board and wages for our civilian trainees. . . . Following such a formula we need neither UMT, military socialism, nor destructive high taxes.[12]

There is no question whatever about the ability of the Army to raise, by volunteering, the number of men it actually needs for combat purposes. And it could do this more economically than is possible under conscription. In 1953 the Army listed the cost of training a recruit for the first six months at $3,200, for the second six months at $2,600, and for the second year at $5,200 or a total of $11,000. This means that at least an average of $5,500 a year per person would be available to pay civilian stenographers, supply clerks, truck drivers and others who are engaged in non-combat activity in continental United States.

It would of course be possible to save the salaries and expenses of a number of generals and other high officers who would not be needed if there were not a large conscript army, to say nothing of the savings if the Selective Service system were eliminated.

So strong is the military control in Congress and the Administration that the kind of civilian initiative demonstrated in Great Britain's modernization of the armed forces is almost totally lacking here. When a largely civilian commission such as the Cordiner Commission makes recommendations that would lead to the abandonment of the draft they are ignored.

A number of Congressmen who opposed the draft and pay raises for officers were defeated when they sought re-election in 1960. While no clear-cut proof has ever been produced connecting their defeat with political action by the military, it has been implied. On November 20, 1960 the Burlington (Vt.) *Daily News* discussed the defeat of a Vermont Congressman who was among "a sizeable group of Congressmen who fought the military draft and some pay raises and other extensions of military organization" and who "were defeated in far-flung districts over the nation this week." The news account stated that "a spokesman for the House Armed Services Committee noted the trend, then said, 'Perhaps in the future we will not have such a hard time getting passed draft extensions and pay bills.' "

The House committee spokesman indicated that "it may have been just a coincidence" but he also indicated that many more military personnel voted that year and that absentee voting by military personnel was particularly heavy in some states. The same news account added: "Rep. Olin Teague of Texas, chairman of the House Veterans Committee and a prodigious watcher of military matters, said 'There were over 400,000 U.S. citizens living in Germany when I was there a few months ago and if no one canvassed them for votes they were missing a good thing.' "

In any event, Congressional resistance to military power is not likely to be encouraged by the assumption that with few exceptions Congressmen who voted against pet military projects were defeated for that reason.

The peacetime draft of men between eighteen and one-half and twenty-six which would have expired June 30, 1963 was extended by Congress for another four years with only three dissenting votes in the House. Before it was formally extended there was an Executive order issued March 14, 1963 providing a mandatory deferment for registrants who are fathers. This order, which reflected a policy of some years standing, was evidence of the growing manpower pool.

In 1962 the Armed Forces inducted approximately 715,000 civilians, including about 157,000 draftees. In 1962 about 1.5 million boys reached the age of eighteen. Because the Armed forces have not been able to take all eligible men even after fathers, students and others have been deferred the average age of the drafted men has risen to twenty-three years.

During the first six months of 1962 only 6.4 per cent of those drafted had graduated from college. Most of them received less than $100 a month pay while in the Army. Their re-enlistment rate has been running less than 15 per cent compared to an overall re-enlistment rate of 54 per cent.[13]

If it is difficult to persuade Congress to end conscription, it will be even more difficult for the Army to abandon a conscript program which for twenty years it has claimed is essential. Undoubtedly Army officers have come to believe their own propaganda that there is something inherently good and democratic in the requirement that every citizen serve his country — the Army way.

The Army leadership also thinks that military training is good for the boys and will teach them a brand of citizenship they won't get in the homes, schools, and churches of America. The National Security Training Commission, on which two military officers served, listed among the advantages of compulsory training "indoctrination . . . upon the principles of duty to country and good citizenship" and "a heightened sense of national unity and purpose." It also said young men would be told "the facts of their world" and the proper "mental outlook, to face the most basic of human challenges." [14]

But aside from such indoctrination there are very practical reasons why the Army wants conscription as a permanent feature of American life. Army officers have a vested interest in maintaining a large establishment which requires a sizable officer trainer corps for every new group of draftees. The larger the establishment the greater are the chances of promotion. The Selective Service System itself provides berths and prestige for additional officers. Moreover, the draft guarantees a steady stream of men for the Army in spite of abuses, poor leadership, and a caste system where volunteer officers are well paid while drafted enlisted men earn too little to support a family.

Peacetime conscription is the basis for a large professional officer corps and hence for an important role in current American militarism. Conscription, in itself, implies a wartime posture no peace-loving people should long endure. It is, as Gen. Jan Smuts once observed, "the taproot of militarism." As such it has no place in peacetime America and should be speedily abandoned.

CONCLUSION

The pattern of militarism in American life cannot be measured solely in terms of military control of foreign policy or economic life or any particular institution. It has pervaded the whole American system of values so that there is no longer an effective counter-force to the military in American political life. Many if not most Americans seem to have accepted the idea that the health of our economy is dependent on military spending, that peace is dependent on the long arm of the Pentagon, that military discipline is good for a young man, that negotiations are useless because our particular enemy can't be trusted to keep an agreement, and that armed might rather than total disarmament is the essence of national security.

These ideas have been sometimes openly and sometimes covertly advanced. They are built into slogans such as "air power is peace power" or statements such as Gen. George C. Marshall's claim that if we had had universal military training the Korean War would not have occurred.[1] They are also the result of the long-drawn-out cold war and the constant advocacy of military solutions to its problems. They have developed because many Americans have identified themselves personally with sons in military service or with the idea of American military might or with jobs that are dependent on military money.

They have developed, too, because a good many Americans have been directly subject to military discipline and indoctrination during terms of military service. One of the "basic ideas" behind universal military training, said an Army pamphlet, *The Fort Knox Experiment,* is that of "developing the 'whole' man . . . in contrast to just exposing them to information."

The Army today is the only organization in America equipped to conduct this kind of efficient training of our citizenry. The civilian institutions willing to accept the responsibility for training the "whole" man constitute but a minute percentage of the educational institutions of America.

The Armed Services have an extraordinary opportunity since they control the time and attention of the trainees 24 hours a day, seven days in the week . . .

To a real degree the armed forces have involved the whole nation in a military educational experience. Hanson Baldwin, the *New York Times* military analyst, summarized the situation shortly after World War II in his book, *The Price of Power:*

With a surge of nationalism — which expresses itself sometimes in the feeling that "America ought to rule the world"; "we must hold to everything we got" — has gone a new respect for our top military leaders and high civilian executives, which complements the latent demand for greater centralization of federal authority, and which has expressed itself in the form of political booms — "Eisenhower for President," "MacArthur for President"; "Marshall for President." However, our population has shown no corresponding gain in respect for representative government or the courts. Put in the words of Dr. Lasswell, all these experiences and attitudes, our increasing dependence upon leadership, our nationalism, etc., which have helped to create the "strong latent demand for executive centralization in governments may well lead to an open demand in the event of any general crisis."

The Armed Forces have even educated civilian leaders and the American people to accept their judgments, frequently without question. They convinced civilian leaders that such important decisions as the frequency and timing of U-2 flights over other nations should be made by local commanders. The U-2 flight that wrecked the summit meeting was sent over the Soviet Union solely for military reasons.[2]

In January, 1960 an Air Force general, Thomas Power, supported by generous newspaper publicity, created the idea that the Soviet Union had moved ahead of us in missile and bomber development — he did so in order to expand the Air Force budget.

President Eisenhower knew that there was no "missile gap" or "bomber gap" and publicly said so. It was generally assumed that he was trying to prevent budget increases. For this reason opposing party leaders and some newspapermen dismissed his denial. Actually, he knew from the photographs of the U-2 flights that not one operational Intercontinental Ballistic Missile base had been constructed in Russia. But Eisenhower could not reveal his authority without endangering the U-2 flight program. So he was captive of the very military machine which for the time being on budgetary and other grounds he was inclined to oppose. It was to photograph the construction of this first missile base before it could be camouflaged that military and intelligence officers sent Gary Powers in the U-2 flight over Russia that resulted in wrecking the summit conference. Significantly, the opposing political party leaders and many other Americans were prepared to trust military officials rather than the President of the United States.

Wise and Ross, the authors of *The U-2 Affair,* wrote: "The U-2 affair revealed the extraordinary extent to which information and activities that are secret to the American people are shaping the nation's destiny. A secret layer of government has established itself, with the power to conceal its mistakes behind a claim of 'national security.'" [3]

The question might well be asked whether the militarization of America is justified because of the power of our present enemy. Short of an extensive analysis of Soviet power and Communist activity, two comments are in order. The first is that the postwar groundwork of the military and its chief successes in militarizing the United States took place in the period from 1945 to 1948 before the Czechoslovakian *coup d'état,* while the Soviet Union was still recovering from heavy losses, before it had developed nuclear power, while it was still without much of a navy, and while its air force was admittedly inferior to that of America. During those years Russia was in no position to engage in war. As Colonel Neblett has pointed out, the Pentagon used Russia as an excuse without any basis in fact for such use. "To gain its constript army," he wrote, "the Pentagon generated in the public's mind fear of an attack by the Russian army and possible destruction of our government by Communist revolution here at home. The fear is shadowy and insubstantial." [4]

Throughout the early postwar period there were repeated indications that the Army high command was interested in the kind of military organization that made the German armies so powerful in World War II. The *U.S. News and World Report* revealed on September 8, 1950 that at the request of American officers the German General Heinz Guderian submitted a survey of the development of Prussian army organization which emphasized centralization of military power and the concept of a single chief of staff. Guderian said:

> General Bradley, who, like many other American generals agreed with my ideas, showed President Truman the manuscript, who, I understand, also shared his opinion. This is how I got tangled up into an argument between the American Navy, Army and Air Force. The resulting tendency toward centralization of power in U.S. defense was, perhaps, the reason . . . for the fact that a U.S. Senator, full of annoyance, said my report seems to constitute a sort of Bible for the majority of American officers.

The second comment is that American military power has not prevented the expansion of Communism in Europe and Asia. All of the conquests in Eastern Europe after German-Russian fighting began were made with American consent or connivance during the second World War. In fact, American military decisions, made against the specific advice of the British, left Eastern Europe open to Russian invasion and occupation.

There have been assertions pro and con that American military power kept Soviet troops from invading Western Europe but there has been no clear-cut evidence to support either contention. The only evidence is that there has been no Russian postwar military effort in Europe even in areas not backed by American alliances. Neutral Finland has not been invaded. Neither Communist Yugoslavia before it was aided by the United States nor Albania after it too left the Russian fold was invaded. Hungary, on the other hand, had Russian troops in occupation which prevented her leaving the Russian orbit. And Russian troops continue to occupy areas conquered during World War II.

In Asia, China went Communist at a time when the United States had a monopoly on the atomic bomb, a Navy larger than the combined navies of the major powers in the world, and what General Marshall called a superior air force. The Chinese civil war was a fact during General Marshall's term as Secretary of State and even then there was no realistic military proposal for saving China nor any likelihood that an American military conquest would have been more palatable to the Chinese than was our ally Chiang Kai-Shek.

Indeed, Communism has continued to make gains in Southeast Asia in recent years, in part because of the byproducts of American military policy described in a preceding chapter.

In Cuba a pro-Communist government developed on the heels of a revolution against Batista whose army was trained and advised by an American military mission.

The one major place where American forces were used against external aggression is the Korean War. That war, however, did not justify either military control in the United States or the maintenance thereafter of a military establishment almost twice as large as in the pre-Korean period. During the Korean war six Army divisions and one Marine division were fighting in Korea. These divisions plus other units totalled about 250,000 men. Before the Korean war the Army totalled 593,000 men. In 1963 the Army numbered almost one million.

Even if it is argued that Soviet military power since the Sputnik is so much greater than in the immediate postwar period, there is still no justification for military dominance in American life. The Soviet Union and Great Britain have both proposed total universal disarmament. This was endorsed in principle by a unanimous vote of the United Nations General Assembly. Our civilian diplomats have indicated that Russia needs and wants disarmament. As early as August 29, 1955 Joseph Alsop reported in the *New York Herald Tribune* that Charles Bohlen, then American ambassador to Moscow, had advised the State

Department to this effect, and on April 3, 1962 Llewellyn Thompson, Ambassador to the Soviet Union, told a closed session of the Senate Foreign Relations Committee that he believed the Russians are interested in pursuing disarmament.

The problem is not one of sincerity or trustworthiness. Nations are not moral units. They make and keep or break agreements according to their national interest. Both the United States and the Soviet Union have broken and kept agreements on this basis. Both have kept mutual agreements such as the neutralization of Austria. And the Soviet Union has kept agreements that have not been backed by American might, such as that regarding Finland.

James J. Wadsworth, President Eisenhower's negotiator at 240 meetings in Geneva, and former Ambassador to the United Nations, said at a news conference: "I think generally, by and large, that the Russian government has every intention of living up to any agreement they may make from the standpoint of nuclear tests or the larger areas of disarmament." [5]

Pentagon and AEC circles have sought to create a contrary impression. Edward Teller, for example, has written of the Russians: "The willingness, despite world opinion, to conduct their bigger tests openly — knowing that they would be detected — was a clear indication that they had already tested the more important small weapons while they could do so in secret." The eight prominent scientists who in the April 14, 1962 *Saturday Evening Post* analyzed and demolished Teller's position, said in response to that statement: "This is a new concept of evidence which would not stand up in any court of law, let alone a scientific discussion. In fact, it is an outright contradiction of known facts."

If American military leaders were sure the Russians did not want disarmament they could easily say, "Go ahead and accept their proposal. Call their bluff." Since the Soviet declaration that they would accept any inspection proposal we make if we accept their proposal for total disarmament it is no longer possible to dismiss the problem out of hand. Moreover, they have already agreed in principle to United Nations inspection and "unrestricted access without veto to all places" as well as to "an international peace force" to prevent violations of the agreement.[6]

The Russian proposal is by no means a perfect proposal and there are still important differences about the implementation of inspection. But here is one great avenue toward national and world demilitarization that needs to be thoroughly explored.

The 1963 treaty banning nuclear tests other than those conducted underground was not viewed by the Pentagon as a step toward disarmament but as preventing the spread of nuclear weapons to other nations and preserving gains already made in our numerous tests.

The issue of disarmament and world security is where the military vested interest is at complete variance with the genuinely civilian interest. The military mind thinks of peace as a result of superior armed might, whereas the civilian mind sees the rival military institutions as a cause of war. War exists chiefly because it has become an institutionalized method of conflict. Often the military mind is so conscious of a specific enemy and the arms race between them that it believes war is inevitable. The world is divided into friend and foe on the basis of military alliances or other military factors. The military mind does not think of processes that might help a totalitarian enemy to liberalize or to become a *status quo* power with a vested interest in peace rather than in revolution.

Military interests involving the achieving or maintaining of a large military establishment make it necessary therefore to build fear or hatred of an actual or potential enemy. From a civilian point of view no foreign policy should start with the assumption of the inevitability of war or with the assumption of a specific and consistent enmity. Today's adversary may be tomorrow's ally. Disputes should be negotiated and victories won by skillful diplomacy wherever possible. The most skillful diplomacy will leave others with the feeling that their security is also important. Friends and allies can be built by recognizing that other nations have vital interests and their people have needs that can be met by mutual assistance. These aims of foreign policy cannot always be achieved but they represent a quite different approach from that of a military-dominated society where the only aim is to defeat the enemy of the moment.

Military interests tend to view foreign policy in essentially military terms. They are unwilling to have civilian leaders take a larger picture into account.

To this end they are prepared to pit civilians of differing political views against each other as well as to manipulate public opinion. In February, 1963, military and CIA leaders "leaked" intelligence about Cuba to right-wing Senators, some of whom were already demanding an invasion which the Administration did not want, in part because of its adverse effect on all of Latin America. A news columnist, Holmes Alexander, on February 24 interviewed Senators Hugh Scott (R., Pa.) and Joseph Clark (D., Pa.) in a statewide radio-TV broadcast in Pennsylvania. Alexander suggested that Senators Keating and Goldwater were "getting their information from what is called 'hard policy' men in the Pentagon and the CIA." Scott confirmed this: "It's coming from people in the very groups you have named. Some of these very people have people working under them who are horrified at the continual weakening of the defense of this country through its foreign policy." [7]

In this nuclear age, when a major war would threaten all mankind, the international community in the form of the United Nations should be consulted on major issues that threaten world peace. In general such approaches are more likely if governments are ruled by civil than by military forces.

Sometimes it is suggested that it is difficult during a cold war in our modern technological age to separate military from foreign policy. Another argument is that the military know what is best in military matters and since the cold war as well as a shooting war involves so many of the nation's resources, all important matters become military matters.

Against this it should be noted that the military man, unlike the businessman or politician, is not accustomed to the bargaining or compromising needed in the give and take of domestic politics and the international situation.

To the argument that military men know how to run a cold war, there is the reply that military control tends to perpetuate rather than end the cold war. When the people seek a relaxation of tension or reduction in taxes, a military scare, whether real or synthetic, is often used to perpetuate control. Enemy submarines are conveniently seen surfacing off an important coastal city at the time military appropriations are being considered. Moreover, military men are often so close to the hostilities that they are unable to retain a larger international perspective and thus may lead the nation into short-term success and long-term disaster. When enemy intentions or ally hesitation and neutralist opposition are seen only or chiefly in military terms, global interests may be threatened by efforts at local military advantage.

Another important reason for the need for civil control of the military is in the realm of domestic liberties. Military men are accustomed to issuing orders and being obeyed. They do not like to have their decisions questioned. Yet the questioning of decisions, the process of free discussion, the right to organize protests, majority rule, minority representation, and especially individual rights of conscience are the life blood of the democratic process of government. Military rule tends to be authoritarian and to neglect or minimize civil liberties, while subordinating civil values to military considerations.

The emphasis on minimizing debate of foreign policy issues under the slogan of a bi-partisan foreign policy is not so much due to delicate or secret matters as to the hesitation to risk public debate when the military decisions have already been made. Secrecy is often the order of the day in America when the same issues are being openly debated in other countries. Colonel Neblett noted that "The citizen officers who were on duty during the war say that *secret* is the Pentagon's synonym for embarrassing. Anything embarrassing to the Pentagon is classified *secret;* if very embarrassing, *top secret* is the classification." [8]

Sometimes the problem is simply military impatience with

the slower processes of democratic discussion and compromise. Drew Middleton, in an article in the *New York Times* Magazine of April 16, 1948, said the military mind has a "dislike of some of the less efficient methods of getting things done that are a part of our political processes . . . "

Militarism is not, of course, confined to professional officers or soldiers. A much wider group of civilians have come to accept the military approach to life. As a result we have already begun to have in America the kind of military control of government with popular support that existed for years in pre-war Japan. There was nominally a civilian government in Japan but real power was exercised by the military. John M. Maki in an analysis of conscription and militarism in Japan wrote:

> The old class barriers . . . were swept away and the war-riors as a separate and distinct class in Japanese society dis-appeared, but the whole Japanese nation became imbued with the psychology that was once held by only a percentage of the population. Universal male conscription, for example, instead of sweeping away the concepts of the once proud military class, really extended to all Japanese the ideals of militarism. The traditions of the military class became the traditions of all Japan.[9]

Although the United States has moved only part way in the direction of universal conscription, our present draft system coupled with the tremendous propaganda and economic power of the Pentagon have accomplished much the same purpose.

Thus it is time for the American people to make a careful appraisal of the degree to which our nation has moved down the military road so that we do not follow that road to where it will ultimately take us. Even if our fears and military ventures do not soon lead to war, the concentration of national power in military hands is always regarded by others as a provocation and threat. Now, when our adversary has proposed total world-wide disarma-ment, we have an unparalleled opportunity to begin serious negotiations to end the arms race and restore to American life the kind of civilian government envisioned by our founding fathers. Democracy can flourish only when the people make their own decisions after full discussion. No people can turn the important decisions of life over to its army without eventually being enslaved.

NOTES

INTRODUCTION

1. *The Federalist,* No. 29, Sesquicentennial ed., p. 179.
2. *American State Papers, Military Affairs* (Washington, 1832-1861), 1, 8, 11.
3. *The New York Times* (August 8, 1947).
4. University of Chicago Round Table (May 25, 1952).

CHAPTER 1

1. Walter Millis, *Road to War* (Boston: Houghton Mifflin Company, 1935), pp. 94-95.
2. Senate Committee on Military Affairs, *Hearings on Compulsory Military Training and Service* (1940), p. 6. For a detailed discussion of the Plattsburg movement and its impact on the country, see Ralph Barton Perry, *The Plattsburg Movement* (New York: E. P. Dutton & Co., Inc., 1921).
3. John McAuley Palmer, *America in Arms* (New Haven: Yale University Press, 1941), p. 197.
4. David A. Lockmiller, *Enoch H. Crowder,* University of Missouri Studies (Columbia, Missouri: 1955), pp. 152-154.
5. Introduction to John McAuley Palmer, *Washington, Lincoln, Wilson — Three War Statesmen* (New York: Doubleday & Company, Inc., 1930), xiv.
6. *Congressional Record,* Seventy-sixth Congress, 3d Session, LXXXVI, Part II, 10027, 12160.

CHAPTER 2

1. *Newsweek* (April 3, 1944), pp. 52, 57.
2. Roscoe S. Conkling, *The Case Against Compulsory Military Training* (New York: Post War World Council, 1945).
3. John McAuley Palmer, "General Marshall Wants a Citizen Army," *Saturday Evening Post* (December 23, 1944), p. 9. *See also* U.S. War Department, Circular No. 247 (August 25, 1944), pp. 4-6.
4. General Milton Reckord, the chairman of the Joint Committee, told the House Armed Services Committee: "He [Marshall] directed me to make the study based on the fact that Congress would give us UMT." (House Committee on Armed Services, *Hearings on Selective Service,* Eightieth Congress, 2d Session [1948], p. 6547.)
5. *Capitol Times* (Madison, Wisconsin: July 16, 1945).
6. House *Hearings on UMT* (1945), pp. 823-824.
7. Ray Tucker, syndicated column for McClure Newspaper Syndicate (July 5, 1945).

CHAPTER 3

1. Donald Nelson, *Arsenal of Democracy* (New York, Harcourt, Brace, & World, Inc.), p. 409.
2. Michigan Labor Committee news release (February 1, 1945); *Conscription News* (February 9, 1945).
3. *The Progressive* (September 17, 1945); *Conscription News* (October 11, 1945).
4. *Conscription News* (July 12, 1945).

CHAPTER 4

1. United Press dispatch from Tokyo (September 6, 1945).
2. *Washington Newsletter* (Friends Committee on National Legislation, February 1, 1946).
3. House *Hearings on Extension of the Selective Training and Service Act*, Seventy-ninth Congress, 2d Session (1946), pp. 7, 162.
4. Associated Press dispatch from Washington (September 26, 1946); *Conscription News* (October 10, 1946).
5. Drew Pearson, syndicated column (October 28, 1945).
6. Action Sheet No. 99 accompanying *Conscription News* (March 27, 1947).
7. *See also* February 4, 1945 *Daily Worker* attacking various pacifist groups for creating the anti-conscription movement.
8. *New Masses* (April 3, 1945); also pamphlet, "Here's Why AYD Supports Military Training."
9. *Conscription News* (August 9, 1945).
10. "What Will We Give Joe on His UMTeenth Birthday?" New York, Youth Division, Communist Party of the U.S.; Discussion Outline on UMT issued by National Youth Commission, Communist Party of the U.S. (December, 1947).
11. John Swomley, *Memorandum* (February, 1948), in files of National Council Against Conscription.
12. Action Sheet No. 129 accompanying *Conscription News* (January 1, 1948); Letter from John Swomley January 15, 1948 to National Council Against Conscription sponsors.

CHAPTER 5

1. *Burlington Free Press* (Burlington, Vt.: June 16, 1947).
2. House *Hearings on Investigation of War Department Publicity and Propaganda in Relation to UMT*, Eightieth Congress, 1st Session (1947), pp. 68, 72, 75.
3. House *Report No. 1510*, Eightieth Congress, 2d Session (1948).
4. U.S. Code Title 18, Section 201.
5. William H. Neblett, *Pentagon Politics* (New York: Pageant Press, 1953), pp. 44-46.
6. *Tribune* (Kokomo, Ind.: February 5, 1948).
7. Cecil Dickson, *Knickerbocker News* (Albany, N. Y.: May 1, 1948).
8. *Philadelphia Inquirer* (January 16, 1948). See also *St. Louis Post-Dispatch* (January 15, 1948), and other papers of the same dates.
9. *Chicago Tribune* (June 19, 1948).
10. House *Hearings on UMT*, Eightieth Congress, 2d Session (1948), p. 339.
11. *The New York Times* (April 26, 1948).

CHAPTER 6

1. Donald Robinson, *Collier's* (April 10, 1948).
2. *The New York Times* (September 10, 1947).
3. *New York Herald Tribune* (December 20, 1947).
4. Drew Pearson, syndicated column in the *Washington Post* (May 18, 1948).

CHAPTER 7

1. *San Francisco Chronicle* (December 18, 1948)
2. Victor Riesel, syndicated column, "Inside Labor," *New York Mirror* (February 4, 1951).
3. First Report to the Congress by the National Security Training Commission (October, 1951), *House Document 315*, Eighty-second Congress, 2d Session, pp. 26-27.
4. *Conscription News* (November 15, 1951).
5. *The New York Times* (February 7, 1952).

CHAPTER 8

1. Walter Millis, Letter to the Editor, *The New York Times* (September 23, 1956).

CHAPTER 9

1. Nelson, *op. cit.* (Ch.3, n.l), p. 363.
2. *Ibid.*, pp. 129, 281.
3. *Ibid.*, p. 409.
4. *Politics* (March, 1944); see also *Army Ordinance Magazine* (March-April, 1944), p. 287.
5. U.S. Congress Joint Economic Subcommittee on Defense Procurement and Supply, Background Material on Economic Aspects of Military Procurement and Supply (February 16, 1960), p. 23.
6. *Ibid.*, p. 25.
7. *The New York Times* (April 6, 1962).
8. Neblett, *op. cit.* (Ch. 5, n. 5), pp. 33, 43.
9. *The Progressive* (April, 1962), p. 9.

CHAPTER 10

1. See *U.S. News and World Report* (June 15, 1951) for detailed description of this technique.
2. Roscoe Giffin, "National Security Seminar of the Industrial College of the Armed Forces," American Friends Service Committee, Philadelphia, Pa.
3. *Idem.*
4. *The New York Times* (April 15, 1951).
5. An office in the Pentagon known as the "Magazine and Book Branch" prepares material for magazines and books and maintains liaison "with magazine and book publishers, editors, staff writers and free lance correspondents." (Secretary of Defense Memorandum, May 19, 1949.) The effectiveness of its work was cited by the Pentagon's propaganda chief in Senate Appropriations hearings in 1953: he reported that the *Saturday Evening Post* had "in the last year carried 57 articles" on military subjects.
6. Senate Appropriations Committee, *Defense Department Hearings* (1952), p. 1762.
7. *Army Information Digest* (September, 1952).
8. Memorandum of Chief of Budget Division of the Army (August 20, 1948).
9. *House Report 1073* (July 24, 1947), Eightieth Congress, 1st Session.
10. Harrison Brown and James Real, *Community of Fear*, Center for the Study of Democratic Institutions, Santa Barbara, Calif., p. 34.
11. *The New York Times Magazine* (June 25, 1961).
12. *Army and Navy Journal* (August 14, 1948)

CHAPTER 11

1. Walter Millis, *Individual Freedom and the Common Defense*, Fund for the Republic (New York: November, 1957), p. 26.
2. John Graham, *The Universal Military Obligation*, Fund for the Republic (New York: June, 1958).
3. *The New York Times* (May 28, 1961).
4. *Ibid.*, September 22, 1959.
5. *Ibid.*, May 10, 1962.
6. Millis, *op. cit.*, p. 23.
7. *The New York Times* (April 7, 1962).
8. *Ibid.*, April 9, 1962.
9. Report in Senate Armed Services Committee, *Hearings on H. R. 6573* (1951).
10. House Armed Services Committee, *Hearings on UMT* (1952), p. 3021.
11. *National Security Training Commission Report* (October, 1951), p. 20.

CHAPTER 12

1. *Senate Report 1179*, Seventy-ninth Congress, 2d Session.
2. Blair Bolles, "Influence of Armed Forces on U.S. Policy," *Foreign Policy Reports* (October 1, 1946), p. 174.
3. *House Report 2361*, Seventy-ninth Congress, 2d Session.
4. *The New York Times* (November 30, 1948).
5. *Ibid.*, May 9, 1951.
6. *Ibid.*, August 4, 1949
7. John W. Masland and Lawrence I. Radway, *Soldiers and Scholars* (Princeton: Princeton University Press, 1957), p. 518.
8. *The New York Times* (May 22, 1961).
9. Arthur Krock in *The New York Times* (February 12, 1959).
10. *Knickerbocker News* (Albany, N. Y.: April 22, 1948).

11. *Saturday Review* (March 26, 1960), p. 26.
12. *The New York Times* (June 9, 1961).
13. *Ibid.*, June 19, 1961.
14. Stewart Alsop, "The Story Behind Quemoy," *Saturday Evening Post* (December 13, 1958).
15. *The Reporter* (November 13, 1958), p. 11.
16. Viceroy Tiao Phetsarath, quoted in *The Reporter* (November 13, 1958), p. 11.
17. *Kansas City Star* (Kansas City, Mo.: November 11, 1962).
18. Homer Bigart, *New York Times* syndicated column in *Kansas City Star* (March 8, 1962).
19. *The New York Times* (July 31, 1948).
20. *Idem.*
21. James Reston in *The New York Times* (November 28, 1948).
22. Thomas F. Hawkins, "U.S. Blunders in Berlin," *U.S. News and World Report* (September 10, 1948).
23. David Wise and Thomas B. Ross, "The U-2 Affair," *Look* (May 22, 1962), p. 142.
24. Hanson Baldwin in *The New York Times* (July 6, 1961).
25. Philip Noel-Baker, *The Arms Race* (New York: Oceana Publications, 1958), pp. 14-22.
26. Chalmer M. Roberts, "The Hopes and Obstinacy of Harold Stassen," *The Reporter* (September 5, 1957).
27. For its services through 1961 it received over $22 million. (*The New York Times*, February 13, 1962.)
28. *I. F. Stone's Weekly* (February 26, 1962).
29. *The Reporter* (June 23, 1960), p. 27.
30. *The New York Times* (March 12, 1958).
31. *Ibid.*, March 10, 1958.
32. *Ibid.*, March 12, 1958.
33. *Ibid.*, March 13, 1958.
34. *Kansas City Star* (July 8, 1961).
35. *I. F. Stone's Weekly* (March 26, 1962).
36. *Ibid.*, March 19, 1962.
37. *The Minority of One* (September, 1961).
38. *I. F. Stone's Weekly* (April 23, 1962).
39. Fletcher Knebel and Charles W. Bailey II, "Military Control: Can It Happen Here?" *Look* (September 11, 1962), p. 21.
40. *The New York Times* Magazine (June 25, 1961).
41. Jerome G. Kerwin, ed., *Civil-Military Relationships in American Life* (Chicago: University of Chicago Press, 1948), p. 66.

CHAPTER 13

1. *The Progressive* (December, 1961).
2. *Congressional Record* (August 2, 1961).
3. Gene M. Lyons and Louis Morton, "School for Strategy," *Bulletin of the Atomic Scientists* (March, 1961), p. 165.
4. *Ibid.*, p. 105.
5. *The New York Times* (April 7, 1962).
6. Lyons and Morton, *op. cit.*, p. 103.
7. *Hearings* of the Special Preparedness Subcommittee of the Senate Armed Services Committee (1961-1962), Part I, pp. 72-73.
8. *The New York Times* (April 7, 1962).
9. See also Glenn Mower, Jr., *But You Can't Trust the Russians* (Philadelphia, Pa.: American Friends Service Committee).
10. *Hearings* of the Senate Preparedness Subcommittee, *op. cit.*, Part III, pp. 1198, 1206 ff.
11. *Ibid.*, pp. 1237-1250. Albert Biderman, in *March to Calumny* (New York: The Macmillan Company) supports Marshall's views.
12. J. Edgar Hoover, *Communist Illusion and Democratic Reality* (U.S. Department of Justice, December, 1959).
13. *Army* (April, 1962).
14. *New York Post* (January 21, 1962).
15. *Army,* (April, 1962).

CHAPTER 14

1. *Pendle Hill Bulletin* (Wallingford, Pa.: February, 1945), No. 60.
2. *Conscription News*, 106, 107, 108.
3. Clyde Weaver and Chalmer Faw, "A Day With the Navy," *The Christian Century* (July 2, 1952).

4. "Spiritual and Moral Resources of the United States Army and Navy," report presented to National Laymen's Committee of the National Council of Churches, Hershey, Pa., April 10-12, 1953.

5. *Army Information Digest* (April, 1952).

6. "The Chaplain at Work," address to Joint Civilian Orientation Conference for Religious Leaders, January 17, 1952.

7. *Congressional Record* (May 15, 1951).

8. John Swomley, *Militarism in Education* (National Council Against Conscription, 1950), pp. 21, 54.

9. Report on Religious Affairs Course No. 7, Battle Creek, Mich., May 18-21, 1959, available from Carl Soule, Methodist Board of World Peace.

10. *Congressional Record* (February 4, 1952).

11. Arthur H. Compton, "God and the Atom," *American Magazine* (October, 1950).

CHAPTER 15

1. *This Week Magazine* (April 4, 1948).

2. President's Report, Emory University, Atlanta, Ga., 1942-1943.

3. President's Report, University of Chicago, 1945.

4. *Business Week* (September 14, 1946).

5. *The New York Times* (November 14, 1948).

6. *House Subcommittee Hearings on Navy Appropriations Bill for 1949*, pp. 964, 967.

7. *Ibid.*, p. 965.

8. *The New York Times* (May 23, 1949).

9. L. V. Berkner, "Government Sponsorship of Scientific Research," *Science* (March 27, 1950), p. 817.

10. *The Reporter* (February 4, 1960).

11. Benjamin Fine in *The New York Times* (May 23, 1949).

12. Letter of September 21, 1949 from George B. Pegram, Vice President of Columbia University, to John M. Swomley, Jr.

13. Letter of September 26, 1949 from L. A. DuBridge, President of California Institute of Technology, to John M. Swomley, Jr.

14. *House Hearings on Defense Department Appropriations for 1963*, Part V, p. 347.

15. Benjamin Fine in *The New York Times* (May 23, 1949).

16. *Idem.*

17. Associated Press dispatch from Palo Alto, Calif., May 3, 1947.

18. *The New York Times* (January 19, 1949).

19. *Bulletin of the Atomic Scientists* (June, 1948).

20. *The New York Times* (December 15, 1951).

21. *American Scholar* (Summer, 1947).

22. *House Hearings on Military Establishment Appropriations Bill* (1950), Part IV.

23. *The New York Times* (May 28, 1961)

24. Dr. J. Herbert Hollomon, the Department of Commerce Scientific Policy Coordinator, quoted in the *Kansas City Times* (Kansas City, Mo., October 4, 1962).

25. *Kansas City Times* (January 24, 1963).

26. *The New York Times* (November 19, 1961).

27. *Idem.*

28. *The New York Times* (April 20, 1962.)

29. Hanson Baldwin in *The New York Times* (August 21, 23, 1960).

30. *The New York Times* (January 11, 1962).

31. Allan Brick, *The Campus Protest Against R.O.T.C.* (Philadelphia, Pa.: American Friends Service Committee), p. 10.

32. Hanson Baldwin in *The New York Times* (August 21, 1960).

33. Gene M. Lyons and John W. Masland, *Education and Military Leadership* (Princeton: Princeton University Press, 1959), p. 104.

34. Hanson Baldwin in *The New York Times* (August 21, 1960).

35. Lyons and Masland, *op. cit.*, p. 110.

36. Hanson Baldwin in *The New York Times* (August 21, 1960).

37. *Idem.*

38. These figures were compiled by Duane Chapman from tables in Lyons and Masland, *op. cit.*

39. Hanson Baldwin in *The New York Times* (August 28, 1961).

40. *Idem.*

41. *Higher Education and National Affairs* (American Council on Education), Vol. IX, No. 10, March 7, 1960.

42. *Idem.*

43. *The New York Times* (August 21, 1960).

44. Lyons and Masland, *op. cit.*, p. 211.

45. *Ibid.*, pp. 198, 199.

46. *Ibid.*, pp. 203, 204.

47. *Kansas City Times* (January 31, 1963).

48. *Kansas City Star* (January 19, 1963).
49. *Kansas City Times* (January 31, 1963).
50. *Conscription News* (November 3, 1955).
51. Senate Appropriations Committee, *Defense Department Appropriations for 1962,* pp. 192-194.
52. Quoted by Arthur Krock in *The New York Times* (May 23, 1958).
53. Letter to College Presidents from Major General T. J. Hanley, Jr., in *New Evidence of the Militarization of America* (National Council Against Conscription, 1949), pp. 27, 28.

CHAPTER 16

1. Letter to *The New York Times* (October 14, 1956).
2. *Ibid.*
3. Albert J. Mayer and Thomas Fort Hoult, *Social Forces* (December, 1955).
4. *Look* (May 27, 1958).
5. Graham, *op. cit.* (Ch. 11, n. 2).
6. Walter Millis, *Individual Freedom and the Common Defense* (*op. cit.*, Ch. 11, n. 1), p. 17.
7. *Journal of Engineering Education* (October, 1951).
8. *The New York Times* (July 22, 1959).
9. Eric Pearl, "The Cannoneer's Hop," *The Nation* (May 10, 1958).
10. *Manchester Guardian Weekly* (November 6, 1958).
11. *Aviation Week* (September 6, 1954).
12. *Congressional Record* (September 3, 1954).
13. *Washington Newsletter* (Friends Committee on National Legislation, January, 1963).
14. *Report* of the National Security Training Commission (October 29, 1951), pp. 10, 28.

CONCLUSION

1. *The New York Times* (January 24, 1951).
2. Wise and Ross, *op. cit.* (Ch. 12, n. 23), p. 141.
3. *Ibid.*, pp. 104, 142.
4. Neblett, *op. cit.* (Ch. 5, n. 5), p. 17.
5. *The New York Times* (January 18, 1961).
6. *Ibid.*, September 21, 1961.
7. I. F. Stone's *Bi-Weekly* (March 4, 1963).
8. Neblett, *op. cit.*, p. 7.
9. John M. Maki, *Japanese Militarism: Its Cause and Cure* (New York: Alfred A. Knopf, Inc., 1945), p. 57.

INDEX

261